THE
WAR
ON
POLICE

THE
WAR
ON
POLICE

HOW THE FERGUSON EFFECT IS MAKING AMERICA UNSAFE

JEFF ROORDA

 WND Books

THE WAR ON POLICE

Published by WND Books, Washington, D.C. WND Books is a registered trademark of WorldNetDaily. com, Inc. ("WND")

Cover designed by Vi Yen Nguyen

WND Books are available at special discounts for bulk purchases. WND Books also publishes books in electronic formats. For more information call (541) 474-1776, e-mail orders@wndbooks.com, or visit www.wndbooks.com.

Hardcover ISBN: 978-1-944229-52-8
eBook ISBN: 978-1-944229-53-5

Library of Congress Cataloging-in-Publication Data

Names: Roorda, Jeff, author.
Title: The war on police : how the Ferguson effect is making America unsafe /
Jeff Roorda.
Description: Washington, DC : WND Books, [2016] | Includes bibliographical
references and index.
Identifiers: LCCN 2016027513 (print) | LCCN 2016040691 (ebook) | ISBN
9781944229528 (hardcover) | ISBN 9781944229535 (e-book)
Subjects: LCSH: Police-community relations--Missouri--Ferguson. | Ferguson
(Mo.). Police Department. | Police shootings--Missouri--Ferguson. | Police
misconduct--Missouri--Ferguson. | Police--Complaints against--United
States. | Police--United States. | Crime prevention--United States.
Classification: LCC HV8148.F47 R66 2016 (print) | LCC HV8148.F47 (ebook) |
DDC 363.20973--dc23
LC record available at https://lccn.loc.gov/2016027513

Printed in the United States of America
16 17 18 19 20 21 LBM 9 8 7 6 5 4 3 2 1

To the men and women of law enforcement

To Darren Wilson, a true "casualty of history"

To my friend and teacher "Mama Doris"

To my little brother Timmy, I miss you

TABLE OF CONTENTS

A lie cannot live.

—DR. MARTIN LUTHER KING JR.

The pursuit of truth does not permit violence on one's opponent.

—MAHATMA GANDHI

No one is born hating another person because of the color of his skin . . .
People must learn to hate, and if they can learn to hate, they can be taught
to love, for love comes more naturally to the human heart than its opposite.

—NELSON MANDELA

If you want to end the war then instead of sending guns, send books. Instead of sending tanks, send pens. Instead of sending soldiers, send teachers.

—MALALA YOUSAFZAI, 2014 NOBLE PEACE PRIZE WINNER (AGE 17)

I don't know how you would characterize the gang leaders who got 13-year-old kids hopped-up on crack and sent them out on the street to murder other African-American children. Maybe you thought they were good citizens . . . You are defending the people who killed the lives you say matter. Tell the truth!

—FORMER PRESIDENT BILL CLINTON TO BLACK LIVES MATTER PROTESTORS

This is not my story. This is not Darren Wilson's story. This is law enforcement's story.

It is a story that ought to be told.

It is a story that *has* to be told.

I figure I'm just the guy to tell it.

While this is unmistakably law enforcement's story, I don't claim to speak for all cops or for any particular group of cops. This book, as I see it, is the police viewpoint of Ferguson and its aftermath.

Indeed, I have a unique perspective to lend to this story. Through an unlikely, almost implausible series of seemingly unrelated events, I landed in the front-row-center seat for one of the strangest, most divisive chapters in American history. Whatever you may call it—chance, kismet, bad luck—I was somehow flung smack-dab into the middle of a fray that, more than any event I've witnessed in my lifetime, polarized public opinion and galvanized social behavior in my community and across America.

Through what can be described as little more than happenstance, I somehow ended up as the de facto national spokesman for law enforcement in the face of perhaps the harshest, most protracted attack police work has ever come under. In hindsight, maybe it was inevitable that the planets would align the way they did. Destiny, as they say, is written in the stars.

I started in law enforcement as a 911 dispatcher in 1986. From there, one police job led to the next—beat cop, detective, undercover narcotics agent, police sergeant—until I ended my police career eighteen years later as a police chief and city administrator.

That's when I successfully ran for public office and was elected to the Missouri House of Representatives. I served four terms in the House, but they were not uninterrupted terms. In 2010, I was benched for two years when the Tea Party wave swept me and other moderate Democrats out of office. I returned to office in 2012 when I cruised to victory in a newly drawn House seat. In the interceding two years out of office, I was hired by Missouri governor Jay Nixon to work in his administration as the special assistant to the director of public safety. I stayed in that job only briefly because a couple of months after my appointment by the governor, the St. Louis Police Officers Association (SLPOA), an affiliate of the Fraternal Order of Police (FOP), the nation's largest police union, offered me a job.

The SLPOA, which represented well over one thousand police officers in St. Louis City, was negotiating a union contract with the police department. They wanted me to come on board as their business manager to help get the deal across the finish line, and then administer the contract once it was inked. I leapt at the opportunity. It seemed like a perfect fit. Even when I won my election to return to the legislature in 2012, the SLPOA asked me to stay on and agreed to let me work a part-time schedule when the House was in session.

The idea of working for the FOP was an enticing one. I was an active, loyal member of the order and had achieved the rare status of life member, although I belonged to the lodge in St. Louis County that represented the suburbs surrounding the city. Around the same time the SLPOA hired me, my FOP lodge asked me to join the board of directors of the Shield of Hope charity they had just created. The Shield was formed to help pay for scholarships and to help officers and their families when they were hurt on the job or, God forbid, killed in the line of duty. So, it was an easy decision; of course I'd help. After all, the charity's annual budget was only supposed to be three to four thousand dollars, and we didn't anticipate having to meet much more than once a year.

Then Ferguson happened, and everything changed in an instant.

The SLPOA and the Shield of Hope both needed a spokesman. I was tapped for the job by both organizations. St. Louis police officers had responded to assist with the riots in Ferguson, and were involved in some high-profile police shootings themselves. The Shield of Hope stepped up to raise money to assist Darren Wilson and other officers in Ferguson with legal, medical, and relocation expenses, and eventually raised around three hundred thousand dollars in a very short time as money came pouring in.

At first, there were a number of us who were associated with the FOP in St. Louis City and St. Louis County, each of whom rotated the duties of making the rounds with local and national media. Ultimately though, the spotlight came to rest on me, which propelled me onto the national stage, not only to speak out about issues connected to Ferguson, but eventually to weigh in on police-related incidents in Baltimore, Staten Island, and elsewhere.

Along the way, I did more than seventy-five nationally broadcast television interviews and also became CNN's "go-to guy" when it came to questions about Ferguson and its aftermath as well as police tactics in other places around the country. In addition to national television, I did hundreds more interviews with print media, radio, and local TV news stations to debunk the false narrative that had emerged from Ferguson, and chronicle the realities on the ground. Reality in Ferguson, it seemed, was slipping through the fingers of history like fine sand.

The other thing I did to chronicle what was happening in the wake of the shooting of Michael Brown was write and write and write and write.

I began recording what was happening almost immediately. Initially, I used those notes to inform my writing for a column I penned each month for the SLPOA newspaper, the *Gendarme*. In the twelve harrowing months that followed the deadly confrontation between police officer Darren Wilson and Michael Brown, I dedicated every column to some topic related to Ferguson and its aftermath. I landed interviews that every journalist in the country coveted—exclusives with the likes of Darren Wilson and three of the St. Louis area police officers who were shot as violence boiled over in our region—interviews you will read in these pages.

The story of post-Ferguson America needs more context than simply a reprinting of the twelve stand-alone op-eds I churned out. That's where the idea for the book came from. It is critical for people to know what really happened on the front lines and behind the scenes in the 365 days of mayhem that ensued after the Michael Brown shooting, along with the fantastic tale that accompanied it and incensed a nation—and continues to infuriate those who reject the undeniable reality of what actually transpired on Canfield Drive that August 2014 day.

Of course, I was not on the front lines in Ferguson. My days of toting a gun and wearing a badge have long since passed. I spent plenty of time on the ground in Ferguson and at other demonstrations in the St. Louis area, but not in a foxhole. I was a correspondent, not a soldier—more Ernie Pyle than Sergeant York.

Like any good war correspondent, my job was simple: cut through the haze of gun smoke and get to the harsh, ugly realities that underlie every war. That was my solemn duty.

And this was most certainly a war. That's why cops on the ground dubbed it "Ferghanistan," and that's why I use that colloquialism in the title of chapter 1. I am well aware, by the way, that employing the sensational moniker Ferghanistan will no doubt roil some. It is not meant to demean the people who live there, nor is it meant to diminish the service of soldiers who fought in Afghanistan. *Stān* is a Persian word meaning "place of." It seems, though, in modern times that every country that has a name ending with *stan* is a place of turmoil, violence, and war.

If you don't believe that the attack on police after Michael Brown's death constitutes a war, you will by the time you finish this book. I accepted it as my personal mission, my divine calling, to share the story of Ferghanistan with the world.

This didn't start out for me as a crusade, but it certainly ended up as one. It has become a crusade to set the record straight and to protect the integrity and accuracy of history even as so many activists, journalists, and politicians try to rewrite that same history right before our eyes. It has become a crusade to hold people accountable for what they say and do. Most of all, it has become a crusade to push back against those who have declared war on cops, on law and order, and on civil society.

While it may be my lips that are moving, I speak with the voice of tens of thousands of everyday heroes, men and women in blue, both here and gone. Their voices have been muted, their noble reputations blemished, and their lives and livelihoods placed in imminent peril. And for far too many cops in post-Ferguson America, their lives have been taken at the hands of the desperate, hopeless souls that lurk in the shadows where we dare shed no light.

I do not abide tyranny or terrorism. I'll not stand for the mistreatment of the brave men and women who patrol our neighborhoods and keep our communities safe. Not now. Not ever. This is my sacred and certain duty as an American.

It is neither a mantle that I pick up lightly, nor a yoke that I wear loosely. While it is weighty, it is no burden. It is a calling, not a curse, and I am humbled to answer its awesome peal.

Unlike the politicians and pundits who hold up their statements about law enforcement in the post-Ferguson era as the irrefutable truth, let me be refreshingly honest: what I say is simply my opinion, my view of the world. But, it is based in fact, not fiction. This book is not about what I want to believe happened that day in Ferguson and in the weeks and months that followed; it's about what actually did happen. It is the untold story owed to the iris of history.

I see things through the eyes of a cop. I make no apologies for that. That's what you'll get here—a frank, honest conversation about how law enforcement officers see what happened in Ferguson and its aftermath. It's a cop's-eye view of things, and I do not purport it to be counterbalanced by or representative of other viewpoints.

I don't claim to understand what was going through Michael Brown's mind or the minds of thousands of other young men who have turned violent toward police officers. I haven't walked in their shoes or suffered what they've suffered. I can't explain how they can rationalize turning what should be a routine encounter with law enforcement into a kill-or-be-killed confrontation, forcing the combatants to fight to the death.

Likewise, I can make little sense of the grievances of those who marched in the street, demanding a "justice" that turned out to be vengeance for an alleged atrocity that was based on a lie, perpetuated by a false narrative, and fueled by gratuitous media and political hype.

I certainly can make no sense of the acts of those who tried to kill and maim police officers after the Brown shooting, or the grand jury findings in that case and others involving deadly confrontations between police officers and their assailants. Nor can I make sense of those who looted and burned the communities they claimed to care about.

Most of all, I don't claim to know the pain that Michael Brown's parents live with. I watched my own parents live through the death of my brother, and I can tell you from watching them that there is no pain—physical, mental, or emotional—that compares to the pain of a parent who has lost a child. I am not unsympathetic to the heartbreak felt by Brown's parents, or the parents of any child who dies during a confrontation with the police. The senseless loss they have to live with is what makes this whole thing so tragic.

That's not my story, though. I am not here to speak for the desperate youths or violent protesters or peaceful demonstrators or mournful parents. I am here to tell you the way we—cops in and around Ferguson and all across America—see it. I'm here to have a candid, raw conversation about policing in our nation, race relations in urban neighborhoods, and the political failures that have imperiled the lives of police officers and black inner-city youths alike.

If you're not ready to have that conversation, and it seems as if much of America is not, then stop here; don't turn another page. This is the blue view . . . the blue line.

The blue line is a fraternity of shared experiences. It is a line of thinking informed by the reality of the asphalt battlefields, not the impenetrable, blue wall of silence encircling the law enforcement profession that our critics so often make it out to be.

If you're unwilling to at least consider the blue view, then close this book now. This isn't some para-masturbatorial academic exercise, nor is it some Pollyanna, pie-in-the-sky, "Can't we all just get along" indulgence of liberal-white guilt. This is the gritty, unabated view from the streets that are made safe by America's greatest heroes: the men and women who pin a badge on their chests every day and place their lives in jeopardy to defend the people of this country.

If you're looking for something else, buy a different book.

FERGHANISTAN

When I awoke on August 10, 2014, I didn't know the world had changed forever for law enforcement. None of us did, at least not yet.

I was awakened that morning by a call from the chief of the St. Louis Metropolitan Police Department, Sam Dotson. I always cringe when I get a call from the chief late at night or early in the morning, and that morning was no different. As the business manager for the union that represents police officers of the City of St. Louis, it wasn't rare for me to hear from the chief at all hours of the day or night. Still, when you're responsible for the lives and livelihoods of more than a thousand police officers, after-hours calls are accompanied by the sinking feeling that one of my cops might be hurt or, heaven forbid, worse.

The chief's words were solemn. "We had a bad night in Ferguson."

I sat up in bed and asked what happened.

What the chief described seemed like pretty significant civil unrest: angry mobs in the street at the scene of the shooting and in front of the Ferguson Police Department, threats of violence against police, and a flurry of shots fired in the air throughout the evening. Little did I know it was mild compared to what would unfold in the next few hours and the next several days.

I asked what our involvement was, and he said he'd sent some St. Louis City Police traffic units to Ferguson to help secure the perimeter, and that he had staged our SWAT unit at the city-county border, standing by in case they were needed for crowd control or tactical support. The St. Louis County Police SWAT unit was already on the ground. That sounded dire, and I was surprised by the rapid spin-up of tensions in Ferguson, a town I considered highly integrated and relatively free of racial tensions.

I wasn't oblivious to the police shooting in Ferguson the day before. In fact, I was watching it closely and was acutely aware that some troubling accusations had been made about the shooting. But the several coppers I'd already talked to who were involved in the investigation assured me it was a "righteous shoot" and that the suspect had tried to take the officer's gun.

It wasn't lost on me, though, that these shootings result in intense media scrutiny and some hard-to-answer questions. I was already watching from afar the media furor over the recent police shooting of John Crawford at the Dayton-area Walmart, and the deadly police encounter in New York that resulted in the death of Eric Garner. Like the shooting in Ferguson, both of those cases involved a so-called unarmed black man (Crawford was holding what turned out to be a BB gun) killed by a white police officer.

After hearing from the chief how bad things had gotten in Ferguson overnight, I remember thinking, *This is bad. The local media is going to have a field day with this. This is the kind of story that could go on for two or three days.*

A miss, as they say, is as good as a mile.

I have to admit, even though the John Crawford shooting happened just four days before the Michael Brown shooting, I hadn't thoroughly read up on it until a couple of days later.

As it happened, the Crawford shooting occurred on August 5, 2014, the same day as the primary election in Missouri. My attention that day was turned toward my own election. I was in my fourth and final term as a Missouri state representative due to term limits. I was running for the state senate in what had turned out to be the hottest election in the entire state.

I was unopposed in the primary, but I had taken the day off to visit with voters at the polls in my senate district. It was a good day. I got a great response from the folks I talked to at the various voting stations. What people seemed most impressed by was my seventeen-year career in law enforcement and my record of standing up for law and order in my eight years as a state representative.

Our campaign plan relied heavily on spotlighting my service to the community as a cop, particularly the five years I spent as a decorated undercover narcotics detective. With all of the popular movies and TV shows about narcs, there was a certain celebrity that went with having done undercover work. The media consultants called it "sexy." The truth is, people in my district and in most places across America respect police work, and their curiosity is piqued by the mystique surrounding clandestine investigations.

Particularly in the St. Louis suburb where I lived, served in office, and had worked as a police officer, the drug problem was a big deal. At one point, my county had led the nation in methamphetamine lab seizures five out of ten years. A fellow lawmaker had once snarked that Jefferson County was "first in meth and last in math." That was a reputation we were desperately trying to shake. The image of needle junkies passed out facedown in a puddle of their own vomit in their dilapidated mobile home was demoralizing to the mostly middle- to upper-middle-class population of the sleepy bedroom community I represented in the legislature.

So, the table was set in my election. The square-jawed, tough-on-crime, "lock-'em-up-and-throw-away-the-key" image would be the central theme of my campaign. The decision to focus on my police bona fides had been made months before, but as the fault lines shifted in Ferguson, the public's obsession with matters of law and order was about to intensify beyond my wildest imagination.

If the first night in Ferguson was a surprise, the second was a complete shock. That second night wrought something unimaginable.

Night two brought looting, arson, shots fired at a police helicopter, and two injuries to police officers. One of my best friends had the windshield of his St. Louis County police car smashed in with a brick as he sat in it. When he texted me the picture, I was aghast. The knot already in my stomach doubled in size. Now it was personal.

As I was writing this book, I seemed to recall that the Quik Trip gas station had been torched by demonstrators on the second night of violence in Ferguson. As I searched the Internet to verify my recollection, the first page that popped up was the Wikipedia article titled "Ferguson unrest."[1]

Easy enough, I thought to myself.

Point. Click. Huh?!

I never made it to night two on the Wiki page. The synopsis of night one made it impossible for me to read on.

There was no mention of either the hostile confrontations with police or the hail of gunfire. Instead, there was only a description of the desecration of a makeshift memorial to Michael Brown. According to the account, officers at the scene allowed their police canines to urinate on the memorial; then officers completed the defilement by running over the flowers and candles with their police cruisers.

"That's not what happened!" I shouted at the computer screen.

The news reports on the following day consistently described the makeshift memorial as having been damaged by vandals. As we all know, the media can be wrong. So, I talked to officers who were there that night. They all said the destruction of the memorial by police canines and police cars was an absolute farce. Some critics of law enforcement would be quick to say that those officers might have a motivation to lie about this if they were involved.

Okay, then how about this? The evening was well chronicled. An abundance of TV film crews and photojournalists were at the scene. Not to mention everyone had their phones out, taking pictures and hashtagging this titillating tweet or Facebooking that provocative post. Yet, not a single word about police dogs peeing on the solemn commemoration. Not one. Anywhere.

The story, as I learned when checking references, didn't appear until August 27, some eighteen days later, on the website of the publication *Mother Jones*.

This is not a story the media would have missed. Nor would they have been reluctant to report on it. Every reporter I know in St. Louis would have knocked over his own grandmother to phone in the story of a police dog literally pissing on Michael Brown's grave, temporary and symbolic though it may have been.

It just didn't happen. As you'll learn in these pages, there were a lot of things that just didn't happen, despite what you may have heard from the press, the protesters, or the politicos.

But there was a narrative to write, a history to forge, and nothing was going to get in the way of that.

Fallacious eyewitness accounts, contrived social media posts, and the unquenchable appetite for sensational breaking news to feed the belly of the twenty-four-hour cable news beast all compounded the problem. The hype-fueled distortions left the truth a smoldering pile of ash. It did the same for the city of Ferguson.

Despite media coverage that demonized police for their so-called bad optics and deified protesters for their "peaceful" pursuit of answers, the truth is incontrovertible: the night of the shooting and the night that followed were defined by wildly violent, reckless demonstrations that endangered citizens, cops, and even the protesters themselves. While those first two nights took their toll on accountability and accuracy, it was the next day that the truth suffered a mortal blow.[2]

That was the day the lantern was kicked over and truth went up in flames.

MRS. O'LEARY'S COW

Michael Brown was a desperate street criminal. I know that seems harsh. After all, he was just a teenager, right? He was just a kid who made a stupid decision that cut his life tragically short, right? He was, in the end, someone's son, someone's grandson. Right?

All true. But what is so often lost in the sensationalized retelling of this story is that in a moment of desperation, Michael Brown turned what has to be characterized as deadly violence against a police officer. While none of us knows for certain what Brown would have done with the weapon had he succeeded in his attempts to disarm Officer Darren Wilson, Darren couldn't risk finding out. Every cop works off the same assumption: If you're trying to take my gun, you're going to kill me with it.

They have to.

Even for those skeptics who deride the grand jury process and criticize the police investigation of the shooting in the name of canonizing Michael Brown, there are some facts that are simply inescapable.

Brown has been described by his adoring fans as a "gentle giant."[1]

Maybe that was an accurate description of Brown before August 9, 2014, but on that day, he was just a giant. He was far from gentle when he swatted the proprietor of the Ferguson Market around like a rag doll as he lumbered out of the store with a handful of stolen cigarillos. And he was far from gentle when he pummeled Officer Wilson and tried to disarm him, and when he charged headlong toward Officer Wilson as Darren pleaded for him to surrender.

Under Missouri law, as it is in every other state I'm aware of, using physical force in the course of a theft is a felony. The crime is colloquially referred to as a "strong-arm robbery," but statutorily it is categorized as "robbery in the second degree." In Missouri, that offense is a Class B felony, which carries a penalty of five to fifteen years in prison. The law sees this as a serious offense because it is a serious offense. That hard-and-fast view of forcible robbery as a serious crime dates back to English common law.

The revisionists would cast Brown as Jean Valjean to Wilson's Inspector Javert in their eagerness to describe Brown's miserable fate as senseless persecution for the mere theft of fifty dollars in perishables. Jean Valjean, by the way, just pilfered the loaf. He didn't knock anybody over in so doing. *Les Misérables* author Victor Hugo labored to create a sympathetic character in Valjean rather than the hulking brute committing a self-benefiting crime that we have in this story.

Aside from the fact that stealing cigars for your own indulgence is significantly less sympathetic than stealing a loaf of bread for your starving family, the theft is not why Wilson stopped Brown, nor is it why he shot and killed Brown.

There has been a lot of subterfuge regarding the actual stop of Brown and his accomplice, Dorian Johnson. The facts are clear. Darren Wilson was leaving a nearby call to assist an ambulance when he spotted Brown and Johnson walking down the middle of Canfield.

Eric Holder's Department of Justice was highly critical of the Ferguson "Manner of Walking Along Roadway" ordinance. Yet, nobody had a problem with the ordinance before Michael Brown was shot. The ordinance was never challenged successfully in court, and it remains on the books despite tremendous DOJ pressure to repeal it. It is on the books because it is dangerous to walk in the middle of a roadway. Ferguson enforced that law because of the pervasive disregard that problem teens had for traffic safety. Some have implied that black youths were being targeted and singled out for the minor infraction of jaywalking. Not so. This wasn't a case of kids cutting across a street, but one of scofflaws walking down the middle of the roadway. Teens would regularly impede traffic on busy streets in and around Ferguson and the Canfield neighborhood. It was their way of thumbing their collective noses at the law and asserting their "ownership" of the streets, their dominion over their territory, their claim to that turf.

I have to ask: Who the hell does that? Who the hell walks down the middle of the street in blatant, cavalier disregard of the law, right after committing a felony? The only logical answer would be: someone who is spoiling for a confrontation.

Some in the media have reported that Darren Wilson knew nothing about the robbery at the Ferguson Market. That's not true. He did in fact hear the dispatch about the robbery. Once Darren saw the cigarillos in Brown's hand, he knew he had spotted the culprits. According to my many conversations with Darren Wilson about this part of the confrontation, it all clicked. The description from the radio broadcast matched Brown to a T.

More important, even if Wilson didn't know it right away, Brown knew he had just committed a felony. There's no other logical explanation for the actions Brown took after Wilson confronted him. That's why he handed his smokes to Johnson and began to batter Wilson. That's why he tried to disarm Wilson with what anyone looking at this objectively must recognize as deadly intent. Brown knew he had been—or would soon be—identified as the culprit, and he didn't want to go to jail. Nothing else makes sense.

Not that there's any sense to be made of this whole thing.

Something in Michael Brown snapped that day. Based on the

physical intimidation he engaged in at the market and the confrontational attitude he assumed the moment he saw Wilson, Brown was clearly agitated and angling for a showdown with law enforcement. His very first words to Wilson were, "F**k what you say."[2]

Kids like Brown live in a tough, eat-or-be-eaten environment. Cops do too. It is what makes these confrontations between inner-city youths and law enforcement so volatile. Both sides of the encounter immediately engage in "territorial pissings," or even unabashed bravado in some cases.

Cops call this "command presence." Street kids call it "survival of the fittest." Both know things can quickly escalate when either side feels threatened. Brown obviously did feel threatened (with certain arrest and ultimate incarceration), and quickly resorted to violence. It was a thuggish response from a young man, who, on that particular day, decided to act like a thug.

I don't mean to speak ill of the dead. My grandmother strongly warned against that. She called it "whistling past the graveyard." And I want very much for Michael Brown to rest in peace and for his family to find some solace, but I also want Darren Wilson to live in peace and his family to find a way forward. That can't happen with Wilson cast as a villainous murderer, despite conclusive grand jury and DOJ findings to the contrary, because as long as Darren is the bad guy in this fairy-tale version of what happened on Canfield, he and his family are in danger.

So, too, is my family, my law enforcement family. As long as post-Ferguson tempers run high, cops are in mortal danger. Not only have criminals been emboldened by the antipolice sentiment being sown by politicians, the media, and militant cop-haters, there is a sick, pervasive urge among some to "settle the score."

The "us against them" fervor that was ginned up by the violent demonstrations, looting, arson, and rioting in the streets of Ferguson and St. Louis has made America's cops more prone to deadly attacks by those enticed by the idea of martyring a police officer or themselves in the name of Michael Brown. It pains me to say it, but most of the people who are spellbound by this "kill or die for the cause" mentality are black men, usually very young black men, as you'll read later in this book.

It is a national phenomenon in the post-Ferguson era, but it is most pronounced in the St. Louis area, where in the eight months following the Brown shooting, eight young black men were shot and killed in deadly confrontations with law enforcement. All of these shootings took place in inner-city neighborhoods in St. Louis City and St. Louis County. It is an unthinkably high, unprecedented number of fatal clashes between cops and the ill-fated, ill-advised assailants who resorted to irrational violence. Eight fatal shootings by law enforcement in eight months is not the norm in the St. Louis area. One would be the norm. Two would be a lot. Eight is a terribly high number that can only be explained by the presence of some new phenomenon.

Of course, this violence didn't start because of Michael Brown. True, Brown did make a terrible, desperate choice—for which he paid dearly. But it all could have ended there were it not for one man.

Dorian Johnson.

It was only a couple of days after the Brown shooting that I coined the phrase "Dorian Johnson is to Ferguson what Mrs. O'Leary's cow was to Chicago." Let me elaborate.

As Windy City folklore has it, Catherine O'Leary left a kerosene lantern burning in her barn on DeKoven Street on October 8, 1871, and dozed off after taking one too many nips out of her little brown jug. That evening, as the story goes, her cow kicked over the lantern, igniting the inferno that would later be known as the Great Chicago Fire.

In the same way that ol' Daisy's bovine bucking reputedly sparked the Chicago *conflagration*, Dorian Johnson's account of the events on Canfield Drive sparked the Ferguson *confabulation*.

It is not easy to call Dorian Johnson a liar. To do so, I'd first have to decide which of his several versions of the shooting he had fabricated. Johnson's story changed so many times in the days and months following the Brown shooting that it is hard to say what he really thinks happened.

The *Washington Post*, one of the first newspapers to get the whole Ferguson story wrong, ultimately got the story right when they published an op-ed about Dorian Johnson's various accounts by former US District Court judge Paul Cassell on December 2, 2014, titled, "Why Michael Brown's Best Friend's Story Isn't Credible."[3] In the piece, Cassell picks apart the credibility of Johnson's implausible narrative by comparing what he told reporters to what he told investigators, to what he told the grand jury, to, most critically, what the physical evidence told all of us. The Cassell op-ed and countless other examinations of the veracity of Johnson's story draw a pretty clear and conclusive picture for anyone interested in those pesky little things called "facts."

So, how can anyone believe Johnson's statements? Let's not forget, he was Brown's accomplice in a violent felony. Johnson's part in the Ferguson Market robbery has never been made clear. We do know that he was listed as a suspect in the robbery in the Ferguson Police Department report.[4] We don't know if he took direct part in stealing merchandise, or if he acted as a lookout, or if he was just there and didn't participate at all. What we know for certain is that Brown handed the stolen cigars to Johnson just before he began to pummel Officer Wilson. Taking possession of the stolen property while Brown tried to make good on their escape absolutely makes Johnson an accomplice who could be charged with the felony robbery. Consequently, Johnson could also be charged with felony murder under a Missouri law that states:

> A person commits the offense of murder in the second degree if he
> or she . . . commits or attempts to commit any felony, and, in the
> perpetration or the attempted perpetration of such felony or in the
> flight from the perpetration or attempted perpetration of such felony,
> another person is killed as a result of the perpetration or attempted
> perpetration of such felony or immediate flight from the perpetration
> of such felony or attempted perpetration of such felony.[5]

I'll never understand why Johnson wasn't charged criminally, but I imagine that the answer contains the words "political pressure."

Even those inclined to empathize with Johnson cannot deny his devastating role in Ferguson and its aftermath here and in other cities across America. His legacy as the AllSpark for a version of events that took on a life of its own cannot be ignored or excused.

I understand the urge to pity Johnson. After all, if he and Brown were as close as he claims they were (and it's not my place to dispute that), then he suffered a tremendous loss, the loss of a close friend. No matter how close they really were, the violent confrontation Johnson saw was certainly emotionally traumatic. And, of course, Johnson didn't ask to be born and raised in an urban war zone where even the best of kids have to struggle with crime, violence, drugs, a broken education system, pressure to join gangs, and countless other challenges I haven't had to endure. Johnson's lot in life—and for that matter, Brown's—should be pitied. We should work together to change the circumstances in which they come of age. It is unfair that kids like them grow up immersed in hopelessness and despair. You can want to make that situation better, while at the same time understanding that Johnson, Brown, and every last one of us should be accountable for the decisions we make under the best of circumstances and under the worst. The stakes are simply too high to let Johnson off the hook for what he did. Actions and words have consequences.

We simply cannot forget that.

By far, the most dangerous words Johnson spoke about the Brown shooting were his first. His story of the execution-style murder of Brown spread through the neighborhood like wildfire. Then he got in front of a camera and repeated those statements to the media on August 11, 2014, setting off a maelstrom. He first spoke to a gathering of local St. Louis reporters; later that night, he went on the cable news circuit, talking to hosts such as Anderson Cooper and Al Sharpton.

In his impromptu press conference with local media, Johnson went through the shocking details of the initial contact with Officer Wilson as if Wilson were the aggressor and Johnson and Brown were merrily skipping down the street, singing church hymns (remember: no one knew about the Ferguson Market robbery at the time of Johnson's press conference, as the damning video had not yet been released).

Johnson accused Wilson of grabbing and choking Brown without provocation. Then he told a story about the actual shooting, that, were it true, would horrify any of us:

> At no time the officer said that, uh, he was gonna do anything until he pulled out his weapon, his weapon was drawn, and he said "I'll shoot you," or, "I'm gonna shoot," and in the same moment the first shot went off and I looked at him [Brown], he, he was shot, and there was blood comin' from him and we took off runnin', and as we took off runnin' I ducked and hid for my life 'cause I was fearin' for my life and I hid by the first car that I saw, my friend he kept runnin' and he told me to keep runnin' 'cause he feared for me too, so, as he was runnin', the officer, uh, was tryin' to get outta the car and once he got out the car he, uh, he pursued my friend but his gu—his weapon was drawn, now he didn't see any weapon drawn at him or anything like that, us goin' for no weapon, his weapon was already drawn when he got outta the car, he shot again and then once my friend felt that shot, he turnt around and he put his hands in the air [mimics the gesture] and he started to get down but the officer still approached with his weapon drawn and, and he, he fired several more shots and my friend died. He didn't say anything to him he just stood over and he was shooting. By then, I was so afraid for my life I just, I got up and I ran.

Wow! Well, that didn't happen.

We know it didn't happen not only because the story has changed so many times since Johnson's first telling, and not only because it so diametrically contradicts the numerous witness statements, but because it is impossible to reconcile his account with the physical evidence, the ballistic evidence, and the autopsies.

As I listened over and over to Johnson recounting the day's events, a quote attributed to Winston Churchill kept playing in my mind: "A lie gets halfway around the world before the truth has a chance to get its pants on." To me, Johnson's story seemed not only rehearsed but heavily coached. I thought that the first time I saw it, and I'm more certain of it every time I watch him reciting the first iteration of his story.

I've interviewed hundreds of suspects in my police career and hundreds more victims and witnesses. After talking to enough people—and I didn't think every suspect was guilty, I toiled to get to the truth—you learn to tell the difference between somebody who is remembering what happened and someone who is reciting a story about what happened. Recollection looks different to the trained eye than repetition does. As time went on, Johnson began to trip up because he seemed to be trying to remember, not the events themselves, but what he'd told people about them. That is what good interrogators look for when they are interviewing a suspect.

Notice how Johnson never called Brown by name, referring to him instead as "my friend." That is not syntax that comes naturally to a person. It appears to be designed to make both Brown and Johnson seem more sympathetic. I doubt Johnson could have devised such a complex verbal tactic himself.

Clearly, someone also told him to use the word *weapon* instead of *gun*. The one time Johnson slipped and started to say, "gun," he corrected and went back to the term *weapon*. It seems awkward and unnatural for a kid from the hood to use such terminology. It was no doubt formulated to make him look a little less "street." Although, speaking in complete sentences and wearing something to the press conference other than a white muscle shirt would have certainly gone farther to accomplish that goal.

I'm not trying to mock Johnson. It's likely that he showed up in a "wifebeater" because that's all he had to wear, though by the time he hit the cable circuit, someone had bought him some nice, new, crisply pressed clothes. How nice for him.

This is no doubt the point in the book where someone is going to scream, "RACIST!" I get called that, or "white supremacist," or "cracker," or "Klansman," by protesters almost every time I speak publicly on behalf of police, because I am an enemy to the false narrative, the most frequent and vocal opponent of that version of history where Michael Brown is an emblematic folk hero embodying black struggle against a universally racist cabal of white cops.

That's fine. Call me whatever you want. My disdain for Johnson drips from these pages; there is no denying that. Let me put it simply: I hate Dorian Johnson; he is nothing but a lying thug.

But I don't hate him because he's black. I spent a career putting thugs behind bars, and the vast majority of them were white. So for me, *thug* isn't some dog-whistle code word used to derogate blacks, as some have suggested; it is simply a synonym for *street criminal* that is worn well by the likes of Johnson.

The reason I hate Johnson is because he told a lie, a lie that has cost so many, so dearly. And not just the shop owners in Ferguson whose lifework was burnt to cinders. Not just the cops in Ferguson who were shot or injured by the rampaging mob. But Michael Brown's parents, who have had to endure a pain worse than they should ever have had to live through.

Yes, Dorian Johnson, I most certainly hate you. Because of your careless words, the lantern you kicked over in Ferguson burns in every city where a black man dies at the hands of a white cop, irrespective of the facts of that particular case. I hate you because that lantern burns in the heart of so many, many young black men who come into contact with the police and let the fires of hatred consume them and compel them to make horrible choices in the heat of that moment. And, if we're being honest, that lantern now burns in the hearts of some cops, too, thanks to you.

I hate you, Dorian Johnson, but I don't want to hate you. I want to love you. I want to love you because that's the way my family raised me. I want to love you because that's what my Christian faith tells me I should do. I want to love you because that is what my heart tells me I should do.

But I can't. We all burn in the fires of our own misdeeds. I want the fire you started to flicker out in the winds of change. I can't begin to tell you how desperately I want that. Instead, your words, and the actions of the people inspired by them, continue to whip that fire into a sweltering, swirling funeral pyre fueled by the hatred and fear and revenge you have poured on it.

You, young man, must burn in that fire.

We all must.

TONS OF ANARCHY

Stoked by Dorian Johnson's inflammatory account, the third night of protests—August 11—was the worst yet. The crowd turned hyper-violent as soon as night fell, and although media reports glazed over it, volleys of gunfire popped off late into the night, with many of the shots narrowly missing police officers working crowd control. The press, the demonstrators, and the politicians essentially ignored the fact that police and protesters alike were in danger from gunfire coming from the crowd, and instead focused on Johnson's fantastical fairy tale and on changing the narrative to one that vilified police. To that end, two new expressions were coined: "police militarization," and "Hands up, don't shoot."

What a farce. Neither of these concoctions accurately reflected what actually happened in Ferguson.

On the same day Dorian Johnson pollinated the seeds of discontent in the streets of Ferguson—and around the world—with his mis-telling of the events on Canfield, two other things happened that should have brought calm to the St. Louis area that night. The first was the Justice

THE WAR ON POLICE

Department's announcements that the FBI was opening an investigation into Brown's death. That should have appeased the elements in the crowd that had been calling for an outside probe in the two days that followed the Brown shooting. It didn't.

The other little nugget that was sure to be heeded by the "peace-loving protesters" was a very public call for calm by Michael Brown's mother, Lezley McSpadden. Why would Ms. McSpadden have to call for calm if the protests were as peaceful as media reports and activist tweets described them?

Nevertheless, the promised probe and the parental plea did nothing to stave off more violence. In fact, the third night was worse than the first two. And that night saw the largest turnout of demonstrators yet.

The protests turned violent quickly, with more gunfire coming from the crowd, along with bricks, bottles, and rocks being hurled at the police. Officers in riot gear fired smoke grenades and tear gas to try to disperse the violent elements within the sea of people. Tactical units from all across the St. Louis region were summoned to the scene to assist with what was rapidly turning into a volatile situation. It was the night that things turned very, very ugly, and things would stay that way for quite some time.

For me, the day started with another briefing from St. Louis Police chief Sam Dotson. He informed me that the number of officers dispatched to help in Ferguson had been increased. He also said that there had been some vandalism to buildings in southwest St. Louis City, and that he was concerned about the escalation he had seen over the first two nights and was worried that the level of violence would continue to increase.

I asked the chief what he was doing to make certain the St. Louis City police officers I represented were safe in case the violence continued to spread beyond Ferguson. He told me he had ordered that all calls, no matter how trivial, be assigned as two-man calls so no officer would go into any situation in the city of St. Louis without backup. He had also directed district captains to "double up" as many officers as possible in two-man cars. The chief even wanted to cancel days off and move officers from eight- to twelve-hour shifts if things got worse, but he was concerned that would violate the union contract.

He and I talked it out and agreed that the most important thing was that there would be sufficient staffing to ensure the safety of both officers and the public. To accommodate that, we decided it would be prudent to utilize an extraordinary clause in the union contract that allowed the chief to suspend the contract in cases of "extreme civil-emergency conditions . . . including . . . riots, civil disorders, tornado conditions, floods, or other similar catastrophes."[1] It was a failsafe provision in the contract, meant to address the most far-fetched circumstances imaginable, and, as such, there we were, neck-deep in just such a doomsday scenario.

Despite all the nasty things you may have read about police unions before or after Ferguson, the labor-management relationship we had in St. Louis was a productive, mutually beneficial one that always put the mission of policing first. That's not true of just St. Louis. I've heard the same thing from police union leaders and police chiefs I've talked to all across the country.

I told the chief I would get the word out to union leadership that the contract had been temporarily suspended. I also suggested to him that morale could use a boost because the tensions in Ferguson and their potential to spill over was unnerving for our officers who were deployed to Ferguson or might be deployed later. The chief agreed and sent out the following e-mail to the entire department to ease concerns about the dynamic conditions surrounding the civil unrest:

> Last night the St. Louis Metropolitan Police Department responded to assist St. Louis County and Municipal Officers as they dealt with events in Ferguson.
>
> I appreciate the efforts of all those who helped restore order in St. Louis County and to those who remained vigilant in our City. St. Louis County Police Chief Jon Belmar, as well as many others, were highly complementary of our assistance. Thank you for your professionalism.

As we plan and prepare for the upcoming days, until further notice, all calls in the City will be dispatched with a minimum of two officers regardless of the call type.

I appreciate everyone stepping up to assist. You continue to do a great job each day.

Be safe.

Chief Sam Dotson

The chief's words were well received by the troops, but tensions remained high, and as the evening unfolded, we all realized trepidation about a prospective third night of violence was well founded.

As I watched the situation unravel on August 11, I couldn't help but think that the politicians joining in the chorus of a rush to judgment of Darren Wilson were doing a great disservice both to the truth and to the community's safety. As these politicians took to the airwaves and to social media with derisive and unfounded allegations, I knew nothing good could come of it. I thought, in particular, black politicians were uniquely positioned to wade into the crowds and plead for peace, while at the same time assuring those who had gathered that justice would prevail.

Instead, far too many politicians basked in the spotlight of the national media attention and used the opportunity for shameless self-promotion. To me, nobody was guiltier of this than St. Louis alderman Antonio French, whose caustic tweets and public comments, in my opinion, fomented violence among the worst elements of the protesters in Ferguson.

I took to the Twittersphere in an effort to call for a more reasoned, responsible approach from Alderman French:

@RoordaJ @AntonioFrench alderman, I implore you to be a community leader during this time of crisis instead of inciting this volatile situation.

10:15 PM - 11 Aug 14

My supplications obviously went unheeded, as the scene in Ferguson devolved into utter bedlam. I watched helplessly as the situation spiraled out of control, with French and other irresponsible politicians leading the charge.

✪ ✪ ✪

On August 12, day four of the protests, so-called civil rights leader Al Sharpton arrived in St. Louis.

Hooray. Just what we needed!

The "Rev" and Michael Brown's family were scheduled to hold a press conference along with the newly hired Brown family attorney, Benjamin Crump.

I have a low opinion of Al "Charlatan." To me, he seems to profit personally from African-American tragedies, while never really doing anything to avert those tragedies, or ease the suffering of those to whom he claims to be ministering. On the other hand, I tried to keep an open mind about Crump, who was renowned for his representation of Trayvon Martin's family.

From my perspective, the Martin and Brown cases were very different. I always found George Zimmerman's acquittal to be an appalling injustice. Then again, everything I know about the Trayvon Martin case, I learned from the media, and after watching the way the media slanted the story in Ferguson, I'm not sure about anything I don't see with my own eyes anymore. Before Ferguson, I didn't buy into the idea of a biased media, but now that I've seen media coverage of a major news event up close and personal, media manipulation of the facts is simply undeniable.

Still, a hired gun like Crump has a job to do, and in this case, that job was to cast Michael Brown as the hero and Darren Wilson as the villain. Unfortunately, Crump's rhetoric was damn near as caustic as Sharpton's, and it ginned up the crowd to fever pitch. Thus, day four continued the pattern of increasing violence. Protests spread to the nearby city of Clayton, the St. Louis County seat, although those protests were largely peaceful as marchers circled the county courthouse, demanding that the name of the officer who shot Brown be released, and that he be charged and prosecuted. It was at this time that calls for St. Louis county prosecutor Bob McCulloch to recuse himself began to really take off.

The main criticism of McCulloch was that because his father was a police officer who was killed in the line of duty by a black man, he couldn't be impartial. Imagine that! Bob McCulloch is an attorney who has been elected to serve an unprecedented seven four-year terms as prosecutor, and, despite twenty-five years in office, his detractors couldn't come up with a single case he had handled to criticize. Instead, the main knock against him was that he, himself, suffered too much because of a violent criminal act. But if Darren Wilson had done what he was accused of doing, wouldn't a staunch, unwavering crime victim's advocate like McCulloch be exactly the guy you'd want prosecuting the case?

While calls for McCulloch to step aside grew, at least the protests in Clayton were, more or less, nonviolent. If all of the protests had gone that way, I probably wouldn't be writing this book; but they didn't. On August 12, events in Ferguson got even uglier.

That was the day the "Hands up, don't shoot" mantra really began to take hold. The proliferation of the myth that Michael Brown had used this phrase or gesture, along with the caterwauling of Sharpton and Crump, whipped the crowd into a frenzy.

That night, the streets were overtaken by the most violent elements of the crowd. While the lion's share of the violence was directed at police, the allure of unabated looting brought out the criminal underworld. Gangbangers and other street criminals from all over the St. Louis metro area flocked to the streets of Ferguson, hoping that crimes of opportunity would present themselves. Some called it "looting tourism." It shouldn't be ignored that the opportunists' only purpose was to use the shroud of the protests to veil their looting, violence, and rioting. These same people would've likely killed Michael Brown for his tennis shoes if they'd had the chance. That the media and others portrayed these miscreants as crusaders for some just cause makes me absolutely nauseous.

As an offshoot, there were some well-armed bangers running into rival gang members in the crowd. It was a perfect environment for settling old beefs or starting new ones. So, fists flew, and ultimately, so did bullets. One of those bullets hit a young girl in the crowd in the head. All of this under the banner of "Black Lives Matter."

✪ ✪ ✪

To paraphrase FDR, "August 13, 2014, a day that will live in anarchy."

Day five was the day the anarchists from around the country arrived in Ferguson in full force. I'm talking about real-live-fist-in-the-air-advocating-for-the-overthrow-of-government revolutionaries, complete with berets, Che Guevara T-shirts, and Molotov cocktails—lots and lots of Molotov cocktails.

Now, I'm not necessarily focusing here on the militant black nationalist groups, like the New Black Panthers (NBP) and the RbG Black Rebels, when I talk about anarchists. The so-called urban militia groups were there, to be sure, and they had their own antigovernment revolutionary bent. They also had a cause, and that set them apart from the purely anarchistic groups that showed their ugly faces in Ferguson. Don't get me wrong; the urban militia groups were dangerous. The RbGs famously put out a bounty for Darren Wilson, which law enforcement took quite seriously. The New Black Panthers were disruptive and intimidating, but they just weren't the old Black Panthers. They also had a lot of internal bickering going on between the national chapter of the NBP and the local chapter that spilled out into the streets.

The bow tie–adorned Muhammadans from the Nation of Islam (NOI) were visibly present as well. Shockingly, they actually had a somewhat calming effect on the protests. They essentially tried to negotiate demands with the police as successful protest groups have done in other places over the years. I'm not saying that the NOI advocated for the sort of passive resistance Dr. King embraced, but their brand of active resistance was organized and purposeful. Had they been able to control the demonstrations, the protests probably would have conveyed an effective, sympathetic message as opposed to the violent, chaotic dissonance that we saw night after night in Ferguson.

Other local African-American groups, like the Organization for Black Struggle and the cynically named Coalition Against Police Crimes and Repression, also contributed to the commotion and misinformation campaign. As an aside, I've had to testify at the same public hearings as the Coalition Against Police Crimes and Repression, and when I do, I always say that I'm testifying on behalf of the Coalition Against Criminal Crimes and Repression. That gets a good laugh, but there is nothing funny about either of these groups. They are all about hate and turmoil, but they are so disorganized that they really didn't play much of a role in Ferguson.

No, the true anarchistic influence on the riots and protests were from the largely white fringe groups. A bunch of real patriots, these guys. A number of these anti-American anarchist groups descended on Ferguson the way the Red Army descended on Moscow a hundred years earlier. Groups such as the Revolution Club out of Chicago, and the Revolutionary Communist Party (more commonly, Rev Com), a national organization based in the San Francisco area, as well as other radical anarchist groups became very conspicuous by day five. And so did the tools of their trade.

Just like their Bolshevik progenitors, these anarchists longed for civil war and saw the chance to co-opt the protesters for their antigovernment purposes as a golden opportunity. The war on police was the perfect proxy for their long-desired war on our government; our American way of life.

For many of these anarchists, nightfall in Ferguson was like happy hour, and the cocktail they served was the namesake of long-ago Soviet diplomat Vyacheslav Molotov. As much as the anarchists wanted to serve these Molotov cocktails themselves, they knew that images on national TV of black protesters launching petrol bombs at white police officers was the quickest way to foment what they were longing for: an all-out revolution. They understood that there is nothing better than a good, old-fashioned race war to divide a nation and bring out the very, very worst in people. According to intelligence I received from interviews, they taught the protesters how to make Molotov cocktails and then provided them with guns and pipe bombs, and showed them "the right way" to burn down buildings so that there would be nothing left but rubble when they were finished.

I know a lot of people saw Ferguson as blacks versus whites. I heard white friends I had never known to say anything remotely racist say some pretty awful things about black people after the looting, rioting, and violence in Ferguson, Baltimore, and elsewhere. Likewise, some of my black friends who had never said a cross word about anyone to me uttered things about white folks that completely shocked me.

The very worst people in Ferguson, though, were these mostly white anarchist groups who stitched the thread of organized violence into the fabric of what could have eventually been peaceful protests aimed at meaningful change. Thankfully, these hatemongers didn't get the race war they were looking for. In many ways, America is just too good to be baited into that.

Even though they were ultimately unsuccessful, these unsavory, radical elements took us to the brink. I shudder to think about how close we actually came to the all-out race war they tried so hard to incite. The post-Ferguson era has been a tenuous, volatile time. At the height of the protests, gun sales in the St. Louis area were reportedly up 50 percent.[2] In and around the Canfield Green Apartments, agents from the Bureau of Alcohol, Tobacco, Firearms and Explosives (ATF) and other federal law enforcement agencies purportedly used undercover operations to buy up as many of the guns and explosives that were pouring into the area as they possibly could. Even though virtually no one was charged criminally for these unlawful transactions because it would "look bad," there can be no doubt of the intentions for those weapons: killing police officers. This was an extraordinarily combustible situation and we were, and are, incredibly fortunate that the rabble-rousers didn't get their way.

We, Americans of all creeds and colors, need to be vigilant that our fears and suspicions aren't co-opted into something worse by the subversive acts of those who want to tear our country apart.

Revcom's slogan is "Revolution—nothing less." We shouldn't let them or any other America-hating group have their way.[3]

As day five turned into night five, the streets of Ferguson looked very much like a revolution. Molotov cocktails hurtled through the air at the wall of police officers with the same "rockets' red glare" that illuminated the ramparts of Fort McHenry as it weathered the fiery onslaught of the bloodthirsty Brits. But "by the dawn's early light" our "star spangled banner," the flag of freedom, had withstood this "perilous fight" in Ferguson, just as it had at old Fort McHenry, and as it shall from now 'til the death of liberty.

✪ ✪ ✪

Day six was all about police tactics and the newly coined term "police militarization."

I like Missouri Governor Jay Nixon and US Senator Claire McCaskill. I really do. They have both been very kind and encouraging toward me over the years, and I am grateful to them for that. But still, I have to ask: *what the hell were they thinking?*

Both Jay and Claire have always been tremendously supportive of law enforcement. Claire was a gritty prosecutor from Kansas City and a no-nonsense state auditor before ascending to the US Senate. Jay served a record four terms as Missouri's attorney general, and nobody who has ever held that office has been tougher on crime. His door was always open to law enforcement during his years as AG, and that continued into his governorship.

Even after Ferguson, I continued to have intimate, earnest conversations with them both about the realities on the ground there. They both listened, but I'm not sure either one heard me. Like so many other politicians, they seemed to go tone deaf to everything but the sound and fury emanating from Ferguson. The din of media sensationalism and protest chants was hard to shout over, but I tried.

I should have probably been more critical of Jay and Claire for so readily buying into the "Hands up, don't shoot" myth, but they'd been so good to me and the entire law enforcement profession for so long, I just couldn't bring myself to harangue them publicly. Besides, hundreds of thousands of other Americans were duped by the Ferguson fairy tale, so why should they be any different?

What really aggravated me, though, was the way they both bought into the whole police militarization fabrication. What a grand distraction. What utter hogwash. Unfortunately, the majority of Americans also bought into the grand distraction about militarization, even though it was only trotted out to pivot national attention away from the unruly, lawless behavior of the angry mob that assembled for the sole purpose of making mayhem each night in Ferguson. And there wasn't a shred of truth to it.

First of all, there was virtually no DOD 1033 program equipment deployed in Ferguson. The vast majority of the armored vehicles, special weapons, and protective gear were purchased by local police departments from private vendors.

Second, and more important, the protective equipment used by law enforcement in Ferguson saved lives, a lot of them. The number of officers that had a solid projectile hit their shields or their helmets numbered into at least the hundreds, quite possibly the thousands. I also saw with my own eyes the MRAPs (Mine Resistant Ambush Protected vehicles) from multiple agencies that had been peppered with gunfire. The sides of the "BearCats"—as they are known in police parlance—were pocked with bullet marks, each representing a police funeral we were able to avert. I've been to plenty of police funerals in my career. They are heartbreaking, gut-wrenching events. Perhaps if more of the many elected officials who attended Michael Brown's funeral had attended a police funeral at some point in their political careers, they would have had a greater appreciation for the solemn duty cops perform, and the sanctity of their sacrifice when they risk their lives in the service of others, all too often with life-ending consequences.

I've appeared on *CNN Tonight* more than any of the other cable news shows. The host, Don Lemon, who is African-American, also did extensive work as a correspondent during the initial civil unrest. Don seemed to me at first to be heavily slanted toward the agitators in the protests, but the longer he reported on Ferguson, the more he got what was happening there, and in the end, I think he did some of the very best reporting that came out of the debacle. His approach seemed more candid than a lot of the other anchors reporting on Ferguson. Don and I talked frequently off camera, far more than any of the other cable guys, and he always seemed more earnest about trying to understand the cops' perspective than anyone else I talked to in the media. On a personal level, you can't help but like him.

I did a panel interview with Don Lemon on *CNN Tonight* live in Ferguson during the riots that followed the grand jury decision. CNN political analyst and Wiki-dubbed "social justice activist" Marc Lamont Hill was still ranting and raving about militarization even as dozens of buildings smoldered behind us at the hands of angry rioters, who were left unchecked because of the timidity over militarization criticism that prevented the full deployment the National Guard.

Marc, as he so often does, sucked the air out of the six-minute interview talking much longer than the other three of us on the panel combined. When they finally got to me, with about twenty seconds left in the segment, I had had enough, "Marc's won me over," I mocked. "I actually now blame the fire department for the fires last night and their over-militarized response. They were wearing helmets and pro-tective gear, and I understand that the fire trucks are the same kind of fire trucks they use in the Army. I mean, this is ludicrous that we keep blaming the police for the actions of the mob." Don had to go directly to commercial to keep a straight face, but the analogy was indisputable then, and it is indisputable now.

It doesn't seem to matter, though. The term "police militarization" appears to be a permanent part of the English vocabulary now, and day six was all about emphasizing that theme. Senator McCaskill pronounced that the police response had "amplified tensions," saying that "militarization of the police escalated the protesters' response."[4] It was an unfair assessment, to be certain. Claire continues to carry forth this demilitarization torch, much to my dismay. When she talks about it, she sounds just like Jan Brady ("Marcia, Marcia, Marcia!"): *Militarization, militarization, militarization.*

She wasn't alone. Even Ferguson police chief Tom Jackson declared, "We're going to talk about not only the tactics but the appearance."[5] The word *appearance* was synonymous with the idea of "bad optics" that had emerged in Ferguson.

I have to admit that even I scratched my head when I saw St. Louis County Police snipers on top of BearCats, fixing their scoped rifles on the crowds in Ferguson during the early days of the protests. It was more than bad optics; it seemed at first blush to be bad tactics. For cops, pointing your weapon at someone usually means you have good reason to use deadly force. St. Louis County police chief Jon Belmar was a former SWAT guy, so I worried he was being a little overzealous, or maybe a lot overzealous.

I sought out some SWAT guys I know to try to better understand what was going on. They looked at me like I was an idiot and told me the snipers could better pinpoint the muzzle flash from the many shots being fired from within the crowd by using the infrared on their scopes.

The explanation made perfect sense, but have you ever heard it? We certainly know the media didn't report it. I still wonder why politicians, or particularly, members of the media didn't do what I did and just ask. In fairness, I suppose Chief Belmar could have explained what he was doing, but maybe he thought that would be giving away too much tactical information. Nevertheless, maybe pulling the scopes off the rifles or moving the snipers to rooftops would have been a better approach. But instead of asking why snipers with scopes were pointing their guns at the crowd, the media turned a logical response to keeping officers—and the public—safe in the midst of multiple shots fired into a Tiananmen Square–like narrative. By focusing so much attention on the snipers and armored vehicles, and so little on the elements fomenting violence and popping off gunshots that endangered officers and innocent bystanders alike, they fed the narrative of the police being in *opposition* to the people, instead of being *protectors* of the people. In the end, though, if it saved a single cop's or innocent protester's life, it was worth it. I've said a hundred times: I'm never going to second-guess the tactical commanders on the ground. They have situational awareness that's just not available to me or anyone else.

The debate over tactics in Ferguson finally ensnared me on day six. St. Louis City police chief Sam Dotson called to let me know he was pulling city SWAT units out of Ferguson because he was concerned about the tactics the county police were using. That was fine; it was his prerogative to do so. He also assured me that he and Chief Belmar were having extensive conversations behind closed doors about the way things were being executed.

Then, the proverbial shit hit the fan. One of the aldermen Chief Dotson briefed about the goings-on in Ferguson leaked the information to the *St. Louis Post-Dispatch*. The story included a quote from Dotson saying, "My gut told me what I was seeing were not tactics that I would use in the city and I would never put officers in situations that I would not do myself."[6]

Both city and county police officers were furious with Dotson about what had become very public criticism of our comrades-in-arms who were then left in harm's way by the second-guessing the article highlighted. Even though I blamed Alderman Kennedy for leaking the information more than I blamed Chief Dotson for making the call to withdraw the troops, I called the chief and told him I was going to have to take him to the woodshed over the now-public remarks. Chief Dotson took it in stride and said he understood why we had to openly criticize the move. The chief has broader shoulders than some people give him credit for.

Ultimately, St. Louis SWAT units were back on the ground in Ferguson within a couple of days in response to the outcry by the FOP.

I spent a lot of time trying to do damage control with the troops that day. I was on the phone all afternoon with the president of the St. Louis County Police Association (who is one of my closest friends), trying to calm him down. I made trips to the command posts in Ferguson and downtown St. Louis. Then, I capped the day off with a summit that state senator Jamilah Nasheed had convened.

Now, as often as I've been called a "racist pig" by the protesters, you would expect me to reflexively despise anyone with a name like Jamilah Nasheed. In fact, Senator Nasheed and I are friends. We served together in the Missouri House of Representatives and were suite mates for two years when I was the minority whip. I liked her moxie and her work ethic, and we often talked late into the night when we were two of the only legislators still at work in our capitol offices.

She being a community activist who grew up in the projects and spent time in juvie for stabbing another girl,[7] and I being a longtime cop, made for a peculiar relationship. We were more like a cat and a dog sniffing curiously at one another, each trying to understand the oddities of the other. But I believe the time we spent together gave us each a greater appreciation for where the other had come from.

Still, I don't want there to be any mistake about this: we agreed on almost nothing when it came to policing in America. She instinctively blamed the cops when something went wrong; I instinctively blamed the crooks. I always considered my way of thinking to be more mainstream, but she seems to speak for the majority in the post-Ferguson era. I guess she's a better politician than I am. I remain unmoved by public opinion in this regard. The cops get it right tens of thousands of times every day in this country for each time they get one thing wrong.

In any event, I gladly accepted the invite to Jamilah's summit. I thought it was productive. It was attended by a bipartisan mix of local and state officials, and the conversation was a cordial, sincere attempt to make sense of what was going on around us. The *Missouri Times*, the premier political publication in the Show Me State, sent a reporter who live-tweeted from the summit:

Collin Reischman @Collin_MOTimes

@SenatorNasheed meeting includes @Eric_Schmitt @pennyhub-bard @ScottSifton @RoordaJ @venglund @SpeakerTimJones @MargoMcNeil #ferguson

Collin Reischman @Collin_MOTimes

@RoordaJ : "we need a bridge between law enforcement and the community. They don't always understand each other."

11:20 PM - 14 Aug 14

If only all of the dialogue around Ferguson had been as sober as the Nasheed summit, tensions there might have eased sooner. But Senator Nasheed ended up being one of the most vocal police antagonists to emerge from the Ferguson movement. I think her heart was in the right place, but the things she said were just downright irresponsible and they endangered the cops that I toiled to protect.

I was furious with the way she conducted herself, but I tried to remember how different her perspective and life experiences were than mine. On November 22, 2014, just before the grand jury verdict was announced, she was returning home from a rally in Ferguson when a young, black man tried to carjack her.[8] Some cops—a lot of cops—reveled in the irony of the number one advocate for young, black males being the victim of a dangerous crime perpetrated by one.

I took no joy in it. I found out about it before the media even got their hands on the story and texted her to make sure she was all right:

Me: Are you okay?

Jamilah: I'm angry right now but I'm okay!

Me: Just be careful. You know I love you despite our differences.

Jamilah: Likewise!

I think that sums it up well. People actually can disagree without their differences turning into hatred.

Governor Nixon's press conference provided the biggest news of day six. Again, in keeping with the anti-militarization theme, Governor Nixon announced he was relieving the Ferguson and St. Louis County Police Departments of operational command and bringing in the Missouri Highway Patrol to take over. He said there would be an "operational shift," and that law enforcement would "step back a little bit," and he installed Highway Patrol captain Ron Johnson to oversee operations in Ferguson. It was reminiscent of the demoralizing feeling the Brits must have felt when General Montgomery was replaced as commander of the Allied ground forces by General Eisenhower during World War II. But, Captain Johnson was no Ike.

Law enforcement in the St. Louis area seethed over the slap-in-the-face change in command. St. Louis County prosecutor Bob McCulloch summed it up well when he carped, "To denigrate the men and women of the county police department is shameful."[9]

My phone rang off the hook with calls from members of the Highway Patrol rank and file gushing apologies for the unforgivable transgression of esprit de corps that the coronation of Captain Johnson represented. They were also mortified by the way Johnson conducted himself.

Johnson, who is African-American, grew up near Ferguson and was heralded as the hometown boy returned to his native land as savior of the masses. What a crock of shit.

Johnson immediately joined in the "Hands up, don't shoot," "anti-militarization," "de-escalation" chorus that completely ignored the dynamics and danger of the swelling mob in Ferguson.

In the early evening hours on day six, Captain Johnson or, as he came to be known by the troops, "Captain Hug-A-Thug," led a march through the heart of Ferguson, walking side by side with some of the very same people who had shot at police and hurled Molotov cocktails at the garrison line. Not to say that there weren't some clergy and peaceful demonstrators walking alongside of him too, but talk about your bad optics! How is a commander supposed to garner the respect of his subordinates when his very first act is consorting with the enemy? Ike wouldn't have walked through the streets of Paris with Pierre Laval, Philippe Pétain, and the other Vichy French.

I know that criticism sounds divisive and hawkish, and the word *enemy* sounds inflammatory. News Flash: THIS WAS A WAR ON POLICE. (Refer to the front cover of the book if you haven't figured that out yet.)

As it turned out, night six was by far the most peaceful night since the Brown shooting. I remember thinking to myself, *I hate Johnson's approach, but if this actually quells the violence and makes it safer for cops deployed to Ferguson, I'm all for it.* Alas, it was a fragile, short-lived détente.

THE MAN WHO SHOT LIBERTY VALANCE

My favorite Jimmy Stewart movie and my favorite John Wayne movie happen to be the same film, *The Man Who Shot Liberty Valance*. I remember thinking about that film when the *New Yorker* published a story (or, more accurately, an ambush hit piece) about Darren Wilson, titled "The Man Who Shot Michael Brown."[1] The similarities were spooky. *The Man Who Shot Liberty Valance* was a story of the collision of wide-eyed idealism with the harsh reality of brute force. Wasn't Ferguson about the same thing?

Stewart's character, Ranse Stoddard, ultimately enjoys fame and success on the strength of his legendary status as the man who gunned down the outlaw Valance. That's where the similarities end. Darren Wilson, it seems, will suffer quite a different fate than Stoddard.

For those of you who have seen the movie, you know that Stoddard didn't actually shoot Valance. It was John Wayne's character, Tom

Doniphan, who did. At the end of the movie, Stoddard reveals the truth about the famous shootout to a newspaperman. After hearing the whole story, though, the reporter trashes the piece, famously saying, "This is the West, sir. When the legend becomes fact, print the legend."[2]

Again, the similarities are eerie, except in this case, the good guy was villainized and the bad guy was immortalized. In Ferguson, the legend most certainly became the "fact" despite all evidence to the contrary.

Day seven was the day that Darren Wilson became "The Man Who Shot Michael Brown."

I don't fault Ferguson Police Chief Tom Jackson for releasing Darren's name. Even though I had unsuccessfully filed legislation in the Missouri House to prohibit the release of names of officers involved in shootings unless they were charged criminally, I understood why Tom did it. The fervor from the crowd to release the name of the officer involved in the shooting seemed to be fueling a lot of the violence by protesters. That placed cops and citizens alike in danger.

Tom didn't yet realize that the protest leaders' lamentations were meant to be intentionally moving targets. Every time he or any other police official tried to kick the football with the intent of mollifying the mob, the goal posts moved. In the end, his placation was lost on the insatiable horde.

I should mention here that I am a big fan of Tom Jackson. We worked together in the 1990s when we were assigned to drug task forces in neighboring counties. He is a good man and a helluva cop who doesn't deserve all of this. In many ways, Tom handled the Brown shooting just as police agencies had handled officer-involved shootings for decades. There was no way for him to know that the ground had shifted beneath his feet, and that the old way of doing things was suddenly unacceptable. Tom Jackson, for all intents and purposes, became the "canary in the coal mine" for law enforcement. And the mine was full of explosive gases.

At the same press conference where Jackson released Wilson's name, he also revealed to the world that Brown and Dorian Johnson had allegedly been involved in a strong-arm robbery at the Ferguson Market.

The throngs of people who had portrayed Brown as an innocent victim now had to reconcile that concocted depiction against the disturbing video of Brown forcibly stealing the cigars and menacing the store clerk.

Whew! That should be the end of all this nonsense, I thought when I saw the damning video.

Boy, was I wrong. The mouthpieces for the protesters immediately screamed, "Character assassination!"

Huh?! I always thought character assassination was when you made crap up about people, not when you showed an unedited, unabridged video of their own unflattering criminal behavior. But what do I know?

Well, surely the good news was that protesters would at least be satisfied that the police had acquiesced to their demands to release the name of the officer and any video the police had.

Ummm, not so much.

Night seven was a colossal shit storm.

Rioting, looting, and arson returned to the streets of Ferguson with a vengeance. The fires weren't just limited to Ferguson this time. Looters also torched five or six buildings in St. Louis that night as the turmoil spilled across jurisdictional lines.

Among the buildings that were set ablaze in Ferguson were a beauty shop, a Domino's Pizza and the Ferguson Market. That's right, the Ferguson Market, the store Brown had knocked over for smokes. *Take that, Mr. Store Clerk!* That'll teach you to have the nerve to report a crime and the foresight to install a camera that captured it on video.

By the way, can you imagine the mob's reaction if Brown had been publicly accused of a robbery and there hadn't been video of the crime? The radical cop-haters among their ranks would have been in complete denial. As it was, there were plenty of folks who claimed, and still do to this day, that the video is doctored or photoshopped. These are the very same people who demand the head of a police officer on a skewer whenever a dash cam or body cam shows something that can be interpreted as bad conduct by the officers. Holy double standards, Batman!

Despite my high hopes, the laissez-faire approach that Captain

Johnson had successfully employed the night before completely back-fired on him on night seven.

Shocker!

To extract their comrades, troopers had to fire tear gas into a crowd of angry demonstrators who had surrounded fellow officers. The Highway Patrol officers were in full retreat on the orders of Captain Johnson. The white flag gambit had disastrous outcomes.

It may sound as though I'm being hypercritical of Captain Johnson. I don't mean to be. While I wasn't happy with his tactics, I don't blame him for the rioting, looting, and arson. I blame the rioters, looters, and arsonists for that. What a novel thought.

Throughout the languishing debate over what precipitated the civil disobedience in and around Ferguson and in other places around the nation, there is this nagging presupposition that the police could have done something different that would have averted the violence, the destruction, and the acrimony.

I've said it a dozen times in TV interviews, but apparently I am the only one keen to this phenomenon: The police changed their tactics almost every night in almost every place that saw post-Ferguson social upheaval, but the outcome—no matter what tactic police utilized—was always the same: violence, arson, looting, rioting, shots fired, and so on.

The proof is in the pudding. The absurdity of suggesting that the crowd's bad behavior stemmed from police being overaggressive or under-aggressive is beyond my comprehension. People are responsible for their own behavior, and they ought to be held accountable for it.

That is what cops do best: hold people accountable for their actions. If you let cops do their job, if you let them perform the essence of what they are called upon by society to do, citizens and communities will be safer and things will be better. If you don't, criminals will act with impunity and, as we've seen in so many places since Ferguson, things will be worse.

This will sound crass or heavy-handed to some, but it is an irrefut-able truth: the world was a better place when people were afraid of their parents, their teachers, and the cops.

5

MICHAEL AHERN
REINCARNATE

Day eight, Saturday, August 16, was the one-week anniversary of the death of Michael Brown, and one thing had become very clear to me: law enforcement was getting its ass kicked in the media.

I had been to the command post on multiple occasions to make sure my officers were well nourished and well equipped. I had also been getting regular situational briefings in both my capacity as a state representative and in my role as the police union business agent. But that Saturday was the first time I had, in the light of day, physically surveyed the area of Ferguson where the protests and rioting had occurred.

It was stunning to see how confined the actual area of involvement was, encompassing no more than three or four blocks on West Florissant Road near the intersection of Canfield. To watch the sensational local and national TV news coverage, you would have thought the entire

9

city of Ferguson, perhaps even the entire St. Louis region, was ablaze. But, there I was, standing on a parking lot, looking up and down the thoroughfare, simply astounded by the very finite area to which the civil unrest had been limited. It was smoke and cameras, an ever-so-slight variation on the phenomenon of smoke and mirrors.

But I wasn't there in the battle zone, behind "enemy lines," to gawk. I was there to set the record straight in the national media.

Brown had died on the previous Saturday, and I didn't hear from anyone but the local press over that weekend. The minute I walked into work at the business offices of the St. Louis Police Officers Association that Monday, though, the situation was very different. The phones were ringing off the hook with calls from national media outlets.

As I explained to those who called, the SLPOA is an affiliate of the Fraternal Order of Police, Lodge 68, to be exact. FOP Lodge 68 only represents police officers with the St. Louis Metropolitan Police Department and the Lambert International Airport Police Department. Our sister lodge, FOP Lodge 15, represents police officers in the Missouri suburbs that surround the city of St. Louis, which includes police officers with the Ferguson and St. Louis County police departments.

Even though I am also a member of FOP Lodge 15, I was in no position to speak on their behalf, so I clarified the distinction in field of membership to reporters who called and gave them the phone number for Lodge 15.

Unlike Lodge 68, which deals with only one employer, the City of St. Louis, Lodge 15 represents officers employed by about one hundred different police departments ranging from crime-plagued urban communities to sleepy rural hamlets. Because of its sprawling, diverse membership, Lodge 15 spends a lot more time in court than Lodge 68, mostly defending its members from unfriendly employers of the police officers it represents. Free legal defense is an included benefit that comes with membership in the FOP. Consequently, in order to handle the high volume of courtroom work, Lodge 15 employs two in-house attorneys rather than a single business manager like Lodge 68.

The reason this is important is because the two attorneys for Lodge 15 do pretty much everything for that union, including acting as its spokespersons. Since Darren Wilson was a member of Lodge 15 at the time of the shooting, both of the in-house attorneys for Lodge 15 would be representing Darren if criminal charges were filed. As a result, they were in no position to speak to the press.

Every media outlet I had ever heard of, and several I hadn't, were calling my office, seeking comment. I would give them the number to Lodge 15, but they weren't talking. The reporters would call me back, begging for me to put them in touch with "somebody."

While I completely understood the position that Lodge 15's attorneys were in, and agreed with their keeping silent, I suggested early on that maintaining radio silence was a very bad idea. With each passing day of lopsided, often slanted media coverage, I became more and more convinced I was right. The leadership of the local, state, and even the national FOP frequently bemoaned the one-sided reporting coming out of Ferguson, to which I would consistently respond, "If we don't speak out on behalf of law enforcement, then no one is going to hear the other side of this story."

It took a while, but once Darren Wilson's name was released on August 15, the reality of my caution against a media blackout finally broke through with those who were initially timid about our organization getting out in front of cameras on behalf of the rank-and-file cops we represented.

With the blessing of Lodge 15's attorneys, we decided to divvy up the duties between Kevin Ahlbrand, president of the Missouri FOP; Gabe Crocker, president of the St. Louis County Police Association; Joe Steiger, president of the St. Louis Police Officers Association; Neil Bruntrager, general counsel for the St. Louis Police Officers Association; and me. All four of my fellow spokesmen are close friends of mine. They are all bright and passionate about defending the good names of police officers everywhere. I trusted each of them unconditionally to do the right thing, and to do well in their advocacy for law enforcement. None of them disappointed me.

The five of us were inundated with requests from print, radio, and television media, both local and national, and particularly from the cable news giants. Fox, CNN, MSNBC, Al Jazeera America, BBC America and more all had correspondents on the ground, feeding the grumbling gut of the mighty twenty-four-hour news monster.

So there I was, in the heart of Ferguson on August 16, surrendering myself to the belly of the beast. I was doing my first cable appearance on a CNN Saturday morning show called *Smerconish*. I had no idea what a Smerconish was. My campaign manager Ryan Burke, who drove me to the interview, quipped that it sounded like a kind of bodily fluid. Eww!

It turns out it wasn't a what; it was a who: Michael Smerconish.

I have to admit that even though I ultimately did more than seventy-five cable news interviews about Ferguson and its aftermath, before the Michael Brown shooting I was never much of a consumer of cable news. It was something I watched when I was walking through a room when someone else had the channel tuned to cable news, not something I ever turned on of my own free will. I generally got my news from print sources.

So, despite his CNN show and his nationally syndicated radio show, I didn't know who Michael Smerconish was. Although not nearly as well known as Anderson Cooper or Bill O'Reilly, Michael ended up being one of my favorite hosts. He had me on his TV and radio show multiple times, and I enjoyed each one. Alas, I suppose there's something special about your first.

Seriously, though, Michael was very kind to me. I eventually learned he had written a book about the murder of Philadelphia police officer Danny Faulkner, one of the most notorious police killings in U.S. history. When I shared with Michael that I was considering writing this book, he not only encouraged me; he went so far as to put me in touch with his agent. Class act, that Michael Smerconish.

That first interview went really well. I was on-screen with Lewis Reed, the president of the St. Louis Board of Aldermen. Lewis, an

African-American politician, and I had always had a warm relationship. We embraced on the parking lot across the street from the Ferguson Police Department as we met on the way to the satellite truck. It was a sharp contrast to the racial divide that had been playing out on that very same street for the seven days that preceded our encounter. Our mutual affection didn't keep me from barely letting Lewis get a word in edgewise on the broadcast. I had a lot to say. Rank-and-file law enforcement hadn't gotten a chance to say much up until that point.

My campaign manager looked on, chomping on his fingernails. He was extremely nervous about me slipping up and having what we jokingly referred to as a "Colonel Jessup moment," and he was quite relieved that I made it through the entire interview without uttering the words "Code red," or "You can't handle the truth," or shouting, "You need me on that wall!"

✪ ✪ ✪

That next day, Sunday, August 17, I got a call from a reporter with the local NBC affiliate in St. Louis. The station had aired a story about Darren Wilson two days earlier and had shown his home on camera. This angered cops and police supporters alike. Within a couple of days there was a "Boycott KSDK Channel 5 News" Facebook page with nearly thirty thousand "likes." The KSDK reporter was beside herself over the station's editorial gaff. She and I had done a lot of stories together over the years, and I trusted her. She told me the station wanted to do a pro-police story to make up for their indiscreet judgment.

I was reluctant at first, but after I thought about it, it occurred to me that it was an opportunity to get some help to the St. Louis Police Wives Association. The wives' organization had traditionally come to the aid of any St. Louis City police officer experiencing a time of need. But two of the police wives worked as dispatchers with the Ferguson Police Department, so it was natural for them to expand their borders after seeing the calamitous circumstances that police were exposed to in Ferguson.

The wives had been feeding and hydrating hundreds of police officers a day in Ferguson for a solid week (little did we know at the time that this would go on for months after). I had raised some money for them, but their funds were quickly dwindling, so I thought that it was a great chance to get in front of a camera and talk about the need for donations to the police wives. I also thought this was a good venue for sharing the police perspective on Ferguson and humanizing police in the wake of the dreadful way they'd been cast in the media.

Knowing this would be a hard sell for my executive board, I sent them an e-mail so they would understand where I was coming from in breaking the boycott of KSDK:

> A KSDK reporter contacted the association tonight asking for an on-camera interview about Ferguson. We initially declined, citing displeasure with the station showing Officer Wilson's home on their newscast. The program manager called later to personally apologize over the broadcast images. He provided us with a written apology that had already been provided to the Ferguson Police and asked us to post it on our website for our officers to see. The station agreed to make the story about the police perspective of the Ferguson situation, and what a great job police had done in using the level of restraint they had in this chaotic ordeal. We saw this as an opportunity to discourage the media behavior that KSDK engaged in, and to put a positive spin on the police response in Ferguson and we agreed to the interview which is scheduled to air at 10 p.m.

I got the go-ahead, and as it turned out, I thought the story was a win-win for police and the police wives.

✪ ✪ ✪

My grandmother was a product of the Great Depression. No matter how long they lived, folks who survived those troubled economic times never wasted anything. My grandma was the epitome of that postdepression "waste not, want not" quality.

As children, we dared not throw away a jelly jar. Those got washed and put into Ruthie's pantry to be used as juice glasses. Oh, and you know those little slivers of bar soap that are left when you've lathered your way to the end of the soap's useful existence? Granny had a plastic bag in the bathroom closet where she kept those. Once she had accumulated enough of them, she would use her herculean strength—she was wiry for such a petite woman—to compress them into a brand-new bar of conglomerated soap slivers. Houseguests would often stare in bewilderment at the multi-colored mosaic in the soap dish that very much resembled a handful of crayons that had been left in the sun too long.

Then, there was the bread; my God, the bread. Never, ever would anyone throw away a stale piece of bread in my grandmother's home and live to tell about it. She had big plans for that bread. Don't get me wrong, if it was just a little bit stale, it could be popped into the toaster in the morning. No one would notice that it was past its shelf life as they smeared it with jelly—"Don't throw away that jar, Jeffrey!"—but if it was too stale, it was repurposed in a whole new way: bird feed.

Grandma would methodically break the bread into bite-size morsels and head to the backyard, where she would cast the scraps about for the nourishment of her beloved birds. Old Ruthie adored birds. She would watch in sheer delight as the delicate winged creatures swooped down toward her stale offerings. They would seemingly come from nowhere. Every size, shape, and color of avian would descend on that tiny south St. Louis yard: sparrows, blue jays, robins, cardinals, wrens, and, of course, crows. Oh, the murder of crows, crowding out the little birdies so they could have the entire booty of crispy crumbs for themselves.

It was a feeding frenzy, with the nimble, smaller birds trying to stay one hop ahead of the larger birds as they all pecked desperately at the desiccated discards.

That's what the makeshift media village that had converged on Ferguson reminded me of. Every media outlet that could afford a tank of gas sent a correspondent, or in the case of some of the big "crows," a fleet of satellite trucks.

Many species of birds eat twice their body weight in a single day. That is the same voracious, insatiable appetite that typified the reporters who dove after every morsel of Ferguson-related news they could get their beaks on. They were very much like the frenzied, desperate peckers that flocked to my grandma's backyard. Yes, I said it . . . the media swarm in Ferguson reminded me of "desperate peckers."

I guess that made me a breadcrumb, because the requests for interviews just kept coming, nonstop. Radio and print were easy. You could do them over the phone. The on-camera interviews, those took some time and required you to travel to war-torn eastern Ferguson.

That's where I ended up on Tuesday, August 19. I had scheduled appearances on two CNN news shows: *The Lead with Jake Tapper* and *AC-360* with Anderson Cooper. I have to say, I was on the defensive when I stepped up to the mic with these two anchors. I expected to be peppered with gotcha questions. That's not what happened, though. There were some probing questions about police tactics; you know: militarization, blah, blah, blah. But by and large, Tapper and Cooper were both courteous and seemed to be genuinely appreciative of the opportunity to get a police perspective from somebody close to the story. There were some real scumbag reporters covering Ferguson, but I found Tapper and Cooper to be legitimate journalists trying to get a true sense of what was unfolding there.

I thought it was a significant victory to finally have a chance to illuminate the law enforcement perspective for a national audience. My campaign manager, however, who also accompanied me to those interviews, was in a blind panic.

First and foremost, he was worried about my safety. I was very unpopular with the protesters, and by the time I finished with *AC-360*, night was falling. The cops deployed to Ferguson called sundown "shift change" because you could see the local Ferguson residents filtering out, and the professional, out-of-town demonstrators shuffling in. These traveling agitators were there to wreak havoc, and you could see that the vast majority of the peaceful protesters who marched during the day headed for the hills when it got dark. Just like the rest of us, they knew trouble was coming.

My campaign manager knew it too, and wanted to get me the hell out of there. Ryan was more than just a longtime member of my campaign staff; he had become one of my best friends. As we walked to the car, he chided me for agreeing to the interviews given the risks to my safety and the dangers to my political career. "No more interviews," he commanded with a determined look on his face.

Then, from behind us came a soft, sultry voice, "Representative Roorda?" We wheeled around to see one of the prettiest women either of us had ever seen. She was a producer for one of the cable morning news shows, and she had just seen my interview on CNN. She begged me to come on the show she worked for the next day.

"Well," I said as I rubbed the back of my neck, "Ryan here just said—"

"Do you have a card?" Ryan interrupted as he moved between me and the pretty young producer. She obligingly handed him her business card. "Why don't you jot down your cell number on the back," he suggested. She did so gladly.

As we drove away in Ryan's car, I stared at him, shaking my head in silent disapproval. He finally saw me out of the corner of his eye, and, without a word, rolled down the window and tossed the card. "No more interviews," he sighed, with a dejected look on his face.

While I continued to do interviews with newspaper reporters and radio hosts along with local TV news, that was the last cable TV interview I did until after my state senate election was over. They kept inviting me on, but Ryan and the rest of my campaign staff thought it was too great a risk to continue to work the cable news circuit. I strongly disagreed, but I ceded to their wishes, a decision I now regret. That's on me, though; it was my decision to make. Mine alone.

For the next two and a half months, I spent a lot of time screaming at the TV as one reporter after another got things wrong in Ferguson. But I felt I could do more to help law enforcement by winning my election than I could by making a few more TV appearances in front of a national audience. Still, it was hard to watch the misreporting that went on in the meantime.

This brings me back to ol' Mrs. O'Leary and her famous cow. Earlier in this book, I used the story of Mrs. O'Leary's cow as an analogy for the carnage Dorian Johnson wrought on Ferguson—and really, America— with the fantastic story that spread like wildfire once he kicked it off.

Comparing Johnson to Mrs. O'Leary's cow seems like the perfect metaphor. There's only one problem: it never happened. The whole story of the pyromaniacal heifer was an artifice. It was made up.

I know, I know; heresy, you say!

The origin story of the Great Chicago Fire is a part of Americana, a beloved passage that has held a prominent place in U.S. history books for more than 150 years. Certainly such a well-chronicled version of events must be true, right?

Unfortunately, the urban legend of O'Leary's ungainly ungulate is just that, a legend, a fable, a canard. It is perhaps America's first urban legend.

I bet you'll never guess how this urban legend started. That's right: THE MEDIA!

In an unprecedented case of yellow journalism, a reporter named Michael Ahern with the *Chicago Republican* fabricated the account of the origin of the 1871 blaze that engulfed the Windy City. Even 144 years ago, it was hard to compete with the big newspaper in town, the *Chicago Tribune*, so stringers with other papers, like Ahern, had to avail themselves of broad editorial license if they were going to scoop the *Trib*.

There is little doubt that the great fire started in the vicinity of the O'Leary homestead on DeKoven Street, so why not just print a headline like: "Destructive Fire Started on DeKoven Street"?

Because it's boring, that's why.

Ahern wanted to pen an article that would grip the hearts and minds of the families of the hundreds of fatalities and the tens of thousands of people who lost their homes. Imagine the provocative imagery of a carelessly unattended lantern left within bucking distance of a cow. Better yet, pin the rap on a drunken old Irish hag.

That's right. This is a case of race-baiting that would put the reporters in Ferguson to shame. The Irish were much despised in post–Civil War America. The open discrimination and hatred toward the recently immigrated "Micks" was unabashed. Where the hell was Eric Holder when the "Paddys" needed him? He could have written a five-thousand-page DOJ report on the pervasive "hibernophobia" that characterized the latter half of the nineteenth century. Heck, he wouldn't have even had to manipulate out-of-context-traffic-stop statistics to issue a scathing report on the "Gaelic-bashing" that went on for decades in America.

It was no accident that Ahern zeroed in on the O'Leary residence as the spark of the fire. He exploited the stereotypes and the dislike of the Irish with a story that implied that the Irish lived in close quarters with their cattle, were careless, and were addled by their whiskey.

Sex sells, but xenophobia zings!

Nevertheless, some forty years later, Ahern, who in his declining years had crawled into a bottle himself, ultimately copped to the false narrative in a story that ran in, of all places, the *Chicago Tribune* in 1911. I guess he had a guilty conscience.

Let's just hope that it doesn't take forty years for the reporters who mischaracterized what happened in Ferguson to have an attack of conscience and cop to their irresponsible reporting.

Despite my newly minted disdain for journalists that resulted from the bedazzled media coverage of the Ferguson story, one of my most enjoyable duties as the business manager for the St. Louis police union was, itself, journalistic.

Each month I penned a column for our newspaper, the *Gendarme* (*gendarme* is the French word for police). The paper goes out to about five thousand active and retired police officers and police widows. Writing my column gave me great personal satisfaction and served as a sort of creative release. I had long written fiction as a personal hobby, but that was strictly therapeutic and self-indulgent, not at all meant for public consumption.

My column, though, was an opinion piece that would be read by my supporters and detractors alike, so I put a lot of effort into it.

The *Gendarme* comes out at the beginning of the month, so I generally tried to have my articles written and in the hands of the editor by the middle of the preceding month to give him time to review my submission and get it to the publisher and the printer.

The Ferguson events had put me way behind deadline, so when I finally sat down to scratch out my September column, I was under the gun. Of course, I was mentally preoccupied with Ferguson, and what I saw as a rewriting of history going on right before my very eyes.

What really happened to Darren Wilson and how law enforcement really responded to the civil unrest in Ferguson, and the realization that both would become casualties of history, was personally very upsetting. As I mused about how the record could be set right, my thoughts turned to my longtime neighbor, famed syndicated radio host Paul Harvey.

I had the opportunity to meet Harvey several times over the years. As the crow flies, he lived about a half a mile away from the house I grew up in. Harvey was a regular fixture in the nearby river town of Kimmswick, where I would eventually become the chief of police and city administrator. Harvey would regularly show up at the Apple Butter Festival to make an appearance as the celebrity churner. He was as mesmerizing in person as he was on the radio.

Harvey had a quirky but captivating way of retelling stories of Americana. He had a hypnotic cadence and a compelling style of weaving a yarn. He retold historical events with more detail, context, and plot twists than anyone I had ever heard before, or since. His tagline rang true with me and seemed apropos to the situation unfolding in nearby Ferguson. I felt compelled to invoke the specter of Paul Harvey in what would turn out to be the first of twelve monthly columns I would write on the subject of Ferguson and its aftermath. Here it is:

THE REST OF THE STORY[1]

Legendary syndicated radio host Paul Harvey used to end his in-depth segments with the tagline, ". . . and now you know the rest of the story."

I can't imagine what Paul Harvey would think of the media coverage of the Ferguson riots that we just lived through.

I say "lived through" because it is amazing that no police officer got killed in the violent aftermath of the shooting of robbery suspect, Michael Brown. There was an organized effort to injure and kill police officers who responded to (not provoked, but responded to) the violent demonstrations in Ferguson. Shots were fired, Molotov cocktails were thrown, and bricks and bottles were hurled at the heads of police officers for over two weeks.

Despite the media coverage that attempted to lay the blame for the vicious attacks on law enforcement at the feet of a "militarized police response," the truth is that the police were on a peacekeeping mission that was an astounding success given the chaos of the mob scene after dark. No rioter, looter, reporter, or peaceful protester was injured as a result of the police response.

The tactical commanders on the ground reassessed their strategic response daily, sometimes hourly, and changed their tactics in response to the aggressive behavior of the crowd that gathered after dark over and over again. The clear evidence that it was the agitators, not the police, who provoked the violence was that no matter what tactics law enforcement employed, the instigators responded the same way, with violence aimed at hurting and killing police, and which placed peaceful protesters and citizens of Ferguson in harm's way.

Despite the deadly force used by the mobs over and over again, police responded exclusively with less-than-lethal force. The restraint used by law enforcement was nothing short of amazing, and every officer who served a tour of duty in Ferguson should be commended.

Rather than commend, the media and politicians chose to condemn. They chose to try Darren Wilson in the streets of Ferguson before even the first detail or piece of evidence was released. They chose to label the protective gear as "militaristic" despite the fact that had they not donned it, police officers would have died.

Have they no shame?!

Despite the relentless, sensationalized coverage of this unprecedented chapter of violence against the police; despite the fact that history will probably remember the police response in a distorted, negative way; despite the fact that the world changed forever for police and the way we do the business of protecting the citizenry on August 9; for the police that took part in the response in Ferguson, it was your finest hour. Hold your heads high and don't let the reporters and the politicians and the cop-haters that you go to work every day to keep safe, tell you any different.

Paul Harvey lived only a half a mile from the home that I grew up in. I had the chance to meet him and talk to him on several occasions. He's gone now, but there will be another Paul Harvey someday . . . a voice of reason that comes across the airwaves with a calm, introspective, honest analysis of what really happened in Ferguson, Missouri, in 2014; of what really led to the shooting of Michael Brown; of what the forensic evidence revealed at the crime scene; of the reality on the ground in the wake of riots, looting, and unprecedented violence against police; of the political failures (not the actions of police) that led to the hopelessness, crime, and violence that characterizes so many communities across the country just like Ferguson.

Someday, a courageous voice will tell the real story of Ferguson with the honest, raw, ferocious dedication to the truth that characterized Paul Harvey's broadcast, and then the world will know "the rest of the story."

6

BROKEN ARROW

et's recap what we knew by August 16, the one-week anniversary
of Brown's death: A hulking, eighteen-year-old black teen had
forcefully stolen some cigarillos from a local convenience store. He
was stopped by a white police officer. The teen was unarmed, but there
were conflicting reports, some saying he was shot trying to surrender,
and others saying he had attacked the police officer and tried to take
his gun. Police and federal authorities were investigating the shooting.
The prosecutor pledged there would be a grand jury inquest.

Similar scenarios have played out over and over in other places
around the country. It's tragic, but it happens, and people in other communities have simply waited peacefully for answers as the investigation
takes its course.

So, what was different about Ferguson?

Wait . . . are you expecting me to answer that? It was a rhetorical
question. I don't have the answer. I've never claimed to understand why
this particular shooting in this particular city at this particular time spun
out of control so quickly and so violently. I asked an African-American

friend if he could explain how the whole situation in Ferguson escalated so rapidly. Of course, he acknowledged that one of the main contributors was the disturbing details of the shooting as recounted by Dorian Johnson, but he said it was more than that.

I'll paraphrase his response: "Jeff," my friend said, "we've been internalizing our anger over black kids, all too often unarmed black kids, dying at the hands of police for decades. When it happened here in our own backyard and there weren't any details from police about what happened, it was easy to believe Dorian Johnson's story, so the anger just came pouring out."

It was a pretty damn good answer, particularly his observation about the void of information from authorities being filled in with Johnson's account.

One of the big takeaways for law enforcement after Ferguson should be that in the age of instant information, complete with social media, the Internet, and twenty-four-hour news channels, police have to be nimbler in getting out the details they know about an incident as soon as they have them. If not, people will peck away on a keyboard until they've pieced together a Frankensteinian version of the truth and unleashed a monster that will menace the proverbial village unrelentingly.

Sometime after my friend and I talked, I was searching for new songs for my iPod when I came across a rare track by my favorite recording artist, Chris Cornell. In addition to producing some amazing solo recording work, Cornell has fronted the bands Temple of the Dog, Soundgarden, and Audioslave. In my opinion, Cornell has the greatest voice in rock-and-roll history (sorry, Robert Plant; you're a close second). Nevertheless, I stumbled on a solo acoustic version of Cornell singing the song "Mind Riot," which he had written and originally released when he was with Soundgarden.[1]

The somber, dirgeful version of the obscure grunge song was a chilling reminder of what my friend had said about blacks internalizing their anger about police shootings over the years. The term "Mind Riot" was an apt description of the pent-up frustration my friend had expressed.

As I listened to the haunting lyrics, it seemed as if the song had been written just for Ferguson, although it was released twenty-three years earlier. Lines about police authority were reminiscent of protester complaints in Ferguson. Likewise, the chorus was incredibly reminiscent of the makeshift memorial to Brown on Canfield Drive and Dorian Johnson's use of the term "best friend." I believe with all my heart that Michael Brown was responsible for his own death, and that nothing Darren Wilson did could have changed the outcome that day. But that certainty doesn't allow me to ignore the human tragedy of Brown's death, and the deaths of so many other desperate, young black men who perish—usually justifiably, but not always—at the hands of police. Likewise, police all too often die at the hands of desperate, young black men.

For the sake of kids and cops—and everyone their lives touch—we have to figure out a way to eliminate these deadly confrontations. We just have to. We can't go on like this.

✪ ✪ ✪

Governor Nixon, realizing that drastic action was necessary, had declared a state of emergency and imposed a midnight to 5:00 a.m. curfew on day eight. I was happy to hear that. A handful of Republican lawmakers and I had been calling for curfews for the entire week of the initial protests. To this day, I still don't understand why they weren't implemented earlier.

That night, police used tear gas to disperse the noncompliant demonstrators who remained as the bewitching hour approached, but the vast majority of protesters just went home rather than face arrest. It was the calmest night of the protests to date. Only seven protesters were arrested, one of the few nights where arrests numbered in the single digits.

Curfews work if done right!

By day nine, I was becoming optimistic that we had turned the corner on the violent protests. The curfew still allowed people to assemble and speak freely, but it permitted them to do it safely, in the light of day, which, for the most part, had been free of the brutality and riotous behavior that characterized the after-hours protests.

We all know the most dangerous viral strains can mutate to over-come your immune system. Apparently, violent protesters have the same characteristic, because the curfews didn't slow them down the second night. Instead, the disruptive elements of the crowd simply spread out and targeted businesses outside of what had previously been the area of involvement.

FICTION	FACT
Michael Brown was a young boy just trying to make his way to college.	In reality, Michael Brown had turned to a life of drugs and crime.
Darren Wilson was a racist cop terrorizing black youths in the neighborhood where Brown lived.	Darren Wilson was in Brown's neighborhood on the day of the shooting responding to a call for a black baby who wasn't breathing.
Michael Brown was minding his own business when Wilson stopped him to harass him for J-walking.	Michael Brown was lumbering down the middle of the street and responded with anger and cursing when Wilson told him to move to the sidewalk.
Darren Wilson didn't have any probable cause to question or detain Brown.	Brown was not only obstructing traffic, he matched the description from the Ferguson Market robbery.
Darren Wilson was the aggressor in the encounter between him and Brown.	Brown pummeled Wilson through the car window and even grabbed for Wilson's gun.
Michael Brown attempted to peacefully surrender with his hands up and his back to the officer.	After exiting his vehicle, Wilson ordered Brown to surrender at which time Brown charged headlong at the officer leaving him no choice but to shoot.
The protests that followed were peaceful displays of civil discourse attended by residents of Ferguson demanding justice.	The violent protests that followed were marred by riots, looting, arson, Molotov cocktails, and shots fired at police, with protesters calling for revenge and anarchy.
The militarized response of law enforcement using federally provided equipment provoked riots.	The rioting began well before defensive equipment, which saved the lives of cops and civ was deployed.
The civil unrest was really a product of years of abuse from a racist police department and court system in Ferguson.	The rioters weren't chanting "hands up, don't write me a ticket;" they were chanting "hands up, don't shoot;" the riots began and ended with a lie.
Darren Wilson murdered Michael Brown.	Darren Wilson was acquitted by a grand jury of his peers and by Eric Holder's DOJ.

The protesters moved north toward the neighboring town of Dellwood, looting businesses and storming a McDonald's, causing employees to barricade themselves in the back of the restaurant. The surging mob had taken siege of the eatery, with the hapless, minimum-wage workers the victims of the harrowing incursion.

To the south, a faction of protesters broke off and tried to overrun the unified command post. When I talked to one of the police supervisors I knew who was in the command post that night, he quipped, "We called 'Broken arrow,' threw our gas masks on, and started dropping tear gas canisters at our own feet to fend off the charge of the crowd." His broken arrow reference was meant to be satirical, but I could tell he was shook-up by the whole experience. It must have felt a bit like the fall of Rome when Alaric's Gothic army came stampeding over the last of the once-mighty empire's defenses.

The scene throughout the night could only be described as pandemonium. Molotov cocktails were once again the *gazole apértif du jour* (a.k.a. the petroleum spritzer special). A police car was shot at, and several shots buzzed over the tops of officers' heads. Shots rang out in the crowd all night long. Three protesters were injured by gunfire, one critically.

Despite all the drivel about police needing to de-escalate, it was clear to me, and anyone involved who had a lick of sense, that we needed to do just the opposite and make a show of force that would quell the violence and get the unwieldy crowd under control.

The wearisome scene was no longer safe for police, neighboring citizens, or protesters.

To my delight, Governor Nixon kicked off day ten with an announcement that he was deploying the National Guard to Ferguson. I know, I know: the last time a guy named "Nixon" called out the National Guard, things didn't turn out so well. To date, though, Crosby, Stills, Nash & Young have not written a song about this one.

This was no Kent State. What happened in Missouri was just the opposite of what happened in Ohio forty-four years earlier. Four died during peaceful protests at the hands of guardsmen at Kent State; no one died during the violent protests in Ferguson. The restraint shown by police and guardsmen in Missouri will likely go unheralded in history, but think about this: according to the *LA Times*, more than sixty people were killed in the 1992 Rodney King riots, ten of them at the hands of law enforcement.[2] Nobody died during the Ferguson riots. Nobody!

What an incredible and unnoticed testament to the self-discipline of the police who answered the call there. By the way, the LA riots lasted only six days. The Ferguson riots continued on and off for a year, and included at least nineteen days and nights of pitched violence. You wouldn't know from all the hullabaloo that came out of the media, but this was a case of law enforcement using unprecedented restraint in the face of unrelenting gunfire and a rain of fiery incendiary devices.

Of course, Governor Nixon was roundly criticized for his "proliferation" of military force. The dirty little secret was that the guardsmen were limited to protecting the perimeter of the command post, and they weren't allowed to load magazines into their rifles. This was far from the military buildup the media made it out to be, but, "This is the West, sir. When the legend becomes fact, print the legend."

I was riding high on the news of the National Guard call-up, thinking that it meant my cops would be safer and a calm would return to the region. Silly me.

The results of an "independent" autopsy of Michael Brown commissioned by the Brown family essentially concluded that the conclusions were inconclusive. I'm no pathologist, so it's not my place to criticize the doctor who performed the autopsy.

Nonetheless, the release of the "independent" autopsy revved up the protesters that night. They boisterously renewed their demands that Darren Wilson be charged criminally. What a bunch of *bullshit!*

Violent standoffs with the police continued in earnest that night, but police employed a new tactic that evening that seemed to work well. They would identify elements in the protest who were engaged in some sort of criminal behavior; take a squad of officers into the crowd, forming a wedge; and apprehend and evacuate the suspect. It was not dissimilar to the military phalanx formation the ancient Greeks used so often in battle. And it was remarkably effective. There were seventy-nine agitators arrested that night. Guess how many were from Ferguson.

Go on . . . guess!

Three. Just three.

The vast majority of the insurgents arrested were professional, out-of-town protesters. We found out later that many of these "Have Gun Will Travel" demonstrators were reportedly being paid (or at least promised payment) by Missourians Organizing for Reform and Empowerment (commonly known as MORE and previously known as ACORN) and other outside "social justice" groups. Between mercenary protesters and looters there to pilfer auto parts and beauty supplies, I wonder how many folks in the crowd were actually attending for some righteous cause rather than their own personal benefit. Perhaps we'll never know.

What we do know is that it was a tremendous setback to the credibility of the protests when the news media reported on the number of out-of-town demonstrators. It took the wind out of the sails of the tired argument that these protests were about the lingering frustrations and racial tensions between Ferguson police and local residents.

✪ ✪ ✪

I had pushed out the story to my media contacts about the stunning number of out-of-town protesters who had been arrested, and I was really pumped to see that it was getting reported when I woke up the next morning, on day eleven of the riots. For the second day in a row, I felt hopeful that we were finally turning the corner on things.

I've got to stop taking those optimism pills every morning.

Around midday, I got a call from St. Louis Police Chief Dotson, who was responding to an officer-involved shooting where two white policemen had shot a young, black male on the city's north side. Oh, that sinking feeling!

The suspect was reportedly armed with a knife and was not expected to survive. I immediately got on the phone with union attorneys and made sure our officers had representation as quickly as possible. One of our attorneys was already on the way to the shooting scene.

Word of the shooting went out over social media, and before the gun smoke had even cleared, a flash mob assembled made up mostly of Ferguson protesters who had rushed to the crime scene. There were immediate allegations that the police had gunned down the young man, later identified as Kajieme Powell, in cold blood.[3]

That narrative would have taken hold except for two important details that emerged pretty quickly.

As I said earlier, one of the big post-Ferguson lessons for police is to tell the press what you know when you know it. Chief Dotson had learned that lesson, and he got out in front of the media right away to share an account of the shooting that included the first important detail. One of the witnesses and 911 callers was a black St. Louis alderwoman, Dionne Flowers.

Ms. Flowers, in my opinion, is the kind of elected leader we need. She is a tireless, no-nonsense advocate for her ward, who works constantly to improve the conditions in which her constituents live, and who cooperates with the police to develop better relationships within her community. We could use more like her.

As Chief Dotson reported to the media, the suspect had walked out of a local market without paying for a beverage and was pacing around outside the market in what appeared to be an agitated state and holding a knife.

When the two officers arrived, he moved toward them with the knife as they shouted commands to drop the weapon. Police training dictates that a person holding an edged weapon can, in some cases, close a distance as great as twenty-one feet before an officer can get a shot off. Nevertheless, the officers continued to bark their commands until the man was upon them. They fired several shots before the man finally collapsed to the ground at their feet, never dropping the knife. He died holding the knife against his chest in what some witnesses described as suicide by cop.

Still, the headlines read like this: "Police shoot and kill mentally ill man." How does that qualify as journalism?! Shouldn't the headline instead read something like: "Knife-wielding maniac shot while trying to kill police"?

This is the new normal, I suppose.

Of course protesters were calling for the officers to be charged criminally—until the next day, when cell phone video that had been taken by a witness emerged. It showed the incident as police had described it and completely exonerated the two officers.

Still, that wasn't enough for some people, and protests continued at the scene of that shooting for a couple of nights.

Meanwhile, as soon as I was done dealing with the Powell shooting on day eleven, I had to rush out to Ferguson because I was scheduled to do interviews with the two CNN shows I mentioned earlier. There was about a three-hour gap between the two shows, so after I finished the first one, I toured Ferguson and then went to the unified command post to mingle with the troops.

I got to talk to several of the National Guardsmen while I was there, including a general I knew. What a great group of men and women working under some pretty horrible conditions. Remember: these weren't a bunch of weekend warriors. Missouri guardsmen had been deployed to Afghanistan and Iraq more times than the Guard has ever been deployed in any previous war, so these were combat veterans, real citizen soldiers.

I also got a briefing in my capacity as a state representative from officials with the governor's administration. I then talked to commanders with the Missouri Highway Patrol, the St. Louis County Police, and the St. Louis City Police. Along the way, I learned that a number of the city police officers didn't have helmets. Then I learned that the Highway Patrol had just gotten a shipment of helmets in, and all of their officers were already equipped with helmets. After a little gentle nudging (I was still a state representative at the time, remember), the city officers were all adorned in shiny new helmets. Yes, I was responsible for increased militarization that day, and I'm damned proud of it.

After the helmet escapade, I circulated among the police officers in the bivouac who were either coming off their tour of duty or beginning it. It was tense. I saw guys there I had known for a long time, and who I knew feared nothing. But there was a look on their faces. It was the look worn by those who are unsure if they will ever see their loved ones again. It is an unforgettable, unmistakable look.

I went back to the makeshift media village and completed my second interview with Anderson Cooper. I stuck around for a little while after the interview, but as night fell, shots began to pop in the distance, and the marchers started getting antsy and paying a lot of attention to me. I didn't have a helmet or any other militarized equipment, so I bugged out.

That night was decreasingly violent, and the number of arrests tapered off.

Likewise, day twelve was characterized by a relatively uneventful after-dark demonstration in Ferguson.

On day thirteen, August 21, 2014, the governor withdrew National Guard troops.

The protests continued that night and the next two nights leading up to the eve of Michael Brown's funeral. Some minor skirmishes and arrests of disobedient protesters continued, but the peak of the protests seemed to have passed.

I was hopeful that Brown's funeral would be a solemn, peaceful event, but the lessons of the protests had become "pray for peace; plan for violence."

7

NO BIKO

On August 18, 1977, Stephen Biko was arrested by police at a checkpoint in Port Elizabeth, South Africa, for engaging in antigovernment activity. The "activity" in which Biko was accused of taking part was limited to speeches and demonstrations in opposition to the Pretorian government's policy of apartheid.

After his arrest, Biko was questioned about his so-called crimes for nearly twenty-four hours in police interrogation room 619. By "questioned," I mean he was beaten into a coma, a coma from which he would never regain consciousness. At a prison infirmary less than a month later, on September 12, 1977, Biko succumbed to the injuries these police thugs—these disgraces to the badge—had inflicted upon him.

In his poignant musical tribute to Stephen Biko recounting the ultimate sacrifice he made in the struggle against state-sponsored racism, British singer-songwriter Peter Gabriel warned that the whole world was "watching" as an admonition to those who would commit atrocities under the belief that they would go unnoticed.

Gabriel's "Biko" is a chilling musical masterpiece that has had a place on my iPod for almost as long as I've owned an iPod. The lyrics are a poignant reminder of what can happen when the world isn't watching.[1]

Just as the world was watching Port Elizabeth in August 1977, so, too, was it watching Ferguson in August 2014. That is where the similarities begin. And, that is where they end.

It is not lost on me that what happened in Ferguson on August 9, 2014, was about more than Michael Brown and Darren Wilson. In many ways, both of them became emblematic of things far greater than themselves. To be certain, Brown became symbolic of a broader black struggle. Likewise, Wilson became totemic of the impossible standards and irrational expectations society demands of police, despite their mortal shortcomings.

We owe some debt to the truth, though. Whether emblematic of the struggle for social change or not, Brown cannot be pardoned of the bad deeds that led to his own demise. It is simply unfair to true agents of social change, to the martyred warriors for good causes, like Stephen Biko, to utter both names in the same breath.

Brown was not an agent of social change. He was a petty criminal. At least he was on August 9. On that day he made a stupid mistake, followed by a deadly mistake. Even if he wasn't a criminal before that day, and I'll give him the benefit of the doubt for the sake of argument for the moment, he wasn't doing the good works in Ferguson that Stephen Biko had been doing in Port Elizabeth.

By the time Biko was Brown's age, he had become prominent in the anti-apartheid movement through activism in student groups. His influence was known far and wide among those who shared his cause. Biko's ideas about improving self-reliance and self-image and taking ownership of one's own fate were taking hold in the collective psyche of downtrodden South African blacks. You may not know the name Stephen Biko, but you most certainly know his words. He is widely credited with popularizing the phrase "Black is beautiful."

Brown wasn't participating in a movement or a cause. He wasn't preaching self-reliance or promoting intellectual discourse about race relations in his country. He was a shiftless street kid moping about with the likes of Dorian Johnson, not doing much of anything to improve himself or his corner of the world.

Michael wasn't born a pothead or a thief or a murderer. He was born an innocent child, as we all were. But by the time August 9, 2014 rolled around, Michael was a drug user, a thief, and, ultimately, a would-be cop killer who pummeled and then tried to disarm Darren Wilson.

I'm sure Michael Brown's parents did the best they could to raise Michael right, but the reality is that no matter how hard you try, kids in economically depressed neighborhoods are, with stunningly few exceptions, raised by the street.

We have to change that. We have to change the world these kids live in. It is a world of hopelessness and helplessness, devoid of opportunity and optimism. Kids deserve better than to be born into that desperation.

All this talk about police reform misses the mark by a million miles. It is not the police we need to change. They are the saving grace of the inner city. Manacling them in the performance of their duties and hindering the order they bring to the asphalt wasteland only makes the world worse for kids born into the urban abyss.

What happened August 9 was unavoidable for Darren Wilson. But it wasn't unavoidable for Michael Brown. He could have made the right decisions; he could've tried to make a positive contribution to the world, like Stephen Biko. But he simply wasn't prepared by his previous eighteen years to make good decisions.

It's unfair to compare Brown to Biko. There is no comparison. Let's all agree to stop it. Brown doesn't deserve to have his name mentioned alongside Biko's or Martin Luther King's or Medgar Evers's or Crispus Attucks's or any other martyr for any other righteous cause. His fate, while an awful waste, was not met in pursuit of a higher purpose. He used physical force and intimidation to steal from a neighborhood market while under the pronounced influence of marijuana, then physically assaulted a police officer, tried to take his gun, and moments later charged headlong at the officer in a murderous rage. What about that makes Michael Brown a martyr for any just cause?

Brown was no Biko. Steve Biko fought for justice. Brown acted on his own selfish impulses from beginning to end. Biko gave his life for a righteous cause and died at the hands of despots who called themselves police officers. Brown lost his by committing a senseless act of violence aimed at a police officer. Brown is no martyr, only a would-be cop-killer.

Stephen Biko deserves the statues erected in his name and the adulation bestowed upon him. Michael Brown does not.

✪ ✪ ✪

What Brown did deserve, was a decent burial. Every man deserves that.

For Brown that came on August 25. For the most part, it marked an end to the violent protests that had been carried out in his name. At least until the imminent announcement of the grand jury decision, that is.

There was also a correlation between the media exodus and the diffusion of the protests. It is very much a chicken-or-the-egg prospect trying to figure out whether the press pulled up stakes because the protests were waning, or if the protests faded because the media headed for the hills after Brown was laid to rest.

To be clear, I'm not blaming the media for the bad behavior that occurred during the pitched media coverage. People are responsible for their own behavior. It is no more fair to blame media sensationalism for the protestors' violent acts than it is to blame police militarization for those acts, the difference, of course, being that there actually was media hype, while the fuss about militarized police was simply a hyperbolic distraction.

That said, there needs to be some accountability on the part of the media for what happened in Ferguson and elsewhere in response to the spectacular spin they put on what occurred on August 9 on Canfield, and what happened on the streets of Ferguson in the days and weeks that followed. Just like Michael Ahern and Mrs. O'Leary's cow, much of what was reported was a fabrication, or, in the very least, a case of selective reporting.

News reporting is done by human beings, with all their flaws and foibles. It is colored by perceptions and bias and emotion and preconceived notions. I guess you could say the same thing about police work. How ironic that that analogy escaped the reporters on the ground as they gently excused their own mistakes when they couldn't avoid acknowledging them, but judged law enforcement harshly for what they perceived as police missteps.

All the media had to do was stop obsessing over the police response, turn their cameras around, and show the behavior of the crowd, and Ferguson would have been a very different story. For that matter, they could have aired the online videos produced by the protesters themselves that showed the deplorable, lawless behavior that permeated the nightly insurrections. While some reporters "played it straight," many, many others tried to make headlines by joining in with the protesters and taunting police or ignoring orders to move to safety, in the hopes of manufacturing some newsworthy confrontation. Still, others twisted the facts to fit into their agenda-driven reporting. Some, and we'll never know just how many, simply made stuff up.

One fact is undeniable: things immediately calmed down once the haze of the national media attention evaporated. Remember what Peter Gabriel said about South Africa. The attention of the world darted off in a new direction once Brown's funeral put some closure, some finality, to the situation. The accompanying media pullout was a welcome respite.

Those of us remaining in the St. Louis region—the people who live here, the people who do business here, the people who police here—were left in the dust of the departing media circus to make sense of the aftermath of the tragedy that had played out on the world stage. Or, perhaps the whole Ferguson saga is a different kind of play, perhaps a farcical Greek comedy. Whatever you call the unrest in Ferguson and the media coverage it received, it was most certainly high theater.

It wasn't just the media that rode off into the sunset after Brown's funeral. The traveling carnival of professional protesters was right on their heels to rain carnage on the next unsuspecting town on the road to anarchy. Not that I wasn't glad to see the national-media types hightail it out of town, but the departure of those who embraced civil unrest as their chosen vocation was particularly good news for our region.

Those out-of-town agitators had left their indelible mark, though, like a tomcat spraying on your drapes. It was more than just the husks of burnt and looted buildings on West Florissant. These Chomsky-loving lunatics had roused the rabble in a profound and pervasive way. The infectious disease that these antigovernment, antipolice social lepers carried with them spread throughout the St. Louis area and remains here as I write about this regrettable chapter in American history.

It is the chapter where reality was replaced with an antipolice mob mentality fomented by anarchists and embraced by those who were, and are too ready to believe the worst about the people who risk their lives to protect them. It is the darkest chapter of American history I have lived through. Darker even than 9/11, because on the fateful day that foreign terrorists attacked our homeland, this country came together as one. But, on 8/9, this country split in two as anarchistic domestic terrorists co-opted the anger of those whose misguided disdain of law enforcement was ripe for manipulation.

The war against police was very real, and I was living at ground zero when 8/9 struck at the American heartland. I lamented this baneful new reality as I wrote my second post-Ferguson *Gendarme* column. It was a call for police under attack from protesters, politicians, and the media to come together and close ranks. I titled the column "The Thick Blue Line," and its dire predictions of worsening attacks on law enforcement was unfortunately prescient. The worst was yet to come.

THE THICK BLUE LINE[2]

It is time for the "thin blue line" to become the "thick blue line."

Detractors of law enforcement have used the term "thin blue line" as a pejorative to conjure up an image of cops belonging to a skull-and-bones-esque secret society that looks out for one another at all cost. And, they say that like it's a bad thing!

We do look out for each other.

We should look out for each other.

And now, more than ever before, that thin blue line needs to be a lot thicker.

For police professionals, the world changed forever on August 9. In the wake of the Ferguson riots and the sensational media coverage that accompanied it, not only was Darren Wilson tried and sentenced in the court of public opinion without the benefit of a single piece of evidence being considered, so, too, was the entire law enforcement profession.

The rush to judgment was accompanied by frantic demands that police strip themselves of the protective gear that saved cops' lives in Ferguson; that police not use deadly force to counter deadly force; that police be subject to a brand of civilian review that provides no due process; and that things like forensic evidence and eyewitness statements be brushed aside in favor of grainy, two-dimensional body camera footage.

This is a brave new world sans the bravery. In this new world, if our cop-hating critics have their way, a policeman's word means nothing; a thug's word means everything; and if it wasn't captured on video . . . it didn't happen. In this new world, your fate is left in the hands of "civilians" who believe that the police are the problem in their crime-riddled neighborhoods, not the violent, well-armed criminals who wreak havoc in their streets.

No doubt, video evidence and civilian oversight have their place. After all, cameras are everywhere now and taxpayers do have a right to know that their police department operates in an effective, lawful way. But, video evidence only tells part of the story. It is taken from one angle; things happen outside the frame of the video; you see people move left-to-right but you don't see them move to-and-fro; and the images can be grainy and, distorted. Of course video evidence should be taken into account, but it is only a piece of the puzzle, and sometimes, a very small piece of the puzzle. And, if the vision for body cameras is the same as it has been for dashboard cameras, like playing gotcha with police officers for silly offenses, like not wearing their hat on a call, or rolling through a stop sign while responding to a 911 hang-up, then there's just no place for them.

Likewise, police should be accountable to outside review by a neutral party. And, we are. In St. Louis, it's called the Civil Service Commission and they are the ultimate authority over discipline and the fate of your career when you're accused of wrongdoing.

But, for too many people, that's just not enough.

So, circle up those blue wagons. Watch each other's back like never before, because there are people watching you and they don't care about justice or peace or living in a safe, crime-free community. They simply care about piercing that blue line.

". . . AND THE REST"

eptember and October saw a dramatic uptick in violence toward police in the St. Louis area, and things got increasingly worse as the Darren Wilson grand jury decision approached in November.

Despite all of the intense attention that was focused on Michael Brown and Darren Wilson after the August 9 shooting, there was a lot more going on around the St. Louis region in the wake of the unabashed lawlessness that followed . . . a whole lot more.

Violent crime spiked all around the region. Homicides in the city of St. Louis skyrocketed to a staggering 159, making St. Louis the deadliest big city in the United States in 2014, with fifty murders per one hundred thousand residents. High-stakes showdowns between emboldened criminals and law enforcement became an almost daily occurrence in and around St. Louis. What was first locally, and then nationally, dubbed as the "Ferguson effect" was a very real phenomenon.

Some laughed it off as a sympathy ploy by beleaguered law enforcement officials, but this force majeure, or, maybe more appropriately, this *force homme* was very clearly present in virtually every aspect of policing in the St. Louis area post-Ferguson.

If tossing a pebble into a body of water causes a ripple effect, then a boulder had been hurled into the police pond. From things as simple as a passersby on the streets, flailing his arms in the air at cops and hollering "Hands up; don't shoot," to things as dramatic as the marked increase in the number of police-citizen contacts where the suspect turned to violence, police work became characterized by never-before-seen dangers. It wasn't just in the St. Louis area, either. This alarming trend was spreading from city to city all across the nation.

The supporting statistics were ample and widely publicized. There were drastic increases in violent crime, murders, and assaults on police. It was most pronounced in cities that had experienced a hyper-scrutinized, police-involved shooting, but it wasn't limited to those cities. Homicides doubled in places like Milwaukee and Houston, which were relatively untouched by Ferguson-like incidents. It was a crime pandemic. The *Wall Street Journal*, the *New York Post*, and a host of other publications documented the undeniable data shift dubbed the "Ferguson effect."

The most alarming trend from my perspective was the precipitous increase in deadly assaults against police officers, which nearly doubled after Ferguson. Some dismissed the irrefutable statistical increase in crime as an unrelated anomaly.

I knew better. Every sensible American did too.

I was invited onto *Fox & Friends* to discuss the alarming trend. Host Steve Doocy asked me if the Ferguson effect was legitimate. I responded, "I don't need a bunch of academic eggheads to tell me we need ten years of crime statistics to tell us whether this is real or not. It's apparent to me; it's apparent to every one of your viewers that this is a very real phenomenon . . . All this anti-police rhetoric that we've heard from protesters and politicians and some in the media has got a gravitational tug to it, and it's just as clear that this is responsible for the spike in crime as it is that the moon is responsible for high tide."[1]

The tidal analogy seemed like the perfect metaphor for what was going on in the wake of Ferguson. Picture for a moment law and order in terms of the celestial relationship between the earth and the moon. The criminal element is represented by one part of the earth, and law enforcement is represented by the other. The moon represents external forces affecting the two parts of the planet. External forces can be a good thing. Take Bill Clinton's funding of COPS grants in the 1990s, which had a profoundly positive effect on law and order. It was high tide for police work.

In the case of Ferguson, however, the moon represents the insidious and unwarranted onslaught against law enforcement by protesters, politicians, and pundits. It also represents the meddling, intimidation, and litigation used by Holder's Justice Department to establish unattainable, elusive standards for law enforcement. Cops can handle high standards. They always have. What they can't handle—what nobody can handle—are impossible standards.

As I said in the interview, these external forces have a gravitational pull to them. As these external influences move into a low orbit, as they did after the Michael Brown shooting, the force of attraction has an irresistible draw on the surface waters of the parts of the planet aligned with the moon, and in this analogy, criminals. The tow of all of the excusing, pandering, mollycoddling bluster from those in positions of responsibility who knew not of what they spoke, emboldened the criminal element. In that emboldened climate, there were suddenly more criminals committing crimes, which meant that those engaged in bad acts were, in turn, less likely to be apprehended. Couple that with the new opportunities to commit crimes as part of a mob; then add in having your covetous looting of televisions or pharmaceuticals described as "social upheaval" or "civil disobedience" by your apologists, and you've got yourself high tide for criminal activity.

On the side of the planet perpendicular to the moon, the external forces have just the opposite effect, pulling surface waters away from those seas. Cops under the constant siege of violent assaults against them, along with the threat of criminal prosecution or civil litigation suddenly become reluctant to do their jobs. Add to that all of the time spent away from normal policing activities working crowd control, reducing the number of patrol units to half due to the shift to two-man cars for officer safety; then you have a natural ebb in enforcement. Some have dubbed the phenomenon "de-policing;" but for the purposes of this analogy, I'll call it low tide for police activity.

Thus, the Ferguson effect.

To me, the most startling aspect of the Ferguson effect was the commensurate hesitation on the part of police officers in the face of deadly violence. I went on to share a story during that same *Fox & Friends* interview about a St. Louis police officer who gave chase of a suspicious person, who ultimately turned and fired a gun at the officer. Here's what I said, "We had an officer here that had a fella pull a gun on him, fire at him several times, and he [the officer] said when he was interviewed afterwards that . . . he knew the guy had a gun, he saw the gun, he knew he should've responded, but because of Ferguson he waited 'til that subject fired on him before he returned fire because he was afraid of being the next Darren Wilson. That is a horrible predicament for cops to be in, and it's a horrible predicament for law-abiding citizens to be in, because the de-policing that follows leaves them vulnerable to crime."

That particular police shooting occurred on October 8, 2014, almost two months to the day after Michael Brown was killed. The armed man in that confrontation was fatally shot by police. The gunman's name was Vonderrit Myers Jr., and he was shot by a St. Louis police officer in the city's Shaw neighborhood.

Instantly, rioting and looting broke out in that neighborhood, and concocted tales that the officer mistook a sandwich that Myers was holding for a gun took hold among the enraptured throng of protesters that had gathered.

The officer involved in the Myers shooting was a member of the police union that I ran, so I was intimately involved in that case.

The officer's union attorney, the union president, and I went on the offensive and called a press conference to set the record straight about the shooting. We pointed out that the bullets recovered at the scene had been fired from where Myers had been standing, that the gunshot residue test concluded that Myers had recently fired a gun, and that Myers had posted a picture of himself posing with the stolen gun that he fired. The column I wrote for the November *Gendarme* describes Myers's shooting and the revelations we brought forward at the press conference:

THE SHAW SHOOT REDEMPTION[2]

They said, "Stop shooting unarmed teenagers."

They said, "We want answers as soon as you have them."

They said, "We want justice."

They said, "If you do these things, there will be peace."

They lied.

They are not peaceful protesters. They are the violent, anti-police agitators that have turned Ferguson into a war zone. We gave them everything they asked for, and still, they tried to bring that same war to the Shaw Neighborhood after Vonderrit Myers Jr. was fatally shot by a St. Louis police officer.

The lies started before the gunsmoke had even cleared. "Vonderrit was unarmed; Vonderrit was only holding a sandwich; Vonderrit had a gun planted on him by the police; Vonderrit was shot in the back of the head by police; Vonderrit was a good boy."

Vonderrit was not a good boy. He was a violent criminal armed with a stolen gun, who, but for the grace of God, would have murdered one of our brethren. At 16, Vonderrit was certified to stand trial as an adult for shooting another teenager. At 18, he was arrested for a firearms violation and was released on bond with an ankle bracelet and other restrictions. And, as he stood on the corner of Shaw and Klemm violating every one of those restrictions, armed with the same stolen gun that he had displayed on Instagram just a few days before, all of the bad decisions he had made had finally caught up with him.

Had he surrendered to the officer, Myers would have certainly gone away to prison for a very, very long time. So, it's no mystery why he thought fight or flight were his only options. What is a mystery is why so many young black men arm themselves and end up on the same proverbial corner, at a crossroads between a life of crime and a life that ends before it really even starts. Maybe it's a mystery that we'll never unravel but there is one thing that is no mystery, this is not a failure of law enforcement . . . it is a political failure.

For the very same politicians that are elected by the people in these troubled neighborhoods—by the mothers and fathers of children like Vonderrit Myers and Michael Brown—to try to capitalize on the deaths of these kids, not innocent kids, but still kids, is despicable. It is sickening; shameless; unthinkable.

How dare you, how dare any of you, fail the people that elected you and then point your blaming fingers at the police. You publicly deride the police and fault them for the crime and the violence in your community and then demand that they do something to stem the violence. What, exactly, did you have in mind when you made that demand? Seems to me that giving chase when a group of men standing on a corner in a crime-stricken neighborhood take off running at the sight of a squad car, one of whom ultimately turned out to be a would-be murderer with a record of firearms offenses who was armed with a stolen gun, was a pretty damn good place to start.

The politicians that spread the mistruths that night; who incited violence; who placed the lives of the constituents they serve and the police they employ in imminent peril, have no business serving in public office.

The proactive tack that we took in pushing back against the false narrative in the Shaw shooting made for a better outcome and a shorter spate of antipolice demonstrations. Hence, another lesson of Ferguson: disrupt the false narrative and stop the hate-filled lies before they start.

During the first season of the iconic sitcom *Gilligan's Island*, the theme song was different from that in subsequent seasons. Reputedly, Tina

Louise, who played Ginger, had a clause in her contract that required that she get final billing in the opening credits, so she was the last one named, with the Professor and Mary Ann relegated to "and the rest" status. Show star Bob Denver, who played the title role, was incensed that two of his costars weren't billed in the show's intro. Denver pressured the show's producers to relent. They did, of course, and the song we all remember from the subsequent seasons names all the characters. No one is left out. Even Gilligan knew that no one should be nameless. No one should be forgotten. No one should be disposable.

In the eight months following Michael Brown's shooting, seven black men, most of them very young, died at the hands of local police in St. Louis County and St. Louis City (another young black man was killed by the FBI). Like Brown, each of them turned deadly violence against police—and each met a dreadful fate for his senseless act.

All of these young men had mothers and fathers and people who loved them. None of them was born evil and none chose to be born into the hopelessness and desperation in which so many young black men grow up. In the end, each of them did make a choice—a horrible, horrible choice—that flung them and a police officer into harm's way.

If you examine the situation in which they found themselves, they all could have made different choices. Every one of them had an opportunity to comply with the officer, disarm, and take a chance in a court of law. Instead, they chose "kill or be killed."

Why?

Well, that is the big question. Maybe the better question is, why so many?

Seven fatal police shootings in eight months is more than quadruple what we would normally see here. But these were not "unarmed men," as the mantra that came out of Ferguson would lead you to expect. Four were armed with firearms, two had knives, and one used his car as a deadly weapon.

We'll never know exactly why they resorted to murderous violence against the police. Each of these young men took the reasons for his actions to the grave with him. It's pretty clear to me that at least a couple of them had mental health issues that contributed to their self-destructive actions. That each of these men opted to try to kill a police officer rather than comply with lawful orders and surrender certainly tells us something.

That something reflects most on the men themselves. It demonstrates horrible judgment. It demonstrates a propensity toward violence. But most of all, it demonstrates sheer desperation.

A sociological theory called "bounded rationality" presumes that people generally act in their own self-interest because it is a rational function of survival to do so. These acts of survival, though, are limited (or "bounded") by the information that is available to us. Sometimes we overreact to a particular stimulus; sometimes we underreact; sometimes we don't process the stimulus at all.

It is innate to the human condition that we do what we must to survive within the confines of our ability to process the information available to us. It is not just instinctive to us. It is the same reason a deer turns and runs in the opposite direction when it hears a potential predator approaching.

That's why it is so hard to understand why young men in the inner city, particularly in the post-Ferguson era, believe it is rational to turn a gun or other deadly weapon on a police officer who is better trained in marksmanship, who is equipped with body armor, who has reinforcements a click of the radio away, whom you will get the death sentence for murdering. It makes no sense when I think about it within the bounds of my understanding as a law-abiding citizen with a good job who lives in a safe neighborhood, and who has made the most of the many opportunities that have been presented to me over the course of my life.

But for many young men—including those who grow up immersed in neighborhoods plagued by violence, crime, and drug trafficking; neighborhoods replete with broken homes, where latchkey kids engage in self-parenting; neighborhoods with schools and other institutions that fail their inhabitants; neighborhoods where one cohabitant after another ends up jobless, drug-addicted, incarcerated, or dead; neighborhoods where the opportunities to make bad decisions outnumber the opportunities to make good ones a hundredfold—their decisions are bounded by a very different reality. What seems completely irrational to you and me may seem to be the only option for survival to someone who thinks he has no future, or that his future is sure to be a dismal one. We, as a society, need to introduce hope into these neighborhoods. This isn't bleeding-heart, welfare-loving, nanny-state liberalism. It is rationalism.

When we abandon such a large segment of our society on an island of hopelessness, we all pay the costs for the plight of these castaways. Crime proliferates, the economy suffers, and people die. Sometimes those who die are young, misguided black men; sometimes they are cops. Either way, the cost is too high.

No one should be a castaway. Life is too precious, too sacred. These seven lost lives and the people who lived them should mean something. They should have some value. We should at the very least learn something from their seemingly senseless loss. We should honor their memory by laying a better path in front of the next young man walking in their footsteps. We should mourn the loss of life and recognize that a police officer very nearly died at their hands, an officer who now carries the terrible burden of taking another life—for life.

If we damn these kids to the anonymity of forgotten mistakes made by those we failed and who failed themselves, then we are damned to repeat our same mistakes over and over and over again.

As I said, even a dunderhead like Gilligan understood that no one should be nameless. We shouldn't remember this chapter in history as Michael Brown "and the rest." The price is too high if we do, because the names of each of these misguided, scared, desperate young men could just as easily be replaced by the name of a dead cop. I name them because it should hurt to hear their names. It should mortify us as human beings to think about the cost of doing nothing.

These are "the rest," the seven castaways. Let's all agree that we as a society should strive for the day that we have no more names to add to this list:

KAJIEME POWELL—DIED AUGUST 19, 2014

VONDERRIT MYERS—DIED OCTOBER 8, 2014

ANTONIO MARTIN—DIED DECEMBER 23, 2014

ISAAC HOLMES—DIED JANUARY 21, 2015

LEDARIUS WILLIAMS—DIED FEBRUARY 3, 2015

THOMAS ALLEN—DIED FEBRUARY 28, 2015

THADDEUS MCCARROLL—DIED APRIL, 18, 2015

9

OBAMANATED

O nce tensions eased in Ferguson following Michael Brown's
funeral, I turned my attentions back to my state senate election.
I had essentially lost the entire month of August to the unrest
in Ferguson, so I hit the ground running as soon as September rolled
around. I called it "racing for the finish line" when I spoke to my campaign staff about our efforts going forward in September and October
in advance of the November 4, 2014, general election date.

Of course, the Vonderrit Myers shooting on October 8 disrupted the
campaign again briefly. I was back on the trail in less than a week, though.

Losing the whole month of August, and a pivotal week in October was
a setback, don't get me wrong, but it was one that I felt I could overcome.

I was very popular in my state senate district. The district was wholly
located in Jefferson County, a St. Louis suburb in the far southern end
of the metropolitan area. It had always leaned heavily toward Democrats,
although in recent years that partisan tilt had been somewhat plumbed.
Still, the district consistently voted for moderate candidates that drove in
the center lane. I was unmistakably the moderate candidate in the race.

I was really well situated to win. I had grown up in Jefferson County and had worked there as a police officer for seventeen years. The last few years I worked in law enforcement, I held the dual position of police chief and city administrator in Kimmswick, a popular tourist destination in Jefferson County. That provided me with a lot of coverage in the local Jefferson County media. That wasn't the first time my name was in the local papers, though.

In 2001 and 2002, I was at the center of a controversy with my former employer, the Arnold Police Department. My former narcotics unit partner and I were the president and vice president of the Arnold Police Officers Association, an affiliate of the Fraternal Order of Police. We had asked the FOP to provide us legal assistance because the police chief had imposed a ticket quota to which we and our members strongly objected. The chief got wind of the legal request and launched an internal investigation into it. When they dragged us into the Internal Affairs Division (IAD), my partner and I asserted attorney-client privilege regarding our request for FOP legal assistance, so the chief backed off on that internal investigation. The retaliation began right away, though.

I had requested leave because my wife was having severe back problems during her pregnancy with our third daughter. By the time I requested that leave under the Family and Medical Leave Act (FMLA), I had worked for the Arnold Police Department for nearly thirteen years and had never used a single sick day. When I asked for the time off, the chief cussed me out and threw me out of his office, refusing to grant the leave. The Arnold city administrator intervened and instructed the chief that FMLA was a federal law. This forced him to give me the time off with pay.

That infuriated the chief. A few days later, his wife, whom I had only met once before, called me out of the blue to report that the chief had violated a court order she had sought, and ran from the police when they responded to the 911 call she had made. She said he was initially apprehended and placed in handcuffs, but when the brass arrived, he was released, and no charges were filed against him. She called it a cover-up.

When I asked her why she was reporting this to me, she said I was "the only one who would stand up" to her husband.

I went into the police station the next day and filed a formal report about the chief's misconduct.

It didn't take long for IAD to exonerate him and accuse me of filing a false police report. Shocker! I was fired as soon as the internal investigation, sham though it was, was complete.

At the next city council meeting, the FOP organized a picket of city hall, which included more than one hundred of my supporters in and out of law enforcement. It got a lot of news coverage even though we didn't loot any stores, burn down any buildings, ignite any Molotov cocktails, or shoot at anybody. Now, that's a peaceful protest!

With the pressure the media brought to bear in the case, the facts that had been concealed in the IAD investigation became public knowledge. That, in turn, led the mayor and city council, most of whom I believe had been misled about the whole thing, to initiate an outside investigation. When that investigation was completed, the city fired both the chief and his second-in-command for some of the very same misconduct I had accused them of in the reports I had filed.

I'm just giving the abridged version here. There were other misdeeds on the part of top police officials that surfaced during the course of the media coverage, but suffice it to say, I was in the headlines for months over the corruption scandal on which I had shined the spotlight. One of the local papers printed a "Top Ten Stories of the Year" feature during the last week in December every year. The story of my whistle-blowing adventures was highly ranked among the top ten features in both 2001 and 2002.

My now public *quixotic* streak made me a popular figure in Jefferson County. Not only did it result in me landing the top appointed post in Kimmswick city government; I also ran successfully for election to the local ambulance district board in 2001, and the local fire district board in 2002.

That was the launch of my political career. I had always been interested in politics. One of my earliest political memories is arguing about Watergate with my dad. I was eight at the time. You see, I am the product of a mixed marriage—my mom is a Kennedy Democrat, and my dad is a Goldwater Republican. At the dinner table or at family functions, you had better be able to defend your position on the hot-button issues of the day or you would get torn to shreds. That politically charged upbringing whetted my appetite to serve in public office. By 2004, I had decided to run for the soon-to-be-vacated state representative seat in the district where I lived.

The year 2004 was not a good year for Democrats. George W. Bush cruised to reelection, and Missouri elected its first Republican governor in twelve years. I won a squeaker by fewer than three hundred votes. My race and a state representative election in Springfield were the only two legislative swing seats Democrats picked up in the entire state of Missouri. While political prognosticators expected Dems to pick up the Springfield seat, my election had been written off by many.

As you can imagine, I was a rock star when I arrived in the Capitol, having provided House Democrats with their only shred of good news in the election. I got a larger office than most freshmen, as well as my pick of the litter when it came to committee assignments. There were a bunch of high-profile, coveted committee spots that I could have picked, but my loyalties were where they'd always been. Even though they weren't nearly as sought after as many of the other committee spots I had to choose from, I opted to get onto the Criminal Law and Public Safety Committee, and the Public Safety and Corrections Appropriations Committee, where I could do more to help law enforcement and other first responders. Despite my lack of seniority and the fact that a number of members on the committee were attorneys, it wasn't long at all before I was elevated to ranking member of the Criminal Law and Public Safety Committee.

In 2006, I cruised to reelection by a nearly 20 percent margin. Then in 2008, I was seen as so strong a candidate that nobody even ran against me in my reelection.

Then 2010 came, and along with it came Barack Obama's first midterm shellacking. Jefferson County gets a bum rap when it comes to matters of race. Even though the county is around 95 percent white, there are long-established African-American communities that largely grew up along the county's railroad and manufacturing corridor. In 2008, Barack Obama won in Jefferson County even though he didn't carry Missouri.

I think most of the predominantly white voters in Jefferson County were much like me: they were excited about Obama's message of hope on the campaign trail, and they didn't much care about his skin color.

Whether you like Barack Obama or not, nobody can say that he is anything short of an electrifying orator who can captivate the hearts and minds of voters with both his commanding delivery and with the message of optimism that defined him as a candidate. The enthusiasm that defined him during the campaign defied him when he came into power, though.

I don't blame this completely on Obama. This is almost certainly the worst Congress that the United States has elected in the post-reconstruction era. The politics of gridlock win the day in every way. It never seems that the nation's well-being is taken into consideration as rhetorical bombs fly back and forth across the aisle, and back and forth between the White House and the U.S. Capitol Building. I often publicly lament the notion that if we had this Congress and this president in 1932, we'd still be in the midst of the Great Depression. The "make sure the other side looks bad" mentality that pervades both parties nationally guarantees that they couldn't have passed the New Deal. They can't pass any deal.

The brunt of the blame must land on Barack Obama's shoulders, though. He ran on a vision of bringing this country together in ways it had never achieved before, but Obama has done nothing but divide this country. He has missed one chance after another to bring Americans together, and has instead opted at every opportunity for the politics of division, the politics of derision. Obama's *Audacity of Hope* had turned into an audacious hopelessness. Ferguson is perhaps the most glaring example of his misguided approach to things.

By the time Election Day 2010 rolled around, I knew I was in trouble. Obama's numbers were in the toilet in Jefferson County, and my House District had become a hotbed of activity for Tea Party aco- lytes disgusted with Obama's divisive initiatives. Even though my fiscal conservatism and tough-on-crime record should've helped me with Tea Party conservatives, the *D* behind my name, the same *D* that Barack Obama had behind his name, was too much to overcome.

When the dust cleared, I had lost reelection, as had thirteen other incumbent Democratic legislators across Missouri. It was a tough loss. But I've learned more from the elections I've lost than the ones I've won. Most of all, I learned I don't like losing, which is a lesson that is all too often missed in our "everyone gets a trophy" society.

It was a mixed blessing in the end. Shortly after I lost the election, the St. Louis Police Officers Association came to me and offered me a job . . . an offer I gladly accepted.

Not only is the job with the SLPOA a great job that I love; it also set me up well for a political comeback in very short order. I had already been a champion of organized labor and public safety groups, but the new position raised my profile higher yet with those constituencies.

I had a couple other things working in my favor too. For one, 2012 was a presidential election year, which meant higher voter turnout, which had always been good for me. More important, though, 2012 was a reapportionment year. District lines were redrawn every ten years after the U.S. Census was complete, and my new House district was a doozy. It included the area where I lived, which was my home turf, where I had always done well, and it added in the strong Democratic area to the north while shaving off the Republican stronghold to the west. It was an open seat, too. Tim Meadows was the incumbent, but was term-limited. He was one of my best friends in the Missouri House, so he came out strong in support of me.

I cruised to victory in 2012. The Police Association even agreed to keep me on and allowed me to work part-time during the legislative session.

The 2010 loss was a mixed blessing in another way too. Had I won in 2010, I would have been term-limited in the House in 2012 (Missouri has eight-year term limits in the House), so I would not have been aligned well to run for State Senate in 2014. Because of my two-year hiatus, I was now very well positioned to run for the open state senate seat in 2014. I was ultimately unopposed by any fellow Democrats in that senate race.

There was also another positive function to the redistricting. Because my old House district and my new one barely overlapped, I had essentially represented two different House districts in the State Senate district. This was a huge advantage. In Missouri, a senate district essentially encompasses five House districts so effectively I had represented about 40 percent of the senate district in the legislature at one time or another. I was only back in office in the House for a few weeks before I announced my plans to run for state senate in 2014.

I got out to a big, early lead in campaign fund-raising, which imbued me with front-runner status among capitol insiders. Early polling showed me ahead of my likely Republican opponent, but there was a real vulnerability that showed up in the polls with regard to Barack Obama's dismal approval ratings in Jefferson County. I disagreed with much of the president's platform and didn't want him tied around my neck like the festering political albatross he had become. The 2014 election was going to be the first midterm in twenty-four years in Missouri that didn't have a U.S. Senate race at the top of the ticket, so I was very concerned that the unpopular president and low voter turnout would hurt my chances in November.

I thought the most effective—and for that matter, the most honest—way to set myself apart from Obama and the Far Left fringe of the Democratic Party that ran things nationally was to localize the election and highlight my moderate record. I was conservative on tax policy, law and order, and social issues. I had a strong pro-life, pro–Second

Amendment voting record. But I was also one of the leading voices in the state on core Democratic issues, like fully funding public education, making college affordable, raising the minimum wage, expanding Medicaid to include the working poor, and protecting union rights and working families.

I routinely emphasized my centrist record and worked hard to separate myself from Obama and the Far Left. As you can imagine, I was wildly popular with moderate Democrats. But I was equally unpopular with the liberal wing of the Missouri Democratic party's legislative leadership. My defense of police and police tactics in Ferguson only further exacerbated the strained relationship I had with the lefties.

That was okay, though. I knew I wasn't going to get any help in my senate race from the lawmakers who landed somewhere to the left of Mao Tse Tung on the ideological spectrum, so I didn't really care that I had ruffled their feathers.

The most important thing was avoiding the anti-Obama sentiment, but once the Brown shooting on August 9 rolled around, there was simply no way to outswim that tide.

In the eyes of voters—Jefferson County voters, at least—Obama had so badly bungled the events in Ferguson and its aftermath that his numbers plummeted even farther. He was even losing Democratic support in Jefferson County and other moderate bastions of suburbia.

Obama's pandering to the most violent elements of the protests, and his (and Eric Holder's) rush to judgment against Darren Wilson and every law enforcement officer involved in any high-profile incident thereafter, was a significant turn-off to the public safety–minded soccer moms and blue-collar laborers that typified the electorate in a district like mine.

What made things worse was the sharp decline in popularity of Jay Nixon. Jay had been one of the most popular governors in Missouri history, winning election twice by atypically high numbers for Missouri. He had served as attorney general longer than anyone else in Missouri history, a whopping sixteen years.

Nixon's popularity had been a real buoy for my political career. Jay also hailed from Jefferson County and had been a political ally from day one. His bipartisan approach to things and his middle-of-the-road record made the idea that there are still some sensible, moderate Democrats a reality in the eyes of much of the voting public in Missouri. There was no place in the state he was more popular than in Jefferson County. Jay had held the state senate seat I was running for before he was elected Missouri AG, so his strong, early support seemed as though it would go a long, long way in the election.

But if Ferguson was Barack Obama's Fort Sumter, it was Jay Nixon's Waterloo. I'm not playing "pile on Jay," like so many other lawmakers of both parties have done since Ferguson. Jay has been a good friend, and I wouldn't beat him up even if he deserved it. He made some mistakes in Ferguson, but in many ways, it was a Kobayashi Maru test for Nixon's helmsmanship as governor (nerd alert: for those of you who didn't spend your entire adolescence and early adulthood watching the various shows that comprise the *Star Trek* universe, Kobayashi Maru is a battle simulation employed in Starfleet Academy testing used to gauge how cadets handle no-win situations). That's because no matter what Nixon did or said, the outside influences that had co-opted the protests in Ferguson were bent on violence and destruction. He just couldn't win.

Jay could have done everything right, or everything wrong, but the outcome would have still been the same: pandemonium. The fact that things didn't end up bloodier in Ferguson is a testament to Jay's leadership; but it is a hollow victory given the devastating damage it did to his legacy as governor.

It damaged his polling numbers too. By September his numbers had taken a nosedive in surveys in my district. He had gone from the most popular figure in either party in my polls, to the depths of disapproval, with near-Obama numbers with likely voters.

"Likely voters": that was the big problem for me. More and more, Democrats and independents were saying that they were unlikely to vote in the November election. Even moderate Republicans, a segment of the electorate with whom I did relatively well over the years, were turning their noses up to the election.

By October, the Obama drag and Nixon's declining numbers were starting to have a noticeable effect on my prospects. Jay had offered to appear in one of my TV campaign commercials early on in the election. It was a huge commitment. Jay had never before done that in a state senate race. But by the time we filmed the commercial in the fall, Jay was so damaged by Ferguson that I joked to the director of the commercial, who also happened to be a good friend, that he shouldn't even take the lens covers off the cameras. We ended up never airing the commercial.

I decided that my best chance of winning was to pivot to an unrelenting narrative about my law enforcement experience and my enduring hard line on law and order as a legislator.

We used robocalls from FOP officials and aired commercials featuring the very popular sheriff of Jefferson County telling voters that I was the tough-on-crime candidate. We also sent out mailers featuring pictures of me when I was a uniformed police officer, as well as other photos from my time as an undercover narcotics detective. People are enthralled by the idea of clandestine deep-cover work. I was lucky enough to have been a narc in the days when we still did a lot of undercover work. I did more than a hundred undercover drug buys, along with the assorted weapons case and vice stings. My political people called it "sexy." I didn't think of the pictures of me with a long, greasy ponytail and a scruffy beard as alluring, but I did get that people are fascinated by it and respectful of the work I did as a police officer. The law-and-order angle seemed to be the best way to inoculate myself from the prevailing anti-Obama sentiments.

None of that mattered, though, because my opponent's polling clearly showed the same thing that ours did: Barack Obama was wildly unpopular among likely voters. My opponent's media team was relentless in barraging voters with photoshopped images of me and Barack Obama together. They unsurprisingly mischaracterized me as a Far Left whack job who supported every bad idea Obama had. The commercials they ran against me were stupendously misleading and were, frankly, poorly done in terms of production value. They were downright kitschy. They resembled those late-night commercials for Zebco pocket fishing poles from the 1970s.

It was all for naught, really. Election Day turnout hit record lows, 20 percent less turnout than the last midterm election, and nearly 30 percent lower than the turnout for the midterm election before that. I was essentially running as a Democrat in a Republican primary because the bulk of the voters who showed up to cast their ballots that day were the same voters who turned out for the GOP primary election.

I made a better showing than just about any of the other area Democrats, finishing with 46 percent of the vote, while other legislative candidates from my party in the county finished with double-digit losses, some as high as 34 percent spreads. I consider the close run to be a reflection of my political moderation and my bipartisan appeal, but it was of little consolation.

I had been Obamanated.

Again!

My grandmother always used to tell me that everything happens for a reason. She was very Calvinistic in that regard. I always relied more heavily on the idea of self-determination over preordained fate.

I would see very soon that Grandma's wisdom, as usual, transcended the ages.

10

BEHIND BLUE EYES

Before the ABC George Stephanopoulos interview, before the *New Yorker* interview, before he sat down for an interview with anyone in the mainstream media, Darren Wilson was kind enough to sit down with me and do an interview for a feature story I did for the little ole *Gendarme*.

It was just another example of how very gracious this kid is. I guess I shouldn't call him a kid. He's proven himself to be a man in every sense of the word in the way he has handled everything that has happened to him. But he's so young and so baby faced, and I'm so, well . . . uh, let's just note for the record that I started my career as a cop before he was born, so it's hard for me to see him or anyone else in his generation of police officer as anything but a kid.

I suppose sitting down with me to do a story for a newspaper that only reaches about five thousand readers (albeit, mostly cops and retired cops) was just Darren's way of saying thank you both to me and to my readers.

The editorial staff at the *Gendarme* and I agreed to embargo my story—titled "Darren Wilson's War," which you'll read here in just a few more pages—until after the grand jury verdict was handed down. Darren taped the Stephanopoulos interview just days after he sat down with me. In fact, he was being prepped for that interview at Fraternal Order of Police Lodge 15 just minutes before I interviewed him. The ABC interview aired right away once the grand jury decision came down. So, because TV gets out faster than a nonprofit-bulk-postage newspaper delivered by U.S. mail, the Stephanopoulos interview was the first one anyone saw. That's okay. The world needed to get to know Darren Wilson as quickly as possible once the cloud of the grand jury proceedings had passed overhead.

I was fortunate enough to get to know Darren a little better than the rest of the world. Not just in learning about him with the probing questions I asked in the interview, but through our frequent interaction afterwards. A few of the cable news outlets described me as Darren's friend. That's not really accurate in the terms that I define friendship. We didn't know each other until after the shooting, we've never been to each other's home, we've never gone fishing together, but I do have a fondness for the kid—er, man. It seems he holds me in high regard as well. Mutual admiration aside, it is more precise to call me a loyal supporter and confidante of Darren's than a friend, although there are few people I'd rather call "friend." I simply don't want to be accused of using the term as loosely as Dorian Johnson did.

So, here's what I've learned about my "friend" and his life.

Darren Wilson's story is an awe-inspiring tale. It is a story of over-coming obstacles and personal tragedies. It is a story of conviction and achievement. It is a story of courage and survival. It is a story of grace in the face of adversity. It is a story of dashed hopes and daring dreams. It is a story of optimism in the darkest of hours. It is, in the final analysis, a story of triumph in the whirlwind of tribulation.

Most important, it is not my story to tell. It is Darren's and Darren's alone.

As I said at the outset of this book, this chronicle is not meant to be Darren's story or my story; it is meant to be law enforcement's story.

We called it Ferghanistan for a reason. In the aftermath of the deadly confrontation between Darren and Michael Brown, war was declared on all of law enforcement. While Darren was the poster child and the unenviable target in this proxy war on cops and justice and law and order, the war was never about Darren. Neither is this book.

What I will tell you, though, is what I know of this man, Darren Wilson. Not his story, but who he is as a person. I will tell you what I know about his character, his heart, his soul. These are the observations he can't make about himself, who he is externally. His internal observations about his worldview and what happened on and after August 9 are his for the telling. I hope his book, when he writes one, sells a hundredfold the copies this one sells. He deserves the chance to be heard and to be given the opportunity to set history back on its natural course.

To meet Darren Wilson, you would never in a million years guess that he has gone through what he has. He is humble and unassuming in a very sort of "aw shucks" kind of way. There is no bluster. There is no sense he's putting on airs. He is simply a genuine, down-to-earth guy trying to move on with his life. He stubbornly refuses to be defined by what happened August 9, 2014.

It has always astounded me that Darren is not more jaded by what happened to him. That's not to say he is unaffected. It clearly touches him deeply. He is steadfast, though, in his conviction that he did what he was supposed to do that day, and that the initiator and the only person that could have changed the outcome of the deadly confrontation was Michael Brown.

People, especially people who work for news outlets, know I am in regular contact with Darren, so they ask me all the time how he's doing. My pat answer is usually, "His world was turned upside down, so he learned to walk on the ceiling." There is a simple truth to that statement. It at once points out what a calamitous chapter this has been in Darren's life, and, at the same time, reminds people how amazing it is that he has handled the whole thing so well.

This is not hyperbole—which I am sometimes prone to. It really is nothing short of amazing.

Here's a guy who didn't want to do anything else but be a cop for the rest of his life. Gone!

Here's a guy who wanted to live a simple, uncomplicated life. Gone!

Here's a guy who doesn't seek attention, who doesn't even like being singled out at his own birthday party. Gone!

Here's a guy who—like every other cop I know—never wanted to have to take a human life. GONE!

Darren's life has been disrupted in every way, turned completely upside down. When we meet in public, he always wears a ball cap even though, like me, he doesn't have a good "hat head" (sorry, Darren; its true). Most of the time, he wears sunglasses too. He engages in nonstop, 360-degree situational awareness. Now, as a former undercover narcotics detective, I find myself looking at every face in a restaurant or bar to make sure I'm not brushing up against an old nemesis. The difference is I'm looking for familiar faces. Darren is looking for anything that might be perceived as a threat: eye contact, whispering, bad reactions, or what I'll call, for lack of a better term, "mean mugging," people snapping pictures, averted eyes, pointing. You name it he has to look out for it. I mean, I'm paranoid and hyperaware of my surroundings, but Darren has got his head on an oscillating swivel.

The vagaries of going out in public are only the tip of the iceberg. Darren essentially had to abandon his home and relocate his family to keep them safe from the incessant onslaught of death threats. Things as simple as having a presence on social media or going to a car wash represent constant challenges, despite the fact that he has been fully and unequivocally exonerated both by a St. Louis County grand jury and the Justice Department. That's Eric Holder's Justice Department. You remember Eric Holder, right? The AG that served as chief justice in the trial of public opinion that convicted Darren of the brutal execution of a gentle, unarmed teen with his hands up and his back to him? Yes, that Eric Holder. You know the one.

I hammer home these points about Darren's good nature and his unshakable resolve and his difficult life and his unfair treatment for one simple reason: he deserves better.

So does America. We deserve better. We deserve unbiased accounts, not media hype. We deserve forthright leaders, not political spin. We deserve reasoned discourse, not the hate mongering of the worst elements of the misguided public protests. We deserve the simple, unabashed truth.

That's all I want to do in these pages, and that's all I wanted to do with the story I wrote about Darren. I wanted to have an honest conversation with my readers, with America, with the world.

I've been accused of being the apologist-in-chief for law enforcement. I've been accused of toiling to make Darren a sympathetic character. Guilty!

I am guilty and proud of it.

My main goal in the exclusive story I wrote about Darren in the *Gendarme* was to show him for the sympathetic character he was, and is. That, and to engage in full-throated honesty, while everyone else was engaged in rewriting history to make Michael Brown into a victim, a martyr.

I'll let you be the judge. Does Darren deserve your sympathy? Does he deserve your respect and praise? As you read my *Gendarme* offering, ask yourself one simple question: would you want to live the way Darren must live, even though you believe in the depths of your heart that you did what you had to do?

If the answer is no, then Darren deserves not only your sympathy, but your abiding praise. I've heard people tell Darren that he is a "hero." He consistently contradicts those people with the humble response, "Not a hero; just a cop." Well, my "friend," that is a difference without distinction. You decide: sympathetic hero or coldhearted monster?

DARREN WILSON'S WAR[1]

The window blinds rustle as he peers into the dimly lit street. A familiar sense of relief quickly replaces the pitched feeling of danger he had experienced just seconds before. The thud that had shattered the stark silence of the wee hours of the night turned out to be nothing more than the slam of a neighbor's car door.

Nowadays, Darren Wilson hears every car door; every trashcan that blows over; every little thing that goes bump in the night.

Darren is not afraid, let's make that perfectly clear. But, he is resolved to the reality that there are those that want to do harm to him and his loved ones. He's equally resolved to the notion that he's not going to let that happen.

Darren runs his fingers across the window blinds to return each slat to its original position. He pushes the buds of his iPod into his ears and tries to lose himself in the song that pops up on his playlist: Lynyrd Skynyard's "Freebird," one of his favorites. He plops down on a chair near the window and starts playing Candy Crush on his phone. Darren knows from experience that it will take him a while to get back to sleep.

It wasn't always like this for Darren. He grew up in a St. Louis area suburb where he felt safe, free of the impending sense of violence and unrest that now plagues not just Darren and his family, but the entire St. Louis region.

As a boy growing up in that middle-class suburb that he describes as "as average as you can get," Darren thought more about hockey and girls than he did about what he wanted to be when he grew up. As a teenager, he loved watching TV shows and movies about police, especially undercover cops, but he didn't really think much about being a police officer someday.

That all changed after the recession hit in 2008. Darren had been working as a carpenter making very good money, much better than a police officer's salary, while the housing market was booming. When the bubble burst, Darren decided to enroll in the police academy. He was uncertain at first if police work was right for him, but he needed to find a new career with the housing market floundering. In just a few days in the academy though, it hit him like a ton of bricks . . . this was the job he wanted to do for the rest of his life.

Before the fateful events of August 9, Darren saw himself working in law enforcement for the rest of his career. But, he had shed his fascination with the Hollywood image of glamorous undercover cops working high profile cases. Uniformed police work was all he wanted to do. With a little luck, he hoped to end his career as a brackish old street cop, a bit grizzled by the job, but with his faith in mankind still fully intact.

That faith, and the trajectory of his career, has been irrevocably altered by the events that followed the fatal shooting of Michael Brown. As I spoke with Darren, the grand jury was still deliberating, so he wasn't at liberty to talk about the shooting itself, but he did say that he's never second guessed himself. It was, as Darren puts it, Michael Brown's actions that led to what happened that day.

I asked Darren if he ever thought he would have to take a life in the line of duty. He answered, as most cops would, that he always knew it was a possibility but never thought it would really happen. Despite the fact that he believes his actions were fully justified and lawful, Darren said he is "sorry that a life was lost; the Browns are still parents who have lost a child."

Darren seems circumspect about what the future holds for him. He appeared optimistic that justice will prevail when the Grand Jury renders its decision. What happens after that is far more elusive. Darren clearly understands that he can't be a police officer again, at least not here in Missouri. That apprehension seems to bother him. A lot.

This is all he ever wanted to do. Darren describes work as a street cop as challenging, interesting, and dynamic. He clearly realizes how cliché it is to say it out loud, but he said that "sometimes you really do get to help people and that feels pretty good." Ironically, it was that yen to help that led him to Canfield Drive on August 9. The call for a sick case wasn't in his beat, but the officer assigned to that neighborhood was tied up elsewhere, so Darren didn't hesitate to volunteer for the call when he heard that someone's baby needed medical attention. It doesn't matter that the three month old was black, or that Darren was there because of his instinctive impulse to help the people in the Canfield neighborhood. What history will remember is what happened next.

For Darren and his family, what happened next has been a surreal experience, a Glass Menagerie of sorts, where the future is a foreboding and uncertain thing. Just like the Tennessee Williams' character, Darren is doing what he can to make a horse out of the broken, hornless unicorn that is his shattered life.

For Darren, every aspect of his daily life has changed. Going out in public presents myriad dangers for him, or whoever might be with him. Running down to the local convenience store to grab a pack of gum has gone from a mundane task to a daunting undertaking. And, when you're in a restaurant or a doctor's waiting room and your picture pops up on the big screen TV, it's time to find the nearest exit.

Darren does his best to cope with his new Salman Rushdie lifestyle, but what he worries about most are his brothers and sisters in blue. For him, it is nearly unbearable to think of not being by their side while other police officers are in harm's way because of something that happened to him. Darren said that he stopped going to church when he was a teenager, but he finds himself praying a lot these days. What he prays for the most is the well-being of his family and other police officers. When I asked Darren if there was anything he wanted to say to the active and retired police officers that will be reading this article he said, "Yes . . . thank you and be safe!" He added that he couldn't have made it through this episode without the help of the Fraternal Order of Police, and said that any cop who's not a member is "out of their mind."

While Darren is hopeful and prayerful that there will not be a violent response to the Grand Jury's decision, it's hard to be optimistic given the civil unrest that immediately followed the shooting. Darren's disappointment in the media and elected leaders was palpable as he spoke about the aftermath of the shooting.

Darren said he understood that there was a history of frustration and resentment in Ferguson, and in other economically challenged minority neighborhoods in the St. Louis area, describing them as "bigger issues that had to be addressed." He believes that the aftermath of the shooting was more of a response to those issues than it was to the shooting itself. He blamed Dorian Johnson's constantly changing and inaccurate accounts of the shooting in the tense hours and days that followed for much of the violence carried out by the worst elements that descended on Ferguson. He agreed that Johnson was to Ferguson what "Mrs. O'Leary's cow" was to Chicago.

Darren worries about what law enforcement looks like going forward. He said that police officers are already under constant scrutiny. He lamented that law enforcement had probably changed forever on August 9. The idea of police officers being held to an impossible standard seemed to trouble Darren deeply. For a guy who simply wanted to help make the community a safer place, and to help people when he could, hobbling the ability of the police to do their jobs is clearly a troubling thought.

These, I imagine, are the things that keep Darren up at night, perched in a chair, peering out the window at every odd noise, keeping silent vigil over his family.

Darren Wilson's war is not some esoteric struggle to find answers to vexing existential questions. It is a very real battle: a battle for justice; a battle for his career; a battle for his safety; and a battle for exoneration. When I asked Darren what his greatest fear was, he was reflexive in his answer, "the fear of the unknown." Despite the grace with which he has handled all of this, that is a burden heavier than any of us can imagine.

✪ ✪ ✪

I wanted to capture the essence of what Darren's post-Ferguson life was like when I wrote my column "Darren Wilson's War." More significantly, I wanted to give people a sense of who he was as a man.

One of the first things you notice when you meet Darren are his deep, soulful blue eyes. I wanted to show people what was behind those blue eyes. I wanted them to know Darren's mind and Darren's heart.

I also didn't want to give too much away. When Darren sat down with me for the interview on November 20, 2014—just four days before the grand jury announced he wouldn't be charged in Michael Brown's death—his one-on-one with ABC's George Stephanopoulos had not been recorded or aired yet. It was important that the nationally televised interview on ABC would be the first time the world was introduced to Darren.

As I said earlier, I'm protective of Darren and I didn't want to preempt the rollout of his personal introduction to America that his legal team was meticulously coordinating. So my column about him was more observational than interrogative.

But now, to a certain extent, America has met Darren through the two national interviews he's done with ABC and the *New Yorker*, but they haven't really seen him in the tender glow that I have. The *New Yorker* interview was a hit piece designed to put Darren in the worst possible light. The Stephanopoulos interview was fair and informative, but it was clear that Darren was cautious and a bit overwhelmed by the bright studio lights.

When he sat down with me, holding his fiancée's hand, he was at ease, candid, and circumspect. I can do his words no more justice than to share them unedited with you. These are Darren Wilson's words. This is the man I know. You should know him too.

THE INTERVIEW

What's life been like since August 9th?

Stressful would be an understatement. It's been very different with an uncertainty of what's going to happen next. I'm always looking over my shoulder. I'm really careful about where I go, where I sit, whether it's a crowded time of the day. My fiancée and I used to sit on the same side of the table when we went out to eat. Now we sit across from each other so we can watch each other's back.

Do you watch the media coverage of the shooting and its aftermath?

Yes. A lot. I don't like hearing all of the negative things people are saying about me. I don't want to watch TV, but I feel like I have to know what's being said.

What do you think of the press coverage of the shooting and the police response to the civil unrest that followed?

Horrible; one-sided. Hard to listen to.

Has anyone got it right?

Some have, not many. Local news hasn't at all.

Did law enforcement change forever on August 9?

Yes. It's even harder for police officers to do their job now than it was before. They're trying to make cops be robotic. Trying to take away their discretion. They're trying to make us afraid to do our job.

Do you fear for the safety of your loved ones?

I do. It's the fear of the unknown, mostly. They don't understand what's happening, why people want to hurt us just because I was doing my job.

Do you fear for the safety of cops who have or will respond to the protests in and around Ferguson?

Yes, daily! I wish I could be right next to them. That's the hardest part.

Have you been followed by reporters or protestors or private detectives?

Yes. We've become very surveillance conscious. We pay attention to everything around us.

What has surprised you most since August 9?

The overwhelming support for not only me but all of law enforcement. Kinda restores your faith in people.

What do you think of Dorian Johnson?

[*Grimaces*] He was involved in something with a friend not understanding what would or could come of it. The situation wouldn't have been nearly as bad if Johnson hadn't made up that story. There wouldn't have been any riots.

Did anything special happen on August 9 before the shooting? Any funny feelings?

No, it was a slow day. I was getting some medicine for my fiancée and was going to meet her for lunch. Another officer was busy, so I took the call in his beat for a three-month-old baby not breathing. That's why I was there [Canfield-Green Apartments] that day.

Where'd you grow up?

In a middle-class neighborhood in the St. Louis area. It was as average as you can get.

Are you a religious man?

No, not really. I grew up Methodist. I've found myself praying more than I ever have lately.

What do you pray for?

That we all make it through this. For the safety of my family. For the safety of other cops.

Where did you see yourself in twenty years before the shooting happened?

Maybe a sergeant. I wanted to be on the road [uniform patrol] my entire career.

Why?

It's real. It's challenging. It's an ever-changing dynamic. Sometimes you really get to help people. That's why I took that sick case [in Canfield] that day.

Where do you see yourself in twenty years now?

It's a mystery. That's what's so hard, not knowing. They stripped away the certainty of life just because I did my job.

If you had turned the other way on Canfield, would there have still been another Michael Brown eventually? That is to say, was the martyrdom that happened here bound to happen someday, somewhere, even if it didn't happen in Ferguson?

Yeah. The tensions that have been exploited here have been brewing for a long time. St. Louis never had race riots in the '60s. It was just our turn I guess.

Did you always want to be a cop? What other professions did you consider?

In middle school, I wanted to be a DEA agent. But after school, I ended up working in construction as a carpenter for five years. It was good money, but I still had a longing for police work. In October of 2008, when the recession hit, I went to the police academy and fell in love with it right away.

I worked with Ferguson Police Chief Tom Jackson and thought he was a good man. Tell me your thoughts on Tom?

Nice guy put in a bad situation. I enjoyed working for him.

Did you have black friends in school, college, on the police department, in your family?

There weren't a lot of black kids in my school, but one of my best friends was African-American. When I was at the Jennings Police Department, I was really close to a black officer that I worked with. I went to his wedding and I was the only white guy there.

What kind of rapport did you have with black youths in Ferguson?

I treated them like everyone else. Working in a poor black community was kind of a culture shock for me but I worked hard to understand their culture.

Did you ever think you would have to take a life in the course of duty?

I always thought it was a possibility, but I never thought it would really happen.

Can a police officer be prepared for what you've gone through after the shooting?

Yes, but you have to be prepared to change everything.

Do you dream about the shooting? Does it always end the same way?

No. I don't dream much. I don't sleep much. I've never second-guessed myself. I didn't make the decision for him to die. He did.

Is there anything good that can come out of what happened in Ferguson?

Yeah. It's a chance to address problems that have been buried; resentment, community distrust. If people would put their faith back in the police, it would be a good thing.

Can you ever be a policeman again?

No. Not in Missouri. Maybe someplace else.

How's your family handling this?

Some good; some not so good.

There are people who think you'll be exonerated who believe you are a hero. Are you a hero?

No. I was just doing my job, doing what I was trained to do.

How do you escape from the unimaginable situation that you're living through right now?

Family and friends.

Do you have any pets? Do they give you comfort?

Yes, we have dogs. One gives me comfort. The other two give me stress.

Do you have any hobbies? Are you able to do those things now?

No. I used to play hockey. Too much tension right now.

What kind of music do you listen to?

Everything really, country alternative, classic rock.

What's your favorite band and song?

I like everything from Jamie Johnson to Poison. "Free Bird" by Lynyrd Skynyrd is one of my favorite songs. The Red Hot Chili Peppers is probably my favorite band. I love all their songs.

What's your favorite movie?

Probably *Top Gun.*

Do you ever feel like jumping in a car and just driving until you felt like all of this was behind you? Who would you take in the car with you?

Yeah [*laughs heartily*]. My family. That's it. We'd just go.

People who have lost loved ones say that some mornings they wake up and in those first few foggy, waking moments they forget about their loss until reality comes rushing back in. Do you ever wake up and forget for a moment that the shooting happened?

No. It's always with you. I'm waiting for the day when I don't have to think about it as much.

Do you feel like you're going to get a fair shake from the grand jury or from the courts if it comes to that?

Yeah, I think they're fair people.

Do you feel like you've already been tried in the court of public opinion?

Yes.

What do you think their verdict is?

Media: guilty. Everyone else: not guilty.

Is what happened in Ferguson after August 9 more about the shooting or race relations, or is it about something else?

I don't think it had anything to do with the shooting. It has to do with bigger issues that have to be addressed.

Do you look out the window every time you hear a car door slam at your house?

Yep [*emphatically*]. Voices, noises, dogs barking, everything. If it wakes me up, it's really hard to go back to sleep. My mind gets going, and it's hard to stop.

Will your life ever be back to normal? What would normal look like?

[*Laughs*] There will be a new normal. We just don't know what it will be yet.

Is there anything you'd like to say to Michael Brown's parents?

I'm sorry that a life was lost. They are still parents who have lost a child no matter what they say about me.

If you could ask Michael Brown one question, what would it be?

Why?

11

WAITING FOR AN IGNORAMUS

loved watching old reruns of *The Three Stooges* when I was a kid. In St. Louis, they were on late on Saturday nights on a local station, so staying up all hours to watch the uproarious behavior of the trio of slapstick icons was a special treat. I picked up all of my best insults from that show: imbecile; nitwit; moron; lamebrain; wiseguy; knucklehead; and my favorite, ignoramus.

I used "ignoramus" as a jibing insult toward my friends throughout my adolescence. Quips like: "Try shuttin' up, ya ignoramus," or, "Why don't ya catch the ball next time, ya ignoramus?" were regular offerings. I know . . . it was fairly mean-spirited, but what can I say? Kids can be cruel.

Because of the way the Stooges used the term, I always took it to mean "an ignorant person." But that loose slang application ignores the true derivation of the word. Like a true *ignoramus* myself, I didn't know until I had been in law enforcement for quite a while that the word *ignoramus* had a very technical, legal meaning.

I worked undercover narcotics for a long time, which meant I would occasionally testify before state and federal grand juries. It was a very informal process. The prosecutor would ask most of the questions, and every great once in a while, you'd get a question from a juror. It was a relaxed atmosphere, more like sitting around a bus station than participating in a judicial process. I was always in and out pretty quick. Drug cases are usually fairly cut-and-dried.

Every grand jury I was ever in front of had an anteroom where you could hang out until the grand jury came back with a finding of "true bill" or "no true bill." Most people's understanding of grand jury deliberations is that they conclude with an indictment or non-indictment. Indictments actually come later. The immediate determination the jurors make is whether there is probable cause to charge, in which case they find "true bill," or that insufficient probable cause exists, in which case they find "no true bill." The process and terminology dates back to English common law.

As a general rule, the door hadn't even fallen completely closed behind me when the prosecutor poked his head out and said, "True bill." That was my cue to go catch the next dope dealer, because this defendant was well on his way to incarceration. On one occasion though, the prosecutor stuck his head out and chimed, "Ignoramus."

Who are you? Moe Howard? I thought to myself. *And what the hell did I do to be called an ignoramus?*

He then chuckled and said, "Just kidding. True bill." Of course it was a true bill. My cases were ironclad, dammit!

My curiosity was piqued, though, so I had to ask him later what he meant by "ignoramus." He told me it was a Latin term used centuries ago that was synonymous with "no true bill." The actual Latin translation I've read since is literally "We do not know."

By November 24, 2014, I had been hoping and waiting for an *ignoramus* in Darren Wilson's case for more than three months. All of law enforcement had.

The grand jury inquiry into the Michael Brown shooting was a long, arduous process. St. Louis county prosecutor Bob McCulloch, described the painstaking deliberations in a public statement he made on November 24: "Fully aware of the unfounded but growing concern in some parts of our community that the investigation and review of this tragic death might not be full and fair, I decided immediately that all of the physical evidence gathered, all people claiming to have witnessed any part or all of the shooting, and any and all other related matters would be presented to the grand jury."

The result of that no-holds-barred approach was hours upon hours of witness testimony, and thousands of pages of documents and reports that had to be meticulously examined by the grand jury.

Bob got plenty of criticism from the media and protest mouthpieces for his full-disclosure approach to the grand jury. They condemned it as a "data dump." Can you imagine the derision that would have been heaped on Bob's shoulders if he had withheld even one piece of evidence? They would've screamed, "Cover-up!" Bob was in a no-win situation, but he handled it like a champ.

We had all known from the beginning that the grand jury process was going to be a long one, but by Monday, November 24, 2014, we were all sitting on pins and needles. On Sunday, November 23, I got a call from someone very close to the grand jury investigation, tipping me off that Monday was going to be the big day, the day we'd find out "true bill" or "ignoramus."

I didn't get too excited initially. It was the fourth time in a ten-day period that somebody reliable had whispered in my ear that the day of reckoning was upon us. Three times, the supposed "big day" had come and gone without a grand jury announcement.

Still, there was a foreboding feeling in the air. The suspense about the decision was settling in over the St. Louis region like a damp, heavy blanket of fog. As the morning progressed, I watched the pieces moving around the chessboard, and I was increasingly certain that it really was going to be the day that the long-awaited announcement would be made public.

The sense of finality that came along with that was both a relief and a concern. I felt confident that Darren would be absolved of guilt, but the apprehension over what havoc such news would bring was disquieting.

I am an optimist by nature, but there was no reason to be optimistic about what the grand jury announcement would bring. I saw people carrying around signs that said "Pray for Peace," but what everyone seemed to have forgotten was, if you pray for peace without praying for the peacemakers, you have squandered your prayers. So I held no illusion that we would be spared the bedlam we saw in August, or worse. I said to one reporter that it was going to be like the Detroit Pistons playing in the NBA Championship: if they win they'll burn cars; if they lose they'll burn cars. I wish they had only burned cars.

In the early afternoon, the prosecutor's office announced that the grand jury findings would be made public later that day. I was on the phone all day talking to union officials, police commanders, Darren's attorneys, and reporters. I was booked up with nationally broadcast TV appearances to comment on the looming announcement.

I visited the command post in St. Louis city, and then headed out to Ferguson to visit with troops in the command post there. I then spent the rest of the evening at the nearby makeshift media village to do a series of live remotes, mostly with CNN. They kept me on the air with their correspondents as the evening unfolded, and various commentators speculated about what the grand jury decision would bring.

Then came the *ignoramus*, although Bob McCulloch never used that word.

Bob did chide the media and others who spread untruths about the grand jury process and the material facts of the case itself. Here are some excerpts from his public announcement:

> The most significant challenge encountered in this investigation has been the 24 hour news cycle and its insatiable appetite for something—for anything—to talk about, following closely behind were the non-stop rumors on social media.

I recognize, of course, that the lack of accurate detail surrounding the shooting frustrates the media and the general public, and helps breed suspicion among those already distrustful of the system. Yet those closely guarded details especially about the physical evidence give law enforcement a yardstick for measuring the truthfulness of witnesses. . . . The grand jury worked tirelessly to examine and re-examine all of the testimony of the witnesses and all of the physical evidence. . . .

They met on 25 separate days in the last three months, heard more than 70 hours of testimony from about 60 witnesses. . . .

They heard from three medical examiners . . .

They were instructed on the law and presented with five indictments, ranging from murder in the first degree to involuntary manslaughter. Their burden was to determine, based upon all of the evidence, if probable cause exists to believe that a crime was committed, and that Darren Wilson was the person that committed that crime. . . .

They discussed and debated the evidence among themselves before arriving at their collective decision. After their exhaustive review of the evidence, the grand jury deliberated over two days before making their final decision. They determined that no probable cause exists to file any charge against Officer Wilson and returned a no true bill on each of the five indictments.[1]

McCulloch pledged to the media and the public that he would take the extraordinary step of releasing the evidence and testimony publicly. He urged that a constructive and peaceful conversation would follow that might help us avoid similar deadly encounters between police and those with whom they come into contact.

As McCulloch was pleading for peace, those among the protesters who longed for anarchy were calling for death and destruction, even as Brown's biological parents joined black clergy and African-American community leaders in urging calm.

The term *mob mentality* is sort of self-defining. It means what it sounds like it means; that is, when you pack a bunch of angry, confused people together and inject the corrosive words of havoc-craving agitators into the mix, it is easy for things to spin out of control very quickly. Add to that the thoughtless words of those who let their emotions get the best of them, like Brown's stepfather, Louis Head, who exhorted the crowd to "burn this motherf----r down,"[2] and you have a powder keg.

The keg was lit and the "motherf----r" burned down.

In all, more than a dozen buildings were looted and set ablaze. Several more businesses were pillaged as well. At least three police cars were torched. Hundreds of shots were fired, and the city of Ferguson lay in ruin when the smoke finally cleared.

Let's be frank. There have been some very bad, albeit extremely isolated examples of police misconduct or overreactions on the part of a handful of law enforcement officers before and since Michael Brown died, incidents that would understandably lead to anger and social upheaval. Brown's death at the hands of Darren Wilson wasn't one of those. There were better martyrs for the cause, whatever that cause is in this case. I don't claim to understand it. There is no excuse in a case where the facts were so irrefutable, for violence and destruction to have boiled over as it did in Ferguson.

There is an explanation, though, and it is undeniable. The point of terrorism is to strike terror in the hearts of your enemies. I have called them anarchists; you may call them terrorists. Call them whatever you like, but the inciters of these riots in the name of Michael Brown know that nothing strikes fear into the soul of a nation like senseless violence. Nothing is more frightening than a threat that you can't make sense of or see coming.

That is why they rioted. That is why they burned and looted and fired shots into the crowd and at police officers—to engender fear, pure, base fear produced by unbridled, senseless hatred.

Those who loved or sympathized with Michael Brown had a right to mourn, a right to demand answers, a right to pray for change. But nobody, NOBODY, has a right to behave like those who decimated Ferguson.

✪ ✪ ✪

Something else horrible happened "the night they drove old Fergy down."

As pandemonium spread across the St. Louis region in the wake of the grand jury acquittal of Darren Wilson, a thirty-three-year-old black man named Major Washington broke into his mother's home a couple of towns over from Ferguson and brutally murdered her.

University City Police Officer Zach Hoelzer and other officers from his department responded to the shooting scene only to be met with gunfire. Zach was hit by gunshots and critically wounded. He barely survived, and the damage done by the bullets has almost certainly ended his police career.

Because all the St. Louis area SWAT teams were tied up with the civil unrest in and around Ferguson, the FBI SWAT team was called in to apprehend Washington when police investigators located him two days later.

It was a high-risk entry, and Washington opened fire on the FBI tactical team, shooting two agents as he tried to evade capture. The FBI SWAT team heroically ended the threat that Washington presented to them and to the community by returning fire, killing Washington.

The FBI SWAT team showed up in an armored vehicle, wearing military-type fatigues; they were equipped with body armor and helmets, and they were carrying automatic weapons. They absolutely, positively should've been equipped with that gear; it likely saved agents' lives. When the press demanded the names of the agents involved in the shooting, the FBI said that they would never release the names of those agents, and rightfully so. The FBI agents who responded to that deadly threat had a right to be protected and a right to be free from the intimidation of having their names made public.

So, too, do local law enforcement officers in this country.

It is utterly confounding that the FBI, the premier law enforcement agency within Eric Holder's Department of Justice, is allowed to keep their men and women safe, yet when local law enforcement employs the same lifesaving protective gear and weapons, or tries to keep the men and women who work for them safe by withholding the names of their officers who are involved in shootings, Holder and his political sycophants scream, "Militarization!" or "Cover-up!" What an unthinkable double standard. Pure hypocrisy.

With all of my focus concentrated on the uprising in Ferguson, what happened in University City the night of the grand jury decision escaped my attention. I feel very bad about that. It wasn't until months later that I got in contact with the injured officer, Zach Hoelzer, to help get him some assistance, and to put him in contact with a network of other officers who had been shot in the line of duty.

Zach's department said that his shooting had nothing to do with Ferguson. I disagree. I think the lawlessness and antipolice sentiment that permeated our region had everything to do with why Washington turned a gun on Zach and the two FBI agents. I believe firmly that Washington was using the turmoil of the grand jury decision as cover for his despicable matricide.

Zach's story is worth hearing and worth telling. It is a cautionary tale, one that should not be forgotten. Here is the column I wrote about my interview with Zach. I'm just sorry it took me so long to write it.

ZACH HOELZER: UNKNOWN SOLDIER?[3]

It was easy to miss. Even for those of us in law enforcement it was just, well, too damn easy to miss. That's not an acceptable excuse. It never should be.

November 24, 2014, was a harrowing night to say the very least. Tensions in the St. Louis area were at an all-time high as the imminent grand jury decision on the Michael Brown shooting death was expected some time that day.

The inevitable trouble that ultimately followed the announcement wasn't anticipated to be limited to Ferguson, so police departments all around the St. Louis area were on high alert. Most departments had cancelled rec days and extended work shifts so that more officers would be on patrol. As a precaution, most departments had their officers riding in two-man cars.

The University City Police Department was no different. Zach Hoelzer, a five-year veteran of the department at the time, was riding in a two-man car with a relatively new officer that he didn't really know well, even though the two had both graduated from the same school, Fox High School, though years apart.

It was Zach's first night back on the midnight shift. He and his partner were listening intently to the police radio as pandemonium unfolded in nearby Ferguson. U City Police had not sent officers to Ferguson to aid the police there in any of the civil unrest that preceded the grand jury decision but Zach thought they might, and hoped that he would be deployed if they did. "I was hoping they would send us if things got bad, since they hadn't before," Zach recalled as I sat down with him recently.

Zach was visibly anxious as we spoke over lunch. After all, he had a lot on his mind.

Zach harkened back to the night of November 24. He had just hit the street when he and his partner got a call to assist on a burglary in progress. Zach and his partner arrived at the scene the same time as his sergeant.

As the three of them approached the house, Zach saw a man standing in a stairwell leading into the basement of the residence. As they made eye contact, Zach pulled back toward cover, but it was too late. The suspect opened up on Zach, striking him in the left arm with two of the shots in the first salvo of gunfire.

Zach was downed and dazed by his wounds. As it turned out, the round that did the most damage entered his left arm and tore through his shoulder, dissecting the brachial artery in two places and severing many of the nerves in his brachial plexus, the nerve bundle often referred to as the "powerhouse for the arm and hand." The bullet then fractured one of his ribs and finally came to rest very near Zach's heart, where it remains lodged today, nearly six months later. Surgically, the dangers of removing the bullet outweigh the benefits.

With essentially no use of his left arm and losing blood fast, Zach

returned fire as he struggled to reach cover. All along, the suspect continued to fire on him. After six or seven rounds, Zach's sidearm stove-
piped. He was able to clear the jam one-handed, but he wasn't able to
re-load the magazine into the gun without the use of his other hand.

He shouted out to the other officers on the scene to let them
know that he was hit, unable to re-load, and losing consciousness
fast. The situation was dire. Zach said he felt like a sitting duck as
his assailant paced back and forth in the cover of darkness, the smell
of gunsmoke wafting through the air.

With diminishing options for survival, Zach knew he had to do
something fast. As the shooter moved east away from him momen-
tarily, Zach made a mad dash for the patrol cars that were parked in
the opposite direction.

He was greeted with bleak expressions from his fellow officers
who could readily see that Zach was critically injured. His lieutenant
threw him in a patrol car and rushed him to nearby St. Mary's
Hospital.

St. Mary's is not a Level One trauma center, but this is where
some divine intervention took form. Zach was crashing. He was
hypovolemic having bled out nearly 8 pints of blood; that's well over
half the blood in a human body. His blood pressure was 40 over 0.
His heart was barely pumping. He was kept alive by assisted breathing
as the ER team rushed to set up a rapid infusion of blood and plasma.

It was sheer good fortune that the Interim ER Director, Doctor
Treaster, was working the floor that night. The doc was an experienced ER physician who had worked in a nearby trauma center where
they had loads of experience with gunshot wounds. Zach believes that
he wouldn't have survived if a lesser-experienced doctor had been on
duty that night.

Zach was stabilized and transferred to St. Louis University
Hospital where he stayed for several days until he was well enough
to go home. He said he felt helpless lying in bed as the manhunt for
his assailant unfolded on TV. It ultimately ended with a spectacular

shoot-out that left two FBI agents shot and the suspect dead in a fiery blaze that consumed the house he was holed up in.

Zach's recovery is far from over. He was scheduled to have neurosurgery just three days after I sat down with him. The prognosis isn't good. The chance of Zach regaining any appreciable use of his left arm is a long shot. At best, the surgery could improve the gripping motion in his left hand. At worst, it could leave him with even further diminished use of his arm and hand. As Zach explained his grim medical outlook to me over lunch, I commented on the way he struggled over simple physical tasks like taking a straw out of its paper wrapper. He responded in stride, "You should see me try to put on a pair of jeans . . . no more button flies for me."

Zach described asking for help even with the simplest of tasks as "very demoralizing." He said he's trying to learn to take the help when it's offered.

Zach described his family with words like "amazing" and "incredible" when it came to helping him through all this. Zach's mom and dad have been stalwarts throughout this traumatic chapter in his life. His dad has been great at answering calls and e-mails, and thanking people for their support. His mom is a cancer survivor who Zach described fondly as "tough as nails." He credited his survival attitude to her, citing the example she set for him through her fight against the deadly disease. "She knows what it's like to be on the brink and pull through." That family trait was clearly passed on to Zach.

Zach's cousin stepped up in a big way, too. Without anyone even asking for his help, he started a GoFundMe page for Zach that has raised $16,000 so far to offset medical bills and loss of income.

Zach beamed as he talked about his new bride, Meg. He called her a "real trooper." The two had only been married for about four months when Zach was shot. "She didn't sign up for this, but she has been a rock. When people ask her how she's doing she says, 'I'm fine; I haven't been shot.'" It is that sort of stoic devotion to Zach that seems to best characterize their life in the aftermath of his debilitating injuries.

He and Meg had planned to jet to a tropical locale for a honeymoon in the winter, but a bullet with Zach's name on it changed all that. The two are making the best of it though and plan to turn their trip to see Zach's sister get married in Colorado into a mini-honeymoon. Zach said they both love the mountains, but the trip will be tough on him because his body doesn't handle changes in the weather very well anymore.

Zach agreed that getting shot just isn't what people expect it to be, based on pop culture portrayals in movies or TV where a cop gets shot in the shoulder, shakes it off, and then karate chops his way through a half a dozen bandits. "Being shot is always bad. It's never a good thing to have an extra hole in your body," Zach observed. Zach was visibly uncomfortable talking about such things. He commented that he just "doesn't like being the center of attention."

That was very clear to me when I attended a fundraiser for Zach just a few days earlier with Joe Eagan. Joe and I both serve on the Shield of Hope, an FOP police charity that presented a check to Zach for $1,000 that night. I also presented Zach with a second $500 contribution from the St. Louis Police Officers Association at the fundraiser.

Zach was clearly overwhelmed by the outpouring of support that night. He doesn't like crowds, he doesn't like being fussed over, and, as he told me, he doesn't think he did anything "heroic or special . . . I just got shot." To the contrary, everyone in the overflow crowd that night obviously thought Zach was both special and heroic. How could you not, given the grace and determination he demonstrated at the moment that bullet seared through his flesh and every moment since?

Zach was particularly appreciative of Joe Eagan. Not so much for the money that Joe has helped raise for him, but more for the inspiration Joe has provided Zach. Joe, you see, is a survivor of a near fatal line of duty gunshot wound himself. Talking to Joe and other GSW [gunshot wound] survivors that Joe has put Zach in contact with has really helped Zach. Likewise, talking to the spouses of those survivors has helped Meg immensely in preparing for what's next.

So, what is next for Zach and Meg? Only time will tell. One thing is certain, though, it won't be easy. Zach acknowledged that saying, "[I]t is what it is, but we [he and Meg] can still enjoy our life together. Reality is reality, you can't wish it away."

It was that matter-of-fact survival attitude that pulled Zach through on November 24. As Zach lay bleeding in that yard in University City, he recalls that "I decided I was going to live through this as I dragged myself to cover and returned fire. I said to myself, 'I really like my life and I really like living'."

As I watched Zach awkwardly greeting the steady stream of well-wishers that filed through his fundraiser, I was embarrassed that it had taken us so long to turn out in support of this reluctant hero.

There is a certain honor in the selflessness of quiet, anonymous service to your fellow man. It is why we hold the unidentified remains of the Tomb of the Unknown Soldiers of foreign wars in such high regard.

But, there is a difference between an unknown soldier and a forgotten soldier.

As Zach was writhing on the blood soaked urban battlefield, scratching and struggling for dear life, the riots, arson, and looting in Ferguson consumed the attention of our city, our country, and really, the entire world. We would serve ourselves better as a nation . . . as a people, to turn our faces away from the bright, hot lights of spectacle and sensation, and honor our true heroes, lest there be another unknown soldier.

12

RAMIFICATIONS

Do you remember where you were at noon on Sunday, November 30, 2014? I do.

It was an unseasonably warm, sunny day for late fall in St. Louis. My grandmother would have called it "Indian summer." The temperature climbed to seventy-two degrees, a record high.

Between my election and the hullabaloo in Ferguson, my yard had been severely neglected. As I surveyed my overgrown backyard, I thought, *I need to mow this one more time before winter gets here.*

I know that guys are supposed to be sprawled out on the couch, watching football, on a late fall Sunday afternoon, but I hadn't caught a minute of gridiron action the whole season because of the slate of other things occupying my time those days. Besides, baseball is my game.

My earliest memories include listening to Cardinals games with my grandpa on a little green transistor radio he had. Televised games were fairly rare back then, so we would strain through the static to hear Jack Buck's and Mike Shannon's descriptions of every pitch, every play on the field. I can almost smell the slight whiff of Lysol in the basement of my grandparents' old brick house as I think about those days now. My abiding love for baseball, a gift from my grandpa, severely suppressed my interest in football.

It's not that I hate football. I really like college football, particularly when I get to actually go to a game. The cool snap in the air, the blustering wind, the hot cocoa, the hotter coeds . . . it's a great time.

Professional football, though? It just seemed too—I don't know— sanitized, too austere. Particularly when played under a dome as it was in St. Louis. I just didn't care about the Rams. Even when they were a great team under the leadership of Kurt Warner, I just wasn't that into them. And in more recent times, well, they just weren't very good.

So the fact that noon was game time for the Rams that day didn't matter to me one iota. Yard maintenance ranked way above that on the list.

I like to listen to my iPod when I'm mowing the lawn. I get lost in the music, and it makes the chore go faster. The only problem with that is, the ring of your phone interrupts the music, and you know you have a call. I made the mistake of answering the call.

"Did you see what the Rams did?" a copper's voice on the other end of the phone barked.

Who cares? I thought to myself. *It's the Rams.*

He went on to explain that five members of the Rams receiver corps came onto the field doing the "Hands up, don't shoot" gesture. I thought, *NFL players make a lot of jack. Don't they own TVs? That myth's been busted.*

Then again I thought, *Who cares? It's the Rams.*

I commiserated about the players' misconception of the reality of the Brown shooting for a minute, and then I got off the phone as quick as I could. Shortly thereafter, I got a second call, then a third call, then a fourth. The more calls I got, the more I realized how offensive the players' misguided gesture was to cops.

I put the lawn mower away with the yard half-finished. After consulting with a couple of my board members, I headed inside and pounded out a press release condemning the players' action. I e-mailed it around to the local media, hoping I'd get the *Post-Dispatch* or one of the local TV stations to bite. They bit, all right.

I never really appreciated the term "going viral," but that story spread like smallpox. The story was up on the AP wire in no time, and then got picked up by media all across the country. Poor Rams. They shut out the Raiders by an astounding 52–0, by far one of their best games in modern history, and all anyone could talk about was the "Hands-up, don't shoot" display and the criticism that followed. I was flabbergasted by the way the story took off. Here is the press release I sent out:

ST. LOUIS POLICE OFFICERS ASSOCIATION CONDEMNS INFLAMMATORY DISPLAY AT RAMS GAME

St. Louis, Missouri (November 30, 2014)—The St. Louis Police Officers Association is profoundly disappointed with the members of the St. Louis Rams football team who chose to ignore the mountains of evidence released from the St. Louis County Grand Jury this week and engage in a display that police officers around the nation found tasteless, offensive, and inflammatory.

Five members of the Rams entered the field today exhibiting the "Hands-up-don't-shoot" pose that has been adopted by protesters who accused Ferguson Police Officer Darren Wilson of murdering Michael Brown. The gesture has become synonymous with assertions that Michael Brown was innocent of any wrongdoing and attempting to surrender peacefully when Wilson, according to some now-discredited witnesses, gunned him down in cold blood.

SLPOA Business Manager Jeff Roorda said, "Now that the evidence is in, and Officer Wilson's account has been verified by physical and ballistic evidence, as well as eye-witness testimony, which led the grand jury to conclude that no probable cause existed, and that Wilson hadn't engaged in any wrongdoing, it is unthinkable that hometown athletes would so publicly perpetuate a narrative that has been disproven over and over again."

Roorda was incensed that the Rams and the NFL would tolerate such behavior and called it remarkably hypocritical. "All week long, the Rams and the NFL were on the phone with the St. Louis Police Department asking for assurances that the players and the fans would be kept safe from the violent protesters who had rioted, looted, and burned buildings in Ferguson. Our officers have been working twelve-hour shifts for over a week, and they had days off, including Thanksgiving, cancelled so that they could defend this community from those on the streets that perpetuate this myth that Michael Brown was executed by a brother police officer, and then, as the players and their fans sit safely in their dome under the watchful protection of hundreds of St. Louis's finest, they take to the turf to call a now-exonerated officer a murderer, that is way out-of-bounds, to put it in football parlance," Roorda said.

The SLPOA is calling for the players involved to be disciplined and for the Rams and the NFL to deliver a very public apology. Roorda said he planned to speak to the NFL and the Rams to voice his organization's displeasure tomorrow. He also plans to reach out to other police organizations in St. Louis and around the country to enlist their input on what the appropriate response from law enforcement should be. Roorda warned, "I know that there are those that will say that these players are simply exercising their First Amendment rights. Well, I've got news for people who think that way, cops have First Amendment rights, too, and we plan to exercise ours. I'd remind the NFL and their players that it is not the violent thugs burning down buildings that buy their advertiser's products. It's cops and the good people of St. Louis and other NFL towns that do. Somebody needs to throw a flag on this play. If it's not the NFL and the Rams, then it'll be cops and their supporters."

Harsh? Perhaps, but the Rams and the NFL had it coming.

I learned quickly that the media loves stories where sports collide with politics. The calls started coming in from print, radio, and TV reporters right away. I really thought I was done with the cable news circuit after the Darren Wilson grand jury decision, but there I was, back again, doing the rounds on cable TV.[1] It wasn't just the cable channels this time; I also got calls from network shows, like *CBS News* and *Inside Edition*. Other shows weighed in too.

Keith Olbermann named me the "worst person in the sports world" on December 1, 2014, on his show *Olbermann* on ESPN2 or ESPN 16 or whatever second-tier station the network had banished him to. Olbermann went on a three-minute blistering tirade about what an awful person I was for challenging the "Hands up, don't shoot" myth and expressing how offensive the gesture was to cops. Of course, the content of his remarks weren't directed at the validity of what I had to say; rather, he engaged in a blathering ad hominem attack against me. Sports fans, I think, see things more from my perspective and the perspective of cops than they do from Olbermann's smug, sanctimonious, self-righteous point of view. I say that because a few months later, on July 8, 2015, ESPN parted ways with Olbermann and cancelled his show. I guess July 8 was the day that ESPN named Keith Olbermann the "worst person in the sports world."

Jon Stewart also lampooned me on Comedy Central's *The Daily Show*. That one stung a bit because I've always liked Stewart and appreciated his groundbreaking brand of satirical political commentary.

Even while watching myself being eviscerated by the news skit on the Rams controversy, I found myself laughing out loud at many of the things Stewart had to say. As he summed things up in his final analysis, he played an interview clip of me and then groused, "So, the St. Louis Police Association is angry and outraged to have been caught in this hail of gestures . . . and feels that the community won't get past this tragic pantomime, unless someone is held accountable. That's the angle they're going with."[2] Oh, Jon.

In twisting the story to his comedic devices, Stewart missed the point that the police in the St. Louis region were caught in an actual months-long hail of gunfire, because this now-debunked gesture advanced a narrative that police were guilty of gunning down Michael Brown and other young, unarmed black men in St. Louis as they tried to peacefully surrender. It just didn't happen that way, and the Rams players knew that by the time they took the field on November 30. That's the angle I was going with.

The dustup with the Rams swirled for a couple of weeks without any resolution. There were ongoing meetings between the police union and the football club during that time. The team's management expressed "regret" that the on-field demonstration had offended the police, but they were unwilling to apologize, and the involved players were indignant at the idea that their antics were offensive to police. In the end, all we asked for from the Rams' management was that they make a public statement saying something like "The opinions of our players are their own and are not necessarily the opinion of the St. Louis Rams management." They were unwilling to even do that, which I found vexing.

The team clung to the position that the league and NFL franchises absolutely do not infringe on their players' freedom of speech and expression on or off the field. Hmmm. That's funny. When the Rams drafted openly gay football player Michael Sam, Miami Dolphins defensive back Don Jones tweeted two comments: "OMG" and "Horrible." Jones tweeted from off the field, from his home, in the off-season. He didn't mention Sam. He didn't mention the Rams. He didn't mention the NFL or the NFL Draft; just the two comments: "OMG" and "Horrible." The Dolphins and the NFL, of course, immediately sprang to the defense of his exercise of free speech. Oh, wait . . . that's not what happened. They suspended him and fined him and *cowed him into making a public apology*!

Listen: I don't mind if you throw me on the ground and smear me in sheep shit; just don't try to tell me it's chocolate syrup.

Before our talks collapsed, the Rams offered to make a sizable donation to the FOP's charitable wing and provide discounted tickets for a "law enforcement appreciation" night at a nationally televised Thursday night game. I suppose that would have served as a symbolic apology, but it would have appeared as though they had bought us off to some. We weren't interested. In the end, the team made a very generous on-field donation to another police charity. That was a nice gesture, I suppose, but the gesture the players made on the field, perpetuating the myth that cops are cold-blooded murderers of innocent kids is not easily forgiven. I don't forgive the Rams that transgression. I know a lot of other cops and former Rams fans that feel the same way.

Actions have consequences. That was the main lesson of Ferguson. It's a shame the Rams couldn't embrace that concept.

✪ ✪ ✪

About five or six years ago, my wife and I decided that instead of buying Christmas gifts for each other, we would buy stuff for ourselves and put a gift tag on it as though each had bought it for the other. I never really knew what she wanted for Christmas, and I couldn't even *think* about returning the hideous-looking shirts and ties she bought me without damning disapproval and a furrowed brow. I guess I'm just a bad husband.

Under our new arrangement, there was still the element of surprise that comes with the opening of presents from under the tree. In our case, it was simply surprise at what we had unknowingly bought for the other. Nancy was extra surprised when I tore open my big gift for Christmas 2014: a Remington model 870, 12-gauge tactical shotgun with pistol grips and a collapsible stock.

Ah, it was like "The Gift of the Magi." Eat your heart out, O. Henry!

She was, to say the least, perplexed. I explained to her, or I should say, I lied to her and said that it was the gun I had always wanted and had decided to spend my Christmas bonus to buy it. She looked at me with a skewed eye, and then opened her gift from me . . . whatever that was. I don't remember. Wow. I guess I really am a crappy husband.

Anyway, what I didn't tell Nancy was that the death threats I'd already been receiving from the "peaceful" protesters in Ferguson and their supporters around the nation had really skyrocketed after the head-line-grabbing coverage of the Rams hands-up debacle. The threats of violence were nothing new in the wake of my very public discomposing of the "Hands up, don't shoot" opus. It was more than just verbal threats; the violent anarchists who had descended on Ferguson wanted to make sure I knew that they knew where I lived. I live on six acres, and I have a billboard on my property. During campaigns, I use the billboard to put up a large Elect Roorda sign. In mid-November, after the election was over, but before I had a chance to remove my sign, these terrorists spray painted a large, red *A* with a circle around it on my billboard just a few hundred feet from my house. The encircled *A* is of course the internationally recognized symbol for "Anarchy," the same symbol that had been prominent at the riotous protests these savage anarchists co-opted in Ferguson. Things only got worse after the Rams story went national.

In the true spirit of the holiday season, menacing hashtags directed at me and my family had taken hold on social media. It was a bit unsettling to open up my Twitter or Facebook account and see #killroorda.

I wasn't terribly concerned, though. In my law enforcement experience, people who really plan to kill you don't tweet about it first. They generally just hop in a car and come blow your brains out without much fanfare and without previewing their murderous intentions. The sheriff was a friend, so his deputies patrolled my neighborhood regularly. And I had a houseful of guns and the training to use them in a firefight. Now I also had a shotgun, which any member of my family could point and shoot at an intruder without much training and with a high likelihood of success. Still, I didn't like to be away from the house, so when I was going to be gone overnight, I had the Sheriff's Department do extra patrols of the house.

I had to do all of this without telling my wife and family, because the point of terrorism is to terrorize. I didn't want the animals threatening me and my loved ones to win. My wife and kids knowing about the threats and the fear it would produce would have been a win for the cowards on the other end of the Internet. I wasn't going to let that happen.

That's why I rushed down to the living room on New Year's Eve to try to turn off the TV before my wife heard the news report about a man being arrested for making online death threats against Darren Wilson and me. Too late. She had already heard enough to know this guy was a serious threat.

The tweet-creep's name was Jason Valentine. He had dubbed New Year's Eve "kill a pig night," and had made specific death threats against Darren and me, offering a bounty if someone succeeded in the dubious call for violence. What an ignoramus.

Valentine's vitriol was more than the harmless musings of a deranged man. To be criminally charged for such hate speech, you have to do more than simply wish harm to someone. You have to take a substantial step toward seeing it through to reality. Valentine was charged with ten felony counts, so I would say his threats were substantial.[3]

I'm generally a pretty forgiving person, especially around the holiday season, but I remember thinking at the time that I hoped they'd not only send Valentine to prison but that they'd build a prison on top of him. Not because I was scared of him but because of the fear and alarm that I saw in my wife's eyes that night. At least my kids weren't in the living room when the story aired.

I reflected on 2014 in my holiday column for the *Gendarme*. It was a dreary piece that I wrote just days after Valentine's arrest. In a play on the title of Aldous Huxley's *A Brave New World*, I bemoaned the "Grave New World" in which we were living in the post-Ferguson era, and what a grave injustice it all was. I talked about the pre-Christmas ambush killings of New York officers Rafael Ramos and Wenjian Liu, and what a sad social commentary that was:

A GRAVE NEW WORLD[4]

I would, just once, love to write my holiday column about what a calm and uneventful year has passed and use this space to wish our members and retirees good tidings in the spirit of the season. But, rather than a Dickensian tale of "peace on earth, good will to men," we find ourselves in the midst of a Huxlian story where "history is bunk."

Just as the forces of evil in Aldous Huxley's seminal novel tried to bend reality by denying history and obfuscating facts, so, too, are we in the midst of a re-writing of history. The post-Ferguson narrative that has emerged is one where police officers are tried and convicted in the court of public opinion by a small but loud group of militant radicals for the most heinous acts imaginable without the benefit of facts, evidence, or reasoned thought.

And, that's not the worst of it.

There is an all-out war against law enforcement afoot. Particularly, here in the St. Louis region where every police-involved shooting, no matter how undeniably unavoidable, is followed by a riot and death threats directed at the officers involved.

We've all heard about the threats of violence against the St. Louis police officers who were allegedly involved in the fatal shooting of Kajieme Powell and Vonderrit Myers . . . Even yours truly was targeted with death threats by Twitter tough-guy "@jdstl314" for the odious offense of publicly speaking out and setting the record straight on behalf of Darren Wilson and other police officers who HAD TO take a life in the line of duty.

Now that jdstl314, a.k.a., Jason Valentine, is in custody, just wait for the cries from the radical cop-haters that his First Amendment rights are being suppressed because the big, bad police want to silence his "public discourse." . . .

But, this isn't just a war of words. While the families of NYPD Officers Rafael Ramos and Wenjian Liu were at home wrapping Christmas presents for their loved ones, those two officers, who were guilty of nothing more than wearing a blue uniform to work, were savagely murdered by a man that took the vitriolic battle cries of the cowards lurking in the shadows to heart.

The novel *Brave New World* ends with the protagonist, John, hanging by the neck in a lighthouse, dejected that his quest to make sense of a senseless world has met such a hopeless end. Let's hope that truth and justice don't meet the same fate in the world we are currently living.

On that grim note, watch out for the people out there who want to do you harm and have a safe and happy New Year.

I'm generally a positive person by nature, but after 2014, my faith in humankind was shaken to its foundation. Surely 2015 was bound to be a better year . . . Right?

13

CHARACTER
CZOLGOSZING

On September 6, 1901, President William McKinley strode boldly into the music hall at the Pan-American Expo in Buffalo, New York, despite his top advisers' repeated warnings of a possible assassination attempt.

Although he is largely forgotten by history, McKinley was a decorated Civil War hero and a popular president. One could easily make a case that McKinley is the most underrated Republican president in US history. Under his leadership, the dollar was stabilized, the country saw a speedy recovery from the Panic of 1893, and McKinley scored a swift and sure victory for our beleaguered, post–Civil War nation in the Spanish-American War. McKinley also greatly expanded US influence abroad by occupying Cuba and territorializing Puerto Rico, Guam, the Philippines, and Hawaii. McKinley, incidentally, was wildly popular with African-American voters, and no Republican, before or since, has captured as much of the black vote as McKinley did.

Despite McKinley enjoying broad appeal and easily coasting to a landslide re-election in 1900, his inner circle was worried about the anti-government zealotry espoused by eastern European immigrants aligned with the anarchist movement (note that anarchists were a problem at the dawn of the twentieth century, just as they were in Ferguson in modern times). McKinley's chief of staff had twice removed the event at the music hall from the president's schedule due to security concerns, but McKinley insisted on making the appearance.

It was a fateful decision. Minutes after entering the hall, a Polish American anarchist named Leon Czolgosz (pronounced Zul-gosh) shot McKinley twice in the abdomen. The nation watched in horror for the next eight days as their beloved leader writhed in pain as his wounds became gangrenous. McKinley finally succumbed to his injuries on September 14, 1901.

In the wake of his murder, the ire of an entire nation turned against Czolgosz and his anarchist ilk. Czolgosz's trial began just nine days after McKinley's death. The next day, after deliberating for just one hour, the jury found Czolgosz guilty of first degree murder and sentenced him to death. Just over a month after his trial, Czolgosz sat in a wooden chair at Auburn Prison with 1800 volts of electricity coursing through his convulsing body.

The American public so despised Czolgosz that his body was entombed in a vat of sulfuric acid on the prison grounds and his writings and belongings were burned to ash so there would be no trace left of the monster that had slain the lauded and laureled president.

McKinley's assassination led to the advent of the Secret Service as the agency charged with presidential security.

The disdain for Czolgosz was so intense that historians believe it to be the origin of mistreatment and derision toward Polish Americans. Some even credit it as the beginning of the "Polack joke."

Thus, the word *Czolgosz* entered the American lexicon as a synonym for treachery, cowardice, and assassination. Hence my use here of the term "character czolgoszing" as a euphemism for character assassination employed by the violent, anti-American anarchists in Ferguson.

Let's make something clear right now. *Character assassination* is a term of art. It has unambiguous meaning when used to describe the maligning and discrediting of those with whom you disagree when you cannot convincingly refute their assertions. It is a subterfuge, a sleight of hand. Character assassination is *not*—despite the nattering of pundits, pols, and protest organizers—the act of releasing the video of a person committing a strong arm robbery.

Here is a quick primer for those confused by the meaning of the term *character assassination*. Character assassination is when you say that someone you're trying to discredit did something wrong, like, oh, let's say using brute force against an unsuspecting shop owner during a cigarillo theft, when he really *didn't* do that at all. There is a completely different term used to describe the release of a speaks-for-itself video of Michael Brown robbing the Ferguson Market. That term is *reality*.

You see, Brown was not the victim of character assassination at all. His disrepute was the product of his own violent, criminal acts.

The term *character assassination* isn't strong enough to describe what happened to Darren Wilson, Chief Tom Jackson, Prosecutor Bob McCulloch, or anyone who had the audacity to question Michael Brown's status as a folk hero—thus, my long-winded treatise on the assassination of President William McKinley by the anarchist Leon Czolgosz.

The derision aimed against anyone who disrupted the "Hands up, don't shoot" narrative needed a stronger, more illustrative expression to describe the caustic personal attacks and physical threats heaped on those of us who tried to set history right. I coined the phrase "character czolgoszing" because it so squarely describes the acrimony and violent intimidation employed by the antiestablishment anarchists and their sympathizers who represent the closest thing we have to Leon Czolgosz in post-twentieth-century America.

The *czolgoszing* took its toll. Darren Wilson resigned from the Ferguson Police Department, even though a grand jury found him innocent of any wrongdoing in the death of Michael Brown. Darren and his family had to put their house up for sale and go into hiding. Sadly, I'm convinced he will never work in his chosen profession of law enforcement again, though he acted properly in the face of Brown's attempts to injure or kill him and was exonerated by not just the grand jury, but by Eric Holder's Justice Department as well.

Tom Jackson was a *czolgoszee* too. The decorated police officer left his post as the Ferguson police chief in disgrace, or, at least, that's how the media spun it. In fact, he left with head held high, performing one last selfless, altruistic act as a police officer when he decided that a concentrated focus on him would only serve as a distraction to the recovery and healing of the city he loved.

The *czolgoszing* of Tom Jackson didn't stop there. The violent, anarchistic elements within the protests weren't satisfied with a pound of flesh; they wanted a gallon of blood too. I know Tom Jackson. We worked a number of cases together when we were both assigned to drug task forces back in the '90s. I can tell you, it weighs heavily on him that the celebration of his resignation ended with two cops shot from the shadows by a *czolgoszesque* coward.

Tom, if you're reading this, please don't blame yourself for the shameless act of yet another terrorist bent on death and destruction. He and he alone is responsible for his despicable acts, and hopefully, he will be judged harshly for them.

Perhaps it seems a bit self-indulgent to say, but Tom and Darren don't have anything on me when it comes to getting *czolgoszed*.

Despite all the evidence to the contrary, protesters believed that Darren Wilson murdered Michael Brown in cold blood as Brown attempted to surrender. Thanks to the specious report conjured up by Eric Holder's Justice Department, they also believed that Chief Tom Jackson lorded over a racist police department whose policies led to bad treatment of people of color, which ostensibly led to Michael Brown's death.

All I was, was a spokesman for the police union, far removed from the actual events of August 9, 2014. Logically, you would expect that, compared to Darren and Tom, I would be the subject of relatively insubstantial disdain. Not so. The vile things that were said about me on social media, and to me in person by protesters and their sympathizers, were every bit as disgusting as what they said about Darren and Tom. Take this Facebook post from "Tim Johnson," for example:

TIM JOHNSON: Officer Darren Wilson should be eating shit and cleaning piss at a Taco Bell while being managed by a 260-pound African American. Jeffrey Roorda should be taken out and shot. December 1, 2014 at 1:25am

What the hell, dude?! How come Darren gets to live out his life in gainful employment at a local fast food eatery, and I get a bullet in the face? You don't even mention Tom Jackson in your post, Tim. What'd I do to earn such fuming rancor?

I'll tell you what I did. I committed the greatest sin of them all, worse than "institutionalizing racism," or "murdering a gentle giant": I engaged in the unpardonable act of disrupting the narrative.

I could see it in their eyes when they came stomping toward me at the scene of protests in Ferguson. Odium seemed to ooze out of their pores as they recognized me and subsequently hurled taunts and threats toward me. I have to admit: I was a bit naughty. My cops had to stand there and take those barrages of hate-filled speech, but I didn't. It was cathartic for me to respond to the cutting barbs with something like "You're a great American," or "F**k what you say." I didn't have to be nice.

Admittedly, I probably shouldn't have responded back. In the end it likely only amplified tensions. But, dammit, it was fun to see the protestors' faces when someone finally came back at them. They were drunk with power from bullying and abusing police officers all those months, and my provocative responses had a sobering effect. They didn't know how to react to my rejoinders, but it was fun watching their heads spin.

Of course, all the animus directed at me was about me meticulously setting the record straight in the media with these inconvenient things called facts. Upending the nice, neat little story that had been concocted

about the Michael Brown shooting and the police response to the protests took some heavy lifting, but in the end, the fabricated narrative was
flipped over on its side by guys like me who were relentless in putting
forth the real story of Ferguson.

That didn't sit well with my detractors. They called me a fraud. They
tried to dredge up dirt from my past. In other words, they engaged in
character assassination, or as I like to call it, character *czogloszing*. They
even threatened me, and my family, with bodily injury.

That wasn't enough though.

When the St. Louis City Board of Aldermen convened a committee hearing to consider a bill creating a Civilian Oversight Board
to investigate alleged police misconduct, I attended the hearing, along
with some of the officers I represented. After hearing about thirty-five
witnesses who maligned the police and used inflammatory rhetoric to
gin up the overcapacity crowd, which included many of the Ferguson
protest leaders, the exceptionally antipolice chairman of the committee
finally allowed a couple of the police officers to testify.

The officers were shouted down as one demeaning slur after the
next was hurled at them. I finally took to my feet and demanded that
the chairman maintain order and that my officers be treated with some
respect. The chairman conveniently found his gavel for the first time,
and then castigated me for having the gall to question his authority or
ability to run a meeting. As I left my seat to approach the witness stand
to give the chairman a piece of my mind, a woman grabbed and pushed
me in the aisle.

A riot ensued in the aldermanic chambers. Papers went flying, chairs
tumbled over, and everyone in the room was on their feet, with a large
number of the agitators in the crowd trying to push and shove their way
toward me. The chambers were cleared and the hearing was adjourned.

The rioters, of course, blamed me for the riot. In particular, they
said the "I am Darren Wilson" bracelet I was wearing caused the riot.
Let me make this clear once again: police protective equipment doesn't
cause riots—and neither do rubber wristbands. *Rioters cause riots.*

The St. Louis media happily joined in the chorus of faulting my bracelet for the riot. These were the very same "champions of free speech" who had defended the actions of protesters who shot at and threw Molotov cocktails at police as a constitutionally protected exercise of inalienable rights, no matter how deplorable their behavior.

There was only one news outlet in town that got the story right. *The Allman Report* is a news-talk show on the ABC affiliate in St. Louis, hosted by longtime St. Louis newsman Jamie Allman. Jamie called out the *St. Louis Post-Dispatch* for allegedly enhancing the photo of me wearing the Wilson bracelet on the front page of their newspaper. He also dissected the account of events given by the woman who had grabbed and pushed me, which other media outlets aired unchallenged. She'd claimed that she was innocently trying to leave the hearing chambers when I knocked her over without provocation. But in a segment using slow-motion video, Jamie showed that the woman, seemingly on cue, got up from her chair very near another exit, walked all the way around the room, and positioned herself at the end of the row where I had been seated, to block my egress. The slo-mo video then shows her grab me and hip check me. You can clearly read my lips when I say, "Excuse me" as I try to exit into the aisle, but the women continues to block my path.

Now, that is czolgoszing at its best!

It should be clear to anyone who watches the *Allman* segment that the woman who assaulted me was placed in the audience to precipitate a physical confrontation to discredit me. At least, it was obvious to me.

What better way to undermine the guy who is disrupting the narrative that you've devised?

Of course there were cries for me to be criminally charged with assault, and indeed, the circuit attorney demanded that a police report be written and provided to her office. About seven months later, she quietly told the woman's attorney that no charges would be issued in the case. I'm still waiting to be notified of the decision not to prosecute me. The circuit attorney never asked me if I wanted to file assault charges against the woman who assaulted me, not that I would have.

So, that is the story of how I was *czolgoszed*. That wasn't the end of it, though. The *Post-Dispatch* invented a story about how I had been muzzled by my union because of my supposed bad conduct at the board of aldermen hearing. I struck back in a column titled "No Muzzle for This Pit Bull":

NO MUZZLE FOR THIS PIT BULL[1]

There are people who want to see me muzzled; gagged; silenced. Apparently, most of those people spend their nights burning down buildings in Ferguson or writing for the Post-Dispatch editorial page (although, I'm not sure which is more dangerous to society at-large). These self-proclaimed crusaders for FREEDOM OF SPEECH don't much like it when someone has something to say that contradicts their world view.

Too bad!

As long as I'm working for the St. Louis Police Officers Association . . . strike that. As long I'm drawing in breath, I'll continue to stand up for the men and women of the St. Louis Metropolitan Police Department.

In the last several months, that job has gotten bigger. As the attention of the world focused on Ferguson and then the Shaw neighborhood, the monologue that we heard from the media talking heads, politicians and "activists" was a destructive chorus of anti-police rhetoric born of a false narrative of what happened here and in other high-profile law enforcement encounters across the country. The silence from objective voices of reason willing to talk about what really happened in all of these deadly encounters was deafening. So, with every opportunity that presented itself, I spoke up and set the record straight on behalf of all of law enforcement.

That "truth to power" approach was heresy to those that were so busily engaged in re-writing history. It disrupted the narrative, as they say. And, the words burned in their ears.

Then the character assassination began. No, there wasn't video footage of me strong-arm robbing a local market. You wouldn't know it from watching MSNBC, but showing video evidence of a crime is NOT character assassination. The attacks against me went back fifteen years ago to when I was fired for "lying" on a police report by the Arnold Police Department. Never mind that it takes, oh, about forty-five seconds on Google to figure out that I was fired by the police chief for filing a police report about a domestic incident where he himself had violated a court order. Never mind the fact that the police chief was eventually fired by Arnold for the very misconduct that I had reported. Never mind that I was hired by the neighboring city as their police chief and subsequently elected four times to the Missouri House of Representatives by the people of those communities. What's important to the media and the "peaceful protesters" they idolize—you know, the ones who shoot at police officers, burn down buildings, light patrol cars on fire, and hurl everything from bricks to Molotov cocktails to human feces at the police—is silencing those who would challenge Michael Brown's status as a folk hero, those who would shed light on what actually happened in Ferguson and the ensuing riots.

It all came to a purulent head at the now infamous Aldermanic Civilian Oversight Board hearing. After listening quietly to a couple of hours of the most insulting, inflammatory, anti-police vitriol that one could imagine, our officers—the guys and gals who put their lives on the line every day to protect the people attending that hearing—were greeted with a deafening clamor of offensive catcalls that made it impossible for them to give testimony on a board bill that directly affected their rights to due process; their livelihoods; their personal safety. I stood up and demanded that the everyday heroes that work for this police department be treated with some respect. Neither the committee chairman nor the agitators in the audience liked that much.

On just about every video of the incident, you can see one of those agitators come from the other side of the room and position herself next to me. Then you see her elbow, hip-check, and grab me right before the rest of the agitators in the room erupt in violence. The choreography of this whole dance leaves no doubt in the mind of the impartial viewer that this physical confrontation was planned by the militant radicals in the room before the meeting ever began for the purpose of discrediting me as a police spokesman. But, who's got time for impartial opinions when you've got a newspaper to print or a newscast to air?

When our attorney testified about the legal flaws in Civilian Oversight bill at the next Aldermanic meeting, the *Post-Dispatch* asked him "Why is Roorda being muzzled?" He told them that I wasn't and that he'd have me call their reporter. I did. The reporter wrote a story where I spoke, un-muzzled, about the Civilian Oversight bill. She even quoted me in the story. Her editors, unable to resist their unsavory impulses, gave the story the headline . . . wait for it . . . w-a-a-a-i-i-i-t for it. "Controversial St. Louis Police Union Leader Muzzled when it comes to Civilian Review." Now that's journalism!

That tremor you feel beneath your feet is Joseph Pulitzer rolling over in his grave.

Here's the irony, the SLPOA hired me because they thought I had a talent for diplomacy and negotiation. The good outcomes we reached on the last two collective bargaining agreements, and on the Local Control Compromise are evidence of that, or, at least I'd like to think so. But, when it comes time to, as Shakespeare put it, "Cry Havoc, and let slip the dogs of war," it is no secret that my bite is worse than my bark. That's because what you do as police officers is so very, very important. That's because the people who do this job are good, hardworking folks answering a noble calling with no consideration for the fact that doing so places them in harm's way.

I'm sorry to disappoint my critics, but no muzzle, either figurative or literal, is ever going to get in the way of me defending what you do. Woof, woof!

14

GET YOUR RED-HOT BURRITOS

Two really great things happened to Darren Wilson in the first week of March 2015. The Department of Justice exonerated him of any wrongdoing in the shooting of Michael Brown, and his baby daughter was born. I won't name his daughter or state her exact birthday because some things aren't anybody else's business. I wouldn't mention the birth of Darren's daughter at all, except that it was already reported in the *New Yorker* interview that he did.

Regardless, these were two closely timed, happy moments for Darren and his wife. Or, at least, they should have been.

But US attorney general Eric Holder couldn't stand to allow Darren the full exculpation of wrongdoing that he deserved. Instead, he obfuscated what should have been irrefutable evidence of Darren's innocence by releasing his "scathing" report on the Ferguson Police Department's patterns and practices at the same time that he released the DOJ's findings in the civil rights investigation of Darren.[1] I'm sure it made the vindication bittersweet for Darren, and certainly distracted from the joy of welcoming his first child into the world.

Darren, as an American, let me apologize to you and your family on behalf of the government that we elect for the injustice they perpetrated on you. You deserved better.

Even if the findings in the DOJ's pattern-and-practices investigation had been legitimate (they weren't, by the way), for Holder to have stolen that moment of final justice from Darren and hijacked that moment of clarity from the American people by ensconcing the findings about the Brown shooting is unforgivable. The haze of innuendo and editorializing about policing in Ferguson served only to further blur reality and more deeply divide our country. For shame, for shame.

General Holder delivered a public address in conjunction with the release of the two DOJ reports that lasted about twenty-four minutes. Amazingly, he only spoke about the DOJ's findings with regard to Darren Wilson's actions for about two minutes, almost to the second. Here is the crux of what he had to say about Darren:

> This morning, the Justice Department announced the conclusion of our investigation, and released a comprehensive 87-page report documenting our findings and our conclusions that the facts do not support the filing of criminal charges against Darren Wilson in this case. Michael Brown's death, though a tragedy, did not involve prosecutable conduct on the part of Officer Wilson.
>
> This conclusion represents the sound, considered, and independent judgment of the expert career prosecutors within the Department of Justice. I have been personally briefed on multiple occasions about these findings. I concur with the investigative team's judgment, and the determination about our inability to meet the required federal standard.
>
> This outcome is supported by the facts we have found—but I also know that these findings may not be consistent with some people's expectations.[2]

That's about all he had to say about Darren. Note that he couldn't bring himself to use words such as *innocent* or *exonerated*, though any reasonable person who reads the report could only conclude that the physical evidence indisputably verified Darren's account of the incident, and refuted every account alleging misconduct, criminal or otherwise, on Darren's part.

But this opportunity to heal a nation was eschewed and, instead, peppered with language implying that rather than Darren being *innocent* of wrongdoing, the DOJ just couldn't meet the evidentiary burden of *proving* he had committed a crime. Take note of phrases Holder seemingly uttered through clenched teeth, like, "the determination about our inability to meet the required federal standard," and "the facts do not support the filing of criminal charges against Darren Wilson in this case." That's pretty general, General. Worse yet, it uses thinly veiled hints that Wilson is evading prosecution on a technicality. The technicality was incontrovertible witness testimony and physical evidence that demonstrated beyond the shadow of any reasonable doubt that Darren was free of guilt and acted as he had to that day, within the unmistakable confines of the law. At the press conference, Holder immediately pivoted to the pattern and practice investigation and went on a twenty-minute diatribe about so-called unconstitutional practices engaged in by the Ferguson Police. Then he did the unthinkable. In the middle of his remarks, he attempted to rationalize the actions of those who had rioted, looted, burned down buildings, shot at police, and otherwise engaged in criminal behavior:

> Of course, violence is never justified. But seen in this context—amid a highly toxic environment, defined by mistrust and resentment, stoked by years of bad feelings, and spurred by illegal and misguided practices—it is not difficult to imagine how a single, tragic incident set off the city of Ferguson like a powder keg. In a sense, members of the community may not have been responding only to a single, isolated confrontation but also to a pervasive, corrosive and a deeply unfortunate lack of trust—attributable to numerous constitutional violations by their law enforcement officials . . .[3]

Blah, blah, blah.

These are the words of a sitting US attorney general: words of sympathy and justification for rioters—would-be cop killers who lobbed bricks, bottles, explosives, and bullets at police officers. They are the most unforgivable words ever spoken by an American law enforcement officer, and they were uttered by the top cop in the nation—our attorney general.

The problem is, the "highly toxic environment" of which Holder spoke simply did not exist. The quantum leaps in logic that it took to criticize, let alone find unconstitutional, the conduct of the Ferguson Police Department would baffle any physicist.

The notion of a toxic environment created by a racist police department was a reverse-engineered, retrofitted version of history. There was never anybody marching around in the street, chanting, "Hands up; don't write me a ticket."[4] People were saying "Hands up; don't shoot." When the grand jury proceedings completely debunked that false "hands up" narrative, a new "biased policing" narrative had to be conceived to justify the mob's actions and the feigned indignation of politicians who joined in the rush to judgment for the sake of political expediency. The story of a hobnailed, jackbooted, occupying police force terrorizing people because of their skin color was backfilled to distract from, and indeed to create doubt about, Darren Wilson's exoneration. Here's the progression of the logic it suggests:

A. Darren Wilson murdered an unarmed black teen in cold blood.

B. Except that he didn't murder an unarmed black teen in cold blood.

C. But he did work for a racist police department.

D. So maybe he really did murder an unarmed black teen in cold blood.

In logic, this is called an *inductive fallacy*. On the street, it is called *wishful thinking* or more colloquially, *horseshit*.

I took to the airwaves to provide a counterpoint to the DOJ reports and the ham-handed manner in which they were rolled out. Of the several appearances I did, the most cantankerous appearance was on CNN's *AC360* with Anderson Cooper.

Anderson first discussed the DOJ findings on the Darren Wilson civil rights investigation with CNN political commentator Van Jones, who is African American. Anderson willingly conceded that the DOJ report exonerated Wilson, but Van couldn't bring himself to do so, saying, "I think it's important to acknowledge some things are possible and some things are provable."[5] The clear implication was that we'll just never know if Darren Wilson murdered a surrendering Mike Brown.

Anderson then turned to me and tried to pivot away from Darren's exoneration with a long, probing question about the pattern and practices report. I wasn't going to answer that without first taking Van's comment to task:

"Well, first of all, Anderson, Van wouldn't be saying we will never know what happened if the Justice Department would have found that Darren was guilty. He would have taken that as being credible and that's the problem. The protesters are unwilling to square up the story that they believed to have happened with the forensic and testimonial [and ballistic evidence]."

Here Anderson interrupted to reiterate "We just acknowledged that was wrong."

I responded, "Well, the justice department report said that. The attorney general couldn't bring himself to say that. Instead, we got a justice department burrito where the meat of the report—that Darren Wilson was innocent of the charges against him—was wrapped in this flimsy tortilla of accusations of racial bias by the Ferguson police department."

Van tried to interrupt, as he so often does, but I continued.

"Van, you get to be on the news every night and be wrong; let me be on the news one night and be right about what happened. . . .

"Let's put it in context, Anderson. So Ferguson is a city that's integrated, 67 percent black, 33 percent white. But it's an island of integration in a very segregated portion of St. Louis county where the entire region together has a population of 85 percent African-American. Those are people that are working and shopping and driving through Ferguson and that's what you would expect as far as police encounters."

Anderson and I went back and forth about those statistics, and then I got to the main point I wanted to make, that there is a profound difference between profit-motivated courts and racially biased policing.

"Well, Ferguson's courts are a problem. There's absolutely no doubt that this report unearthed some problems with Ferguson's courts. . . . But this problem that we have with these profiteering municipal courts in Missouri is not just a problem with black communities. We've got it all over the state. There's a law called the [Macks C]reek law, advancing through the Missouri legislature, named after a white town in outstate, Missouri and [the Fraternal O]rder of [P]olice supports [that] bill that cracks down on this [profiteering by these courts]."

As I spoke, Anderson became apoplectic over the idea that I wasn't going to buy into the new, false narrative about biased policing any more than I had bought into the old "Hands up, don't shoot" myth. The picture of Anderson with his hands over his eyes, with me talking on the other side of the split screen, is priceless. To this day, it remains the cover photo on my Facebook page.[6]

There is something insidious about that picture if you look at it closely, though. The on-screen caption reads: "Hands Up Account Questioned."[7] It wasn't questioned; it was completely and utterly refuted by the St. Louis County Grand Jury and Eric Holder's Justice Department. The way cable news networks use the subliminal scrolls and captions that flash on your TV screen is a very dangerous thing. They have the potential to plant subtle, contradictory messages that register in your subconscious more than you realize. To paraphrase Ike, "Beware the cable news industrial complex."

Before I got off the air with Anderson, I made sure to acknowledge how horrible I thought the racist e-mails were that three Ferguson employees had sent out on city computers. I commended Mayor

Knowles for taking swift action to terminate or suspend all three employees. All three eventually quit or were fired from the city of Ferguson.

But the tasteless and wildly inappropriate content of the e-mails that three autonomous employees sent out of their own volition doesn't at all prove that the entire organization was racist, or that there was some culture of bias there. If you snooped around the e-mail boxes of any corporation in America, you would likely find about the same percentage of inappropriate e-mails sent out by their employees. If 4 percent of General Electric's or Walmart's employees were found to have sent out racially charged e-mails, would that make GE or Walmart a racist corporation? Again, the DOJ conclusions are a case of faulty logic.

To underscore my comment to Anderson about kangaroo courts, it really is a problem all over Missouri, and probably all over the country. People are disproportionately disadvantaged by citation-for-profit practices because of their economic status, not their skin color. In Ferguson, the vast majority of people living in poverty are black, so they are the predominant victims of profiteering courts there. In other towns in Missouri, the bulk of poor people are white, so it's white people who suffer the most at the hands of profiteering courts in those towns. It's not about skin color; it's about geography and economics. The Justice Department knew that. They didn't care.

Then there is the disparity in traffic stops that the DOJ made such a big deal about in its pattern and practices report.[8] Here is a look at the towns adjacent to Ferguson and their racial makeup as of the 2010 U.S. Census, and the disparity index for stops involving black drivers through 2013 (or the most recent previous year of data):[9]

JURISDICTION	% BLACK	DISPARITY INDEX (BLACK)
MISSOURI	11	1.59
FERGUSON	67	1.37
Berkeley	79	0.80
Calverton Park	36	1.79

JURISDICTION	% BLACK	DISPARITY INDEX (BLACK)
Cool Valley	83	0.92
Dellwood	76	1.23
Florissant	24	2.92
Jennings	81	0.59
Kinloch	97	0.87
Normandy	64	0.89

Wow! Kind of puts it in perspective, doesn't it?

First you'll notice that Ferguson is well below the state "disparity index" for stops involving black drivers (Missouri = 1.59; Ferguson = 1.37). It is also below the national disparity index for stops involving black drivers.

To understand disparity indices, it helps to operationalize the numbers. A disparity index of 1.0 means that relative to a proportion of population of a particular race in a given jurisdiction, they make up the same proportion of traffic stops for that race in that jurisdiction. If the number is higher than 1.0, people of that race are stopped more frequently than their relative percentage of population would dictate; if the number is lower than 1.0, then they are stopped less frequently.

So, in Cool Valley, for instance, where the disparity index for black drivers is 0.92, blacks are stopped at just below their relative representation of the total population of that city.

Statewide in Missouri, where blacks make up only about 11 percent of the population, the disparity index is 1.59, so they are stopped about one and a-half times more often than their percentage of population would dictate. By the way, statewide, whites have a 0.96 disparity index, and all minorities combined have a disparity index of just over 1.0, which means that in Missouri, whites and nonblack minorities are stopped at almost the exact same rate as their percentage of population. Not bad, huh?

The more important statistics are the percentage of population represented by blacks in and around Ferguson. First of all, let's remember that the census numbers only tell us about the makeup of the population who reside in a given jurisdiction. In other words, who lays their head down on a pillow there at night. It doesn't tell us how many people who live in that jurisdiction drive a car in that jurisdiction. More important, it doesn't tell us anything about the driving population; in other words, the race of the people who work, eat, shop, go to school, or drive *through* that jurisdiction. That's why it is so important to examine the population figures of the surrounding towns.

As I expressed on *AC360*, this is a heavily African-American portion of northern St. Louis County. The DOJ makes a huge deal of the fact that Ferguson's population is only 67 percent black, while 85 percent of traffic stops involve African-American drivers. There are a few details that they leave out. Look at the surrounding towns. Five of the eight surrounding towns have considerably higher African-American populations than Ferguson, from Dellwood, with 76 percent black, to Kinloch, with 97 percent black.

On the other hand, Florissant, with only a 24 percent black population, would seem to drag the numbers back to the middle, but Florissant is a bit of a statistical outlier. It is the most populous city in St. Louis County and is geographically expansive as well. Only a small corner of Florissant is contiguous to Ferguson. That part of Florissant has a significantly higher concentration of African-Americans than the rest of the city.

So, if you drew a circle around Ferguson, you would have a donut hole of a relatively integrated population of about two to one, black to white, surrounded by a heavily African-American population in neighboring towns. Again, the significance of this is that Ferguson has more places to work, eat, shop, and so forth, so the people coming into Ferguson from nearby communities are bound to influence the racial mix of drivers. Those people are largely African-American.

The other issue that is glazed over in the patterns and practices report is that these are decennial census numbers, which means they reflect the makeup of the population as of 2010. The DOJ's own report acknowledges that the African-American population in Ferguson has been increasing by about 1.5 percent to 2 percent per year over the last twenty years.[10] That means that by 2014, when Michael Brown was shot, the percentage of blacks living in Ferguson could have been as high as 75 percent.

Taken together, these numbers give you a lot more context and a better understanding of the racial makeup of the motoring public who came into contact with the police in Ferguson. The Justice Department, in their "scathing" report, doesn't seem to care much about context.

Take, for example, the big deal they make in the report about the fact that 95 percent of the summonses for the offense of "Manner of Walking" are issued to black pedestrians.[11] The report implies that these were simple jaywalking tickets, but that's not what was happening in the streets of Ferguson.

There was a turf war going on there, and young, black males exerted their claim on the streets of Ferguson by boldly walking down the middle of busy thoroughfares, blocking traffic and demonstrating to everyone that they reigned over the city streets. Police had to deal with the problem, not just because it was unsafe, but because when you're policing a community, you can't allow scofflaws to run roughshod over you as they seek to establish their dominion over the law-abiding folks in the community. Let's not forget that this flagrant exercise of strutting down the middle of the street as if they owned them was exactly the behavior that Michael Brown and Dorian Johnson were exhibiting even though they had just committed a cigarillo heist. Now, that's chutzpah!

Let's also remember that when Darren initially contacted them, rather than writing them a summons, he merely told them to get out of the street. This is quite different from the racially biased policing the DOJ accuses Ferguson law enforcement of practicing.[12]

It wasn't until Michael Brown said, "F**k what you say," and refused to get out of the street that Darren noticed the stolen smokes he was carrying.

Maybe mentioning *that* somewhere in a DOJ report would put the whole story into context.

But, "this is the West, sir. When the legend becomes fact, print the legend."

US V. THEM

After going back and re-reading the DOJ report on Ferguson months after it had been released, I thought it would be interesting to turn the tables on Eric Holder's Justice Department and Barack Obama's administration, to let *them* read in black and white the criticism that I and so many other Americans have for their conduct in Ferguson and the countless other American cities where they have interfered with our local, sovereign right to maintain law and order and some semblance of security. To that end, I decided to issue my own "Patterns & Practices Report," focusing on how the DOJ has engaged in an identifiable, systematic course of conduct that violates not just the civil rights but the natural rights of law-abiding American citizens to be free from the dangers posed by those who would threaten our safety and infringe on our liberties.

I modeled my missive after the same format the DOJ used in the Ferguson report and the myriad other pattern and practice reports issued during the Obama administration. My report is harsh but fair and accurate, in contrast with the DOJ reports, which have only been harsh.

I hope you enjoy it. It is meant to be both earnest and entertaining. And I hope somebody at the DOJ—even some low-level functionary—has the gumption to read it and to understand how most Americans view their unforgivable assault on American law enforcement.

THE PEOPLE V. THE DOJ: PATTERN & PRACTICE REPORT

I. REPORT SUMMARY

The Common Sense Division of the People of the United States (hereafter "US") opened its investigation of Eric Holder's Department of Justice, also known as "The Hypocrites Engaged in Misinformation" (hereafter "DOJ" or "THEM"), on March 4, 2015, the day the DOJ released its report on the Michael Brown shooting and the Ferguson Police Department.

This investigation was initiated under the pattern and practice provisions of the Violent Crime Control and Law Enforcement Act of 1994, 42 USC § 14141, the Omnibus Crime Control and Safe Streets Act of 1968, 42 USC § 3789d ("Safe Streets Act"), and Title VI of the Civil Rights Act of 1964, 42 USC § 2000d ("Title VI").

Although these statutes are meant to empower THEM, not US, there is a principle in English common law known as *qui tam*, which is short for the Latin expression *qui tam pro domino rege quam pro se ipso in hac parte sequitur*, which means, "He who sues in this matter for the king as well as for himself." Qui tam lawsuits are brought in federal court all the time when an individual files suit on behalf of the government. That's when it benefits the government though. Unfortunately, this investigation and its findings have no force of law because the people apparently have no authority to investigate the government, while the government seems to have unbridled authority to investigate the people and those who protect them.

This investigation has revealed a pattern and practice of unlawful conduct within the DOJ that violates the First, Fourth, Tenth, and Fourteenth Amendments to the United States Constitution, federal statutory law, and especially, the "Life, Liberty and the pursuit of

Happiness" clause of the Declaration of Independence.

Over the course of the investigation, we watched in disgust as the media, misguided politicians, and protestors—both peaceful and violent—distorted reality and used the DOJ as an instrument of division. We pored over every one of the twenty-three politically motivated Obama administration investigations of local law enforcement agencies, whose distinct autonomy and separate power are a now broken promise of the United States Constitution.

We thank the officials of the Department of Justice for their openness and honesty with the American people. Yeah, thanks for nothing.

In short, we don't trust THEM, we don't like THEM, and we don't want THEM undermining our safety with any more attacks against the law enforcement heroes that patrol our streets every day in this country and protect *our* rights.

FOCUS ON GENERATING REVENUE[1]

The twenty-three jurisdictions against which the Obama administration has launched a so-called unconstitutional policing investigation are funded almost exclusively by taxes collected from the citizens. The federal government is funded in much the same way, the difference being that in economically challenging times, the federal government simply borrows and/or prints more money. Local jurisdictions, on the other hand, are forced to turn to other sources to generate revenue. The city of Ferguson did just that and increased enforcement of traffic ordinances and other city laws that produced fines.

This is a sensible model for revenue generation that places the onus for funding police and municipal court services on those who are creating the most work for law enforcement, to wit, lawbreakers.

The irony here is that economically challenging times are almost always the result of faulty federal policies, so the need for local jurisdictions like Ferguson to rely on new sources of revenue, such as traffic fines, was the direct result of the Obama presidency's sluggish economic recovery effort.

But rather than concentrating on the need to produce funding that local jurisdictions have experienced in this post-recession economy; this report will instead examine the Obama administration's "focus on generating revenue" not for itself but for its political allies.

It is critical to understand that these pattern and practice investigations into the policing strategies of local jurisdictions are patently unconstitutional. The United States Constitution is peppered with intentional separations of power that serve as checks and balances on one part of the government to prohibit them from exercising too much dominion over the other parts. The three branches of the federal government, the bicameral Congress, and the presidential veto power are examples of this. But the most important separation of power exists in the Tenth Amendment, which limits federal power and guarantees the sovereignty of the states. This was, in fact, the deal that united the colonies and made the republic possible. It is printed here since the DOJ hasn't read it in a while based on their caprice in recent years: "The powers not delegated to the United States by the Constitution nor prohibited by it to the States, are reserved to the States respectively, or to the people."

The Tenth Amendment isn't meant to render the federal government is powerless. To the contrary, the framers meant for the national government to have a great deal of authority, and they were methodical in delineating that authority in the Constitution. They even provided for a mechanism for the people through their state governments to expand the power of the feds through amendments to the Constitution, which Americans have done numerous times throughout the history of this nation.

But that's it. There is no pronouncement either explicit or implicit in the Tenth Amendment that provides for any extra-constitutional powers of the federal government. The feds overreach a lot in this arena, very often relying on the interstate commerce clause to justify their encroachments. Every federal law enforcement agency is engaged in some expansion of federal power reliant on an overly broad interpretation of the interstate commerce clause. Don't mistake this as me joining in the war on police. This is not an attack on our brothers and sisters in federal law enforcement. They do a whole bunch of good, constitutionally allowed enforcement work that I and local police agencies support and appreciate. But their bosses in the White House and Congress foist a lot of duties on them that are "reserved to the States."

Certainly, enforcing their own laws and keeping the peace within their own borders are distinct functions of the states and their political subdivisions to whom they have delegated police powers. The founding fathers were loath to the idea of a national police force and were meticulous in their crafting of the Tenth Amendment to avoid just such overly expansive federal powers. Lyndon Johnson, who advanced the most liberal agenda of any president in U.S. history, including Barack Obama, once observed: "Unlike most other countries, America has no national police force. And it desires none. Our founding fathers were very careful to see that none was provided for."[2]

Of course, federal courts have taken a different view of the Tenth Amendment, one that eschews the plain reading of the constitutional provision. The U.S. Supreme Court has called the Tenth Amendment a "truism,"[3] meaning that it is a self-evident statement, like, "I'm always early except when I'm running late." Evidently the high court thinks the authors of America's great social contract were just musing when they penned the amendment that defined federalism.

In fact, in the last eighty or so years, there have only been two or three cases where the U.S. Supreme Court embraced a Tenth Amendment argument by a state or local jurisdiction, and in all those cases, the court ruled in favor of the locality only because the feds were attempting to require local enforcement of federal statutes. Such unlawful conduct by the federal government is known as "commandeering" in constitutional parlance.

Isn't that what the DOJ is attempting to do in these coercive preemptions of local authorities to regulate the local provision of police services? Aren't they commandeering local law enforcement and trying to force them to police in compliance with federal statutes? How is this different from the very federal government conduct the high court has prohibited in other Tenth Amendment cases?

The DOJ bases all of these unconstitutional policing investigations on a single federal statute, Title 42 USC § 14141, more commonly known as the Violent Crime Control and Law Enforcement Act of 1994. President Bill Clinton pushed hard for this law during the crime spike of the early 1990s. Clinton is oft criticized because the law is said to disproportionately target African-Americans because it took aim at the crack cocaine dealers who were responsible for the proliferation of drive-by shootings and other gang violence in that period. The Crime Control Act was a tremendous success though. It was directly responsible for a sharp decline in violent crime.

But the act had another component that the left edge of the Democratic Party in Congress insisted on including in the wake of the much ballyhooed arrest of Rodney King. The provision created the ability for the feds to take action against "any governmental authority, or any agent thereof . . . engag[ing] in a pattern or practice by law enforcement officers . . . that deprives persons of rights, privileges, or immunities secured or protected by the Constitution or laws of the United States."[4]

Before the Violent Crime Control and Law Enforcement Act of 1994, the federal government had no constitutional authority to investigate local law enforcement agencies and had never done so in the preceding two hundred–plus years. That's because their authority to do so was limited by the Tenth Amendment. The Violent Crime Control and Law Enforcement Act of 1994 changed federal statutes, but it *did not* change the Constitution. So if police powers were reserved to the states by the Constitution before the Crime Control Act and the Constitution was unchanged by the act, how then did the federal government suddenly have the authority to regulate local law enforcement?

Chew on that for a moment, all you Madisonians.

The answer is, it didn't. The feds' incursion into local law enforcement is blatantly unconstitutional. It is the federalization of law enforcement one police department at a time. And it is a billion-dollar industry.

That takes us back to my earlier point about the Obama administration's "focus on generating revenue" for its cronies. When the feds take a local law enforcement agency to task, the outcome is always expensive for the jurisdiction being targeted. When the outcome is a consent decree or some other court-approved settlement, the financial consequences are crushing for the police agency. Capital outlays such as purchasing body cameras or early alert system software are costly, but nothing compared to the personnel costs associated with a settlement with the DOJ. Agencies that capitulate and sign a consent decree spend a lot of money on lawyers and consultants, but the big bucks go to outside monitors.

You see, these settlements are not supervised by the judge who okays them, nor are they supervised by the DOJ. Instead, the Justice Department forces the local jurisdiction to pay outside monitors to look over the jurisdiction's shoulders to evaluate compliance with the decree.

What a racket!

Ferguson got off relatively cheap. They only expect to spend about $3 million a year to comply with their consent decree. That's a lot for a small town to absorb though. Bigger cities pay much more to comply with consent decrees. Cleveland anticipates that it will spend about $13 million a year in compliance. That's probably a pretty good guess since that's about what New Orleans has been spending to toe the line on its DOJ settlement. Seattle won't get by so easy. The "Queen City" expects to spend a whopping $40 million a year to conform with the requirements of its consent decree. That estimate may be low. Los Angeles spent $40 million in the first year of implementation of its settlement with the feds, but that number climbed to as high as $50 million per year. Detroit, by contrast, got off cheap, or at least the mayor did (pun intended).

Detroit spent about $10 million per year on compliance with its decree that included just under $2 million on an outside monitor. That was all fine and good until it was learned that Detroit mayor Kwame Kilpatrick was having an affair with the monitor. There is a name for a person who has sex for money. Oh yeah: consent decree monitor.

Even without the sexual favors, the going rate for the monitors tends to be between $1.5 and $2.5 million per year. These consent decrees are open-ended and can drag on for years and years. Los Angeles's decree lasted for twelve years, and the New Jersey State Police, for ten years. Detroit's is still open and it started in 2003. The costs of these monitors and other expenses really start to take a toll on a city after years and years of outside meddling.

The local taxpayers are the real losers. More than a billion dollars in local funds have been spent to satisfy the gnashing teeth of DOJ automatons and the court-mandated overseers. It really is like a bad George Orwell novel.

Whenever there are losers, there are winners. It's not just the monitors, attorneys, and the consultants in this case, politicians are almost certainly enjoying some gain. (NOTE: To my knowledge, nobody has successfully followed the money trail on these consent decrees yet but I can assure you of one thing after serving in the state legislature for eight years and watching fellow politician constantly putting their hands out, a bunch of this money is coming back to elected officials. This is the game that's played in the halls of government. Some slimy opportunist gets rich off of some ill-conceived activity the government engages in and those "entrepreneurs" and their lobbyists dump tons of money and gifts on politicians to keep their gig going. I'll bet my bottom dollar that a bunch of elected officials are getting rich off this new cottage industry of decrees for profit).

No elected officials in Ferguson made any money off of the citations that were written to people who were, by the way, breaking the law. They used that money to keep the lights on and to keep cops on the street. Yet the mighty Justice Department and the politicians who lord over it have the gall to criticize the city of Ferguson for its "focus on generating revenue."[5]

Unbelievable.

COURT PRACTICES

The DOJ report also scolded Ferguson for its municipal court practices, saying:

> Ferguson has allowed its focus on revenue generation to fundamentally compromise the role of Ferguson's municipal court. The municipal court does not act as a neutral arbiter of the law or a check on unlawful police conduct. Instead, the court primarily uses its judicial authority as the means to compel the payment of fines and fees that advance the City's financial interests. This has led to court practices that violate the Fourteenth Amendment's due process and equal protection requirements. The court's practices also impose unnecessary harm, overwhelmingly on African-American individuals, and run counter to public safety.[6]

How do the federal courts stack up to those criticisms when it comes to lawsuits against police agencies filed by the DOJ? Focus on revenue generation, check. Failed to act as a neutral arbiter, check. Advancing the federal government's interests, check. Imposing unnecessary harm to a particular race, check. Acting in a manner that runs counter to public safety, big *FAT* check!

Seriously, the essential criticism of the Ferguson municipal court seems to be that it acts as little more than a rubber stamp for the city's law enforcement agency. Isn't the Justice Department a law enforcement agency? Aren't the federal courts acting as a rubber stamp for them in every cause of action that they bring against a police department? The DOJ has brought sixty-eight actions against local police agencies, and in only one case has the local agency prevailed in federal district court. The DOJ appealed that case and will almost certainly win at the appellate court level. Wow!

RACIAL BIAS

The DOJ criticisms against the city of Ferguson regarding racial bias were inferential, derivative, and anecdotal.

This was covered in great length in chapter 14 which demonstrated how statistically flawed the racial profiling numbers used by the DOJ were. The numbers, put in the proper context of the larger region, showed the impact on black motorists of Ferguson's enforcement activity was only slightly disproportionate based on the driving population of the city. Yet, the DOJ report concluded, "Ferguson's law enforcement practices overwhelmingly impact African Americans."[7]

This is going to sound garish, but so what?

Here is the dirty little secret that nobody is supposed to talk about: African-Americans commit crimes, particularly violent crimes, more frequently than members of other races according to any number of studies including a 2012-2013 study by the DOJ's own Bureau of Justice Statistics.[8] It's what the Supreme Court calls a truism.

It is *not* because of their skin color though. African-Americans are disproportionately born into poverty in this country, and the poor are simply more likely to commit crimes. That goes for every crime, from traffic violations to murder.

The socioeconomic plight of blacks that lingers on 150 years after the end of slavery is not the City of Ferguson's fault. You know who could be spending more time addressing the issue of institutionalized black poverty and less time undermining local law enforcement?

The federal government.

Chirp, chirp, chirp. Nothing but crickets.

It seems we'll just have to wait another 150 years for the federal government to do something about a broken socioeconomic system then.

In the meantime, yes, you're right, Mr. Holder. Blacks are disproportionately the subject of enforcement activity by Ferguson PD and by every police department in the country that patrols poverty-stricken inner-city neighborhoods. It's not racially biased policing; "it's the economy, stupid."

There is one more thing about race and Ferguson that people shouldn't miss. In virtually every other pattern and practice investigation that has been launched by the DOJ, there have been allegations of rampant and excessive use of deadly force being disproportionately used against blacks. Those are serious allegations although they've been conflated by the DOJ in almost every investigation they've launched. In Ferguson though, there were no such complaints. There was only one case of deadly force against a black man being investigated by the DOJ in Ferguson, and they announced the same day they released the pattern and practice report that the use of deadly force in the case of Michael Brown was justified.

This shouldn't be lost on people. All of these DOJ investigations are witch hunts to one degree or another, but the Justice Department probe into Ferguson made Salem look like Disneyland.

COMMUNITY DISTRUST[9]

As a member of a community, I just want to say, I don't trust the Department of Justice!

Do you?

'Nuff said.

II. BACKGROUND

DOJ pattern and practice investigations into local law enforcement agencies are a fairly new phenomenon in this country. The practice is very much a post–Rodney King response, a solution in search of a problem, so to speak. The feds claim that their authority in these matters springs from Title 42 USC § 14141, which was created out of whole cloth and without constitutional foundation by the Violent Crime Control and Law Enforcement Act of 1994.

Nevertheless, it's illuminating to look at the background of the law's implementation and its abuse under President Obama.

As of 2015, sixty-eight pattern and practice investigations had been launched by the Justice Department. Twenty-five were initiated under President Bill Clinton, twenty under President George W. Bush, and twenty-three under President Obama. That seems to show consistency, almost evenhandedness, among the three presidents who have served since the law's inception.

It's important to note, however, that the Holder Justice Department began using the threat of pattern and practice investigations in 2011 to bully local law enforcement agencies into ceding their authority to operate autonomously of the federal government. By 2015, a dozen police departments had capitulated to intimidation by the feds and entered into what are known as *collaborative reform agreements*. The non sequiturs that the DOJ employs are hilarious: "consent decrees" as if someone is actually consenting to them; "collaborative reform agreements" as if any collaboration took place.

The Justice Department has the unmitigated nerve to imply not only that collaboration takes place but that local law enforcement actually came to them, begging for this outside intrusion into their agencies' operations. Here is a tidbit from the DOJ's COPS office website:

> The U.S. Department of Justice (DOJ), Office of Community Oriented Policing Services (COPS Office) created the Collaborative Reform Initiative for Technical Assistance (CRI-TA) in 2011 in response to requests from the law enforcement community for a proactive, nonadversarial, and cost-effective form of technical assistance for agencies with significant law enforcement-related issues. It provides the DOJ with a middle ground between formal investigation and consent decree monitoring through the Civil Rights Division and smaller-scale resources and assistance currently provided by the department.[10]

Requests from law enforcement agencies?! Nonadversarial?! Cost-effective?! You've gotta be frickin' kidding me!

On a personal note, I only have an inkling about what's happened elsewhere, but I have firsthand knowledge of what precipitated the Collaborative Reform Agreement between the St. Louis County Police Department and the DOJ. The feds cowed, cajoled, and corralled the county police into relenting to federal pressure to reshape that agency. The county police pushed back as long as they could, but eventually, everyone says, "Uncle" to Uncle Sam.

The point is, the Obama administration has been far-reaching in its incursions into local law enforcement, and it doesn't stop with consent decrees or collaborative reform agreements. Every police department in America that patrols communities of color trembles at the thought of having Uncle Sam's boot on their neck, and as a result, they have all backed away from proactive policing. That more than anything else explains the precipitous spike in violent urban crime we have seen in the post-Ferguson era. These jaunts into local policing by the feds are meant to pander to Black Lives Matter and African-American voters, but because blacks are disproportionately the victims of violent crime, the result has been a stunning loss of life, mostly black lives. How does that make their lives "matter" more?

To those who would say the Obama administration's response is appropriate to current social conditions, think about how the last two presidents responded to similar claims of excessive force and police brutality. Although each of the three presidents launched roughly the same number of pattern and practice investigations during his term in office, the results between Obama and his predecessors vary widely.

Both Clinton and Bush had three DOJ probes each that ended in consent decrees during their presidencies. Obama's administration has had a staggering fifteen investigations end in consent decrees or some similar court-approved settlement agreement. That's two and a half times as many as Clinton and Bush combined (see chart that follows).[11]

JURISDICTION	STATE	PRESIDENT	DATE	DISPOSITION	STATUS
PITTSBURGH	PA	Clinton	4/16/1997	Consent Decree	Closed
STEUBENVILLE	OH	Clinton	9/3/1997	Consent Decree	Closed
NEW JERSEY STATE POLICE	NJ	Clinton	12/30/1999	Consent Decree	Closed
LOS ANGELES	CA	Bush	6/15/2001	Consent Decree	Closed
DETROIT	MI	Bush	6/12/2003	Consent Decree	Active

PRINCE GEORGE'S CNTY	MD	Bush	3/1/2004	Consent Decree	Closed
US VIRGIN ISLANDS	VI	Obama	3/23/2009	Consent Decree	Active
WARREN	OH	Obama	1/26/2012	Consent Decree	Active
SEATTLE	WA	Obama	7/27/2012	Consent Decree	Active
EAST HAVEN	CT	Obama	11/19/2012	Consent Decree	Active
NEW ORLEANS	LA	Obama	1/11/2013	Consent Decree	Active
SAN JUAN	PR	Obama	7/17/2013	Consent Decree	Active
PORTLAND	OR	Obama	8/29/2014	Consent Decree	Active
ALBUQUERQUE	NM	Obama	11/14/2014	Consent Decree	Active
LOS ANGELES CNTY	CA	Obama	4/28/2015	Settlement Agreement	Active
CLEVELAND	OH	Obama	5/26/2015	Consent Decree	Active
MARICOPA COUNTY	AZ	Obama	7/17/2015	Settlement Agreement	Active
MERIDIAN	MS	Obama	9/17/2015	Settlement Agreement	Active
MIAMI	FL	Obama	3/10/2016	Settlement Agreement	Active
FERGUSON	MO	Obama	3/17/2016	Consent Decree	Active
NEWARK	NJ	Obama	3/30/2016	Consent Decree	Active
COLORADO CITY	UT	Obama	N/A	Open Investigation	Active
VILLE PLATTE	LA	Obama	N/A	Open Investigation	Active
EVANGELINE PARISH	LA	Obama	N/A	Open Investigation	Active
BALTIMORE	MD	Obama	N/A	Open Investigation	Active
CHICAGO	IL	Obama	N/A	Open Investigation	Active

And Obama's presidency isn't over yet. His Justice Department stooges are busy putting the screws to five other police agencies who are the subject of open investigations. It is highly likely that all five of those DOJ proctological exams will end with a decree or a settlement upping Obama's total to twenty. That's because wrongdoing has been a foregone conclusion of every investigation undertaken by Eric Holder's Justice Department, and there's no reason to think his successor, AG Loretta Lynch, will be any different. Every Obama-era "unconstitutional policing" case has resulted in some sort of sanction, if not a consent decree or settlement agreement, at least a memorandum of agreement or technical assistance letter.

By contrast—sharp contrast—twenty-two of the forty-five DOJ probes launched by Presidents Clinton and Bush were closed without any sort of agreement. That's the way it should be. George W. Bush once said, "I do not believe the Justice Department should routinely seek to conduct oversight investigations, issue reports or undertake other activity that is designed to function as a review of police operations in states, cities and towns."[12] Under Obama's way of thinking though, every police agency in America by virtue of their very existence is guilty of unconstitutional policing. He just hasn't gotten to them all yet. Now, that, folks, is real, live "implicit bias." Hell, scratch that. It's explicit bias.

There is one glaring exception though, "the mouse that roared" as it were, to borrow from the title of the old Peter Sellers movie. The tiny Alamance County Sheriff's Department in Graham, North Carolina, which employs only 123 sworn deputies, was the first law enforcement agency to post a win against the crushing weight of the federal government's brawn.[13]

The Columbus, Ohio, police department fought mightily, by the way, and scored some victories in court, but in the end, they still ended up under a memorandum of agreement.

Not so for Alamance sheriff Terry Johnson, who leads one of the smallest law enforcement agencies that the Justice Department has ever targeted with a civil rights suit. The allegations were specious at best and entirely based on hearsay and circumstantial evidence. They consisted of little more than a whiff that the sheriff and his men had used racial epithets in referring to Hispanics. The U.S. District judge in the suit saw right through the onionskin case against the tiny hamlet and dismissed the suit in a scathing 249-page ruling that eviscerated the government's case. He called the DOJ's methodology in bringing the charges "seriously flawed" and essentially laughed the Civil Rights Division's cabal of attorneys out of his courtroom.

Obama and Holder should pick on someone their own size, because this particular David kicked their Goliath asses.

The punch line, of course, isn't very funny because the feds are sure to have the last laugh. They took the case up to the federal court of appeals, where they will get another bite at the apple. The way the federal courts are stacked against the little guy, I suspect that the DOJ will ultimately prevail in the case. Even if they don't, the joke is on the people of Alamance County, who will pay for both sides of the lawsuit, funding the Alamance County attorney with their local taxes and the DOJ's legal team with their federal income taxes.

When you say your prayers tonight before bed, throw in a little vesper for the folks down Alamance way and their Davidian battle for justice. While you're at it, pray that the U.S. Court of Appeals awards attorney's fees to the defendant in the case of *United States of America v. Terry S. Johnson.* The purpose of all of this background about the conduct of the Obama administration is to demonstrate two things about the way the president and his Department of Justice have discharged their duties: a "pattern" and a "practice."

The prez and his minions are trying to force change, and they are using excessive force in the process. The federal government is an expansive, powerful thing—tens of thousands of times more powerful than even the largest of local law enforcement agencies. There is an awesome responsibility that goes along with the exercise of that much might, and the Obama administration has abused it in every situation. That is their pattern. That is their practice.

But what is it that underlies this gross abuse of authority? Clearly, President Obama holds American law enforcement in very low regard. Perhaps he was stopped once when he was still Barry Obama the college student and questioned or searched or ticketed when he didn't think he had done anything to warrant such attention. He concluded, no doubt, that it was his skin color that triggered the unbearable harassment he endured. It seems he's bent on showing law enforcement who's boss.

Let me make an observation, Mr. President. I worked as an undercover narcotics detective for five years. I had long hair, multiple piercings, and a grizzled appearance. Every shirt I owned was either made of flannel or had the name of a grunge band emblazoned on it. I drove around in a series of jalopies that no doubt attracted the attention of law enforcement even though I was careful to obey all the laws of the roadway. I was stopped dozens and dozens of times during my tenure as a narc. It might have been because of my appearance, but it certainly was not because of my skin color. The thing is, I'm disappointed that I wasn't stopped more often. I was always carrying around a gun and usually carrying around large sums of money or drugs that I had just purchased in the course of my duties. Very often, I was accompanied by some of the seediest, most low-down human beings on the planet, some black but most of them white. And the police should have stopped me. They should have stopped and questioned and searched me over and over and over again, not because they were engaged in some illegal pattern and practice but because that's what cops are supposed to do.

I'm sorry that you and thousands of other African-Americans have been stopped and inconvenienced, and I'm sorrier yet that you leapt to the conclusion that you were racially profiled and that your petty slight amounted to some colossal intrusion into your civil rights. But get over it.

American law enforcement has a job to do. In the process they have to balance the public's need for safety and security against the sacred, guaranteed rights of the citizens with whom they come into contact. It's a tough job. You should be law enforcement's partner in this job, not its adversary.

That is your obligation as the president of the United States of America, and in the discharge of this solemn duty, you have failed.

III. VIOLATIONS OF FEDERAL LAW & CONSTITUTIONAL RIGHTS

In the Ferguson report, Eric Holder and his Justice Department identified two chief criticisms of the city which the feds characterized as unlawful: (1) "Ferguson law enforcement efforts are focused on generating revenue" and (2) "Ferguson law enforcement practices violate the law and undermine community trust, especially among African Americans."[14]

First things first. Ferguson *law* enforcement efforts are not focused on generating revenue. Ferguson *traffic* enforcement efforts are focused on generating revenue. That is the case, like it or not, in every police department in the country.

I don't like it much either. I believe that writing tickets has become an acceptable substitute for real police work to the detriment of law enforcement and the people we serve. Police chiefs across the country have become obsessed with numbers, and they can't distinguish between a traffic stop where you write a forty-five-year-old soccer mom in a minivan a speeding ticket for going eight miles per hour over the speed limit and a felony car stop where you seize a bevy of knives, guns, and crystal meth from a carload of outlaw bikers.

I agree with you, Mr. Holder: it is wrong that policing in America has pivoted from law enforcement to traffic enforcement. But it ain't illegal. It ain't unconstitutional. And it ain't racially motivated.

No, it's economically motivated. Poor people get stopped more than people who are well off. Poor folk don't keep their cars in good working condition, so they have a lot of equipment violations. They don't always have the money to properly license their cars or renew their license plates, so they stick out like a sore thumb to cops. They don't have the dough to keep their insurance paid up or to pay off traffic fines from previous stops, so they very often have warrants out for their arrest.

While that does seem unfair, Mr. Holder, and it does as you say in your report trap low-income people in a perpetual cycle of encounters with law enforcement and the courts,[15] again it's not illegal. In fact, it is the fault of people like you that this is happening.

You and your Justice Department goons and the civil rights groups that you coddle have made cops fearful to do the tough job of legitimate criminal law enforcement, and you have simply scared the panties off of police chiefs. You are the reason that police agencies have retreated to this strategy of traffic enforcement busy work. It's much safer than locking up real criminals, because those cases can get nasty. I can tell you from firsthand experience that people engaged in serious unlawful activity who know that they're going to prison want to escape from, fight, and even kill the people attempting to apprehend them. The police response in those situations can be messy, messy business, a lot of blood and sometimes, a lot of lead. Because of people like you, Mr. Holder, cops have increasingly removed themselves from those situations and turned to traffic enforcement, which disadvantages poor people, which disadvantages black people.

So, congratulations Dr. Holderstein. Meet your monster.

On your second point, that Ferguson law enforcement practices violate the law and undermine community trust, especially among African Americans, I say, "Huh?!"

You claim in your report, General Holder, that just about every city ordinance on the books in Ferguson is unconstitutional. In particular, the DOJ took umbrage with the Failure to Comply, Disorderly Conduct, Interference with an Officer, Resisting Arrest, Misuse of 911, and especially, the Manner of Walking ordinances.[16] You declared these laws unconstitutional, but you didn't say what made them constitutionally repugnant other than in a town that is majority African American, African Americans were more likely to get arrested for them. The inverse is also true. I policed in an almost all-white town that had pretty much all of these same ordinances, and whites were disproportionately charged with these crimes there. That doesn't make the laws race-based or constitutionally repugnant. Why don't you just say you don't like these laws instead of trying to play judge?

You know who has played judge with respect to these ordinances? Judges.

That's right. The ordinances that you labeled as unconstitutional are on the books in substantially the same form in just about every municipality in the country. They have been tested time and time again in courts and have withstood judicial scrutiny from honest-to-goodness, real-live judges. And you know what else? These ordinances that you don't like are still on the books in Ferguson because no judge has said they're unconstitutional. So, just because you say they violate civil rights doesn't make it so, General.

You do try to make the case in the Ferguson Report for generational mistrust of the local police by people of color in the community, noting:

> Our investigation showed that the disconnect and distrust between much of Ferguson's African-American community and FPD is caused largely by years of the unlawful and unfair law enforcement practices by Ferguson's police department and municipal court described above. In the documents we reviewed, the meetings we observed and participated in, and in the hundreds of conversations Civil Rights Division staff had with residents of Ferguson and the surrounding area, many residents, primarily African-American residents, described being belittled, disbelieved, and treated with little regard for their legal rights by the Ferguson Police Department. One white individual who has lived in Ferguson for 48 years told us that it feels like Ferguson's police and court system is "designed to bring a black man down."[17]

Say whattttt?

That sounds pretty anecdotal and more than a little hyperbolic. But not as anecdotal as this passage from your report:

> In December 2011, for example, an African-American man alleged that as he was standing outside of Wal-Mart, an officer called him a "stupid motherf****r" and a "bastard." According to the man, a

lieutenant was on the scene and did nothing to reproach the officer, instead threatening to arrest the man. In April 2012, officers allegedly called an African-American woman a "bitch" and a "mental case" at the jail following an arrest. In June 2011, a sixty-year-old man complained that an officer verbally harassed him while he stood in line to see the judge in municipal court. According to the man, the officer repeatedly ordered him to move forward as the line advanced and, because he did not advance far enough, turned to the other court-goers and joked, "he is hooked on phonics."[18]

Anecdotes can be very entertaining, and they are fun to embellish, particularly when you have a captive audience of bloodthirsty feds. You know what's missing from the anecdotes I just excerpted from the Ferguson report or the scores more that intertwine your narrative and undergird your findings? The other side of the story. It is amazing that you took all of these fish stories as gospel yet never, by all appearances, made any attempt to get the account of the officers involved. That is just hilarious.

You did unearth one very serious finding, and it is no joking matter. There were some racially offensive e-mails culled from the accounts of three police and court employees that were downright disturbing. I've read them, and they were hurtful and in extraordinarily poor taste. Those employees were dealt with harshly by the City of Ferguson as soon as you brought the e-mails to their attention. I sincerely thank you for doing so.

But let's exercise some clarity here. There was no evidence of authorship by the three employees. They simply received and/or forwarded those e-mails. I don't mean to sound like I'm downplaying that. As I said, the e-mails were offensive. Answer this though. Has the Department of Justice ever gone through a thorough audit of all of its employees' e-mails as you did in Ferguson? If you did, would it surprise you if roughly 3 percent of your employees had received or forwarded an inappropriate e-mail? It wouldn't surprise me, not at all. It also wouldn't make the Department of Justice a racially biased law enforcement agency, just as the bad e-mails in Ferguson don't constitute a racially biased organization there. These things happen, and they happen in a vacuum. They are unfortunate, but they amount to bad acts of the individual, not the whole.

Get back to me after you've audited all of the DOJ servers and we'll talk.

IV. CHANGES NECESSARY TO REMEDY THE DOJ'S UNLAWFUL LAW ENFORCEMENT PRACTICES AND REPAIR COMMUNITY TRUST

Here is the first sentence from the remedies section of the Ferguson report: "The problems identified within this letter reflect deeply entrenched practices and priorities that are incompatible with lawful and effective policing and that damage community trust."[19]

Boy, if that doesn't describe the Department of Justice to a T, I don't know what does.

Clean your own house before you go peering through the windows of your neighbors' houses.

V. CONCLUSION

Our investigation concludes that the Department of Justice has the capacity to reform its approach to law enforcement. Just not under this president . . . never ever under this president.

The true victims of the federal overreach in these pattern and practice investigations under the Obama administration aren't the cops that have been targeted; it's the law-abiding citizens whom they serve and protect. We law-abiding citizens don't stand out as much as some groups who claim discrimination, but we've been discriminated against by this administration nonetheless.

Some of us wear badges; some don't. Some of us are white; some of us are black. We are young, old; rich, poor; man, woman; urban, rural. Most of all, we are vulnerable—vulnerable to the threats posed by the criminals you have sided with over cops and law-abiding citizens.

It was noted at the outset of this chapter that the Justice Department violated the natural rights of us law abiding citizens to "Life, Liberty and the pursuit of Happiness" expressed in the Declaration of Independence. Safety is inherent among those God-given rights guaranteed to us as American citizens. In fact, Jefferson originally wrote *"preservation* of life, & liberty, & the pursuit of happiness."[20] The word *preservation* was dropped before the document was sent onto the Continental Congress, but the intent is clear.

Preserving life is the awesome responsibility of the cops who patrol our neighborhoods all across America. They do it with undaunted courage and unrelenting devotion. They are doing God's work. Leave them be . . .

Lest you be judged for your trespasses.

16

THERE WILL BE BLOOD

I never watched the TV show *The New Normal*. It got canceled in its first season before the show ever got off the ground. Frankly, I just don't watch sitcoms anymore. They kind of bore me.

Despite the show's lack of success, the term "the new normal" has become a widely used buzz phrase in a world that changes more rapidly than it has at any time in human history. I frequently use it myself to describe the post-Ferguson world. If I'm being honest, I still haven't figured out what the new normal is in this burgeoning age of violence and pervasive antipolice sentiment.

One of the things I superstitiously avoid saying anymore is "Things are starting to get back to normal." Uttering such words is self-comforting because the idea of a return to predictability is something I desperately long for. Saying such things ignores the reality, though, that there is no back to normal; things are never going to be back to the way they were.

Some people would say that's good. They didn't like the way things were the day Michael Brown died. They didn't like that normal. I didn't either. A cop almost got killed that day. But the new normal of post-Ferguson violence has been even deadlier for young black men. It has been far more dangerous for police officers too.

In March 2015, that new normal was about to become even more evident.

A week had passed since the release of the two DOJ reports. I expected the protests that accompanied that release to be much more violent and to last much longer than they did. Thankfully, I was wrong. The protests never got nearly as hairy as they had in August or November. They petered out pretty quickly, and things calmed down after a day or two.

By March 11, 2015, which marked one week since the DOJ reports had been aired, I remember saying to people that I thought things were finally "getting back to normal." That's what you call jinxing yourself.

In the early afternoon on March 11, the news broke that Ferguson police chief Tom Jackson had tendered his resignation to the mayor and city council. It was an unceremonious end to a prestigious, celebrated career. I mentioned earlier that Tom and I had worked dope cases together in the '90s when I was an undercover cop, and I held him, and still hold him, in high regard. His reputation preceded him. He was a decorated SWAT operator who himself had been shot in the line of duty during a high-risk entry. Even before I ever worked with Tom, who was a sergeant with the St. Louis County Police Department at the time, I knew his reputation, and all of the county cops I knew thought highly of him. I quickly adopted the same opinion of him, and that opinion has never changed. In the end, Tom resigned because he thought it would make life safer for the officers of the Ferguson Police Department and other cops who were still assisting with the simmering unrest there.

Would that it were.

I expected that the news of Tom's retirement would've assuaged the concerns of the protesters in Ferguson and elsewhere, that it would be a celebratory moment for them. But when you feed red meat to lions, they are immediately hungry for more red meat.

Hold the phone, protesters! Before you once again tweet that I'm a racist and that my whole family should be brutally killed, let me put my comments into context. If you are a protester who took to the streets to express your feelings and demand answers about the shooting of Michael Brown or any other police shooting around the country, and you never threw a brick, rock, bottle, or Molotov cocktail; never fired a gun; never set fire to a building or car; never looted; never rioted; and never encouraged the bad acts of others, then you should be very proud of yourself. But you should not be proud of the protests themselves, because they were marred by the bad deeds of others standing in your midst and you did nothing to stop them, nothing to separate yourself as a peaceful protester from the violent insurgents who turned the protests into something of which no one should be proud.

Of all the protests that have been held in Ferguson, the one on March 11 is the one people should be least proud of. That was the protest that ended with two police officers being shot in front of the Ferguson Police Department. One of them is a friend of mine. I take that very personally. He was targeted strictly because of the badge he wears on his chest. That should be an affront to every single American. Instead, I watched in sheer disgust as some protesters, far too many protesters, celebrated the near-fatal shooting of two of my brothers in arms. It affected me deeply, it bred more violence, and it damaged forever the cause of anyone who really wants to avoid the next Michael Brown scenario.

I've said it before, but I just can't say it too many times: *some people want resolution; some people want revolution.* We saw that in bright, crimson Technicolor on March 11.

Of course, I was back on TV right away, talking about the double shooting of my law enforcement brethren. One of the first shows I appeared on was *The Lead with Jake Tapper* on CNN. Jake was live on the scene in Ferguson, and his show kicks off CNN's prime-time coverage, so my interview with him would set the tone for the rest of the evening, an evening when I was booked on all of the prime-time CNN shows, in addition to scheduled appearances on Fox and other networks.

Jake, who had done extensive correspondent work on the ground in Ferguson in August and November, acknowledged that gunfire was a regular occurrence during past protests. He then described this one as a "different kind of incident" as he asked about the physical evidence that had been recovered so far in the investigation. My response was terse:

> Well, first of all, I don't know how different this is. There've been active attempts to shoot officers for months here in August and November. Officers were shot at. By the grace of God, they weren't hit, but last night, the violent elements of these protests got what [they] wanted, which was officers laying in the street bleeding.[1]

Saying the protesters got what they wanted started a fierce debate. The antipolice wing of the media seized on that comment like grim death. They wanted to divert the attention from the protester who'd shot and nearly killed two police officers by focusing on my "broad" characterization of protesters as thirsty for police blood. The demonstrators who marched with signs that read, No Justice, No Peace didn't seem to understand that you can't write the word "peace" in the blood of your enemies. Indisputably, though, history is on my side. So, I stood by my comments. If you had seen the celebrations in the streets by protesters who'd finally got their pound of bloody flesh, you would see it that way too. You didn't see those celebrations, because the media turned a blind eye to them.

After a long day of interviews—more than fifteen of them, including on-camera interviews with the foreign press, I was back up early the next day doing the circuit on the morning shows. I was unwavering in my defense of the remarks I had made the day before. When asked about the comment on *Fox & Friends*. I replied, "I kept hearing yesterday the protesters finally got what they wanted. Chief Jackson stepped down. They didn't get what they wanted when Tom stepped down. They got it late last night when they finally, successfully shot two police officers."[2]

I hadn't done *Morning Joe* on MSNBC yet at that point and really hadn't done many appearances on MSNBC at all because the network's coverage was heavily slanted toward the protesters, and they didn't seem to care much about including a local police perspective in their coverage. One of the anchors, Mika Brzezinski, couldn't wait to sink her teeth into me. After one of the other anchors asked about the condition of the two officers, Mika quickly tried to put me on the spot about my comments about the protesters: "You said they wanted dead cops," she said. "There are a lot of protesters out there who want to protest peacefully, and who want change and have legitimate concerns. Are you sure your words were exact?"

I fired back.

> First of all, the shooter or shooters were peaceful protesters 'til they decided to pull a gun out and try to kill two cops. There are certainly peaceful elements within the crowd along with these violent elements, but those folks were placed in jeopardy, too, by these shooters. . . . It ceases to be a peaceful protest the minute somebody in the crowd engages in violence, and that protest then becomes something very different, and you can't hear the complaints of these protesters—the story that they want to get out to the world—over gunfire, and that's the point I was making.

Mika was unrelenting as she sighed aloud throughout my response and tried repeatedly to interrupt me. She finally carped, "Okay, I'm trying to help you out. All those protesters do not want dead cops. I think what you did was perhaps lump them all together in a way that was a little ham-fisted."

I wasn't having any of it. I was going to set the world back on its axis and history back on its rightful course (by the way, I didn't think for a second that she was trying to help me out).

> And, you know, a problem with the media coverage of this has been "Oh my gosh, we have this isolated incident where police officers were shot." This is an ongoing phenomenon. In August for two solid weeks we had shots being fired at police officers. For the two nights following the grand jury verdict, there were shots being fired at police

officers, and all along, the media [were] criticizing officers for wearing protective gear. Ballistic shields would have kept those two officers from being shot the other night, so I'm a little concerned about the rewriting of history here, and I think we need to report accurately what's going on out there.

It was a very diplomatic way of saying, "Kiss my behind."

Then, to my delight, Joe Scarborough jumped in. It was a sort of Popeye "That's alls I can stands; I can't stands no more" moment.

Joe launched into a pro-police monologue that evoked looks of unadulterated horror from the cast of his coffee nook. Joe had been unflaggingly pro-police in his previous post-Ferguson commentary, but the denunciation of the false narrative that spewed forth from him that morning was a refreshing departure for a network like MSNBC that had been getting the story of Ferguson and policing and race relations in America wrong month after month after month. The producers were pushing to go to commercial, but Joe relentlessly forced his cohosts to eat crow over their now-discredited reporting on Ferguson. The segment went on for twelve minutes, which is an extraordinarily long segment for morning prime-time TV. I stayed on mic the entire time and got some more jabs in, but Joe did yeoman's work in taking the false narrative of the Brown shooting and its aftermath to task.

I'm not going to recount the entire interview here, but it's easy enough to find on the Internet, and is certainly worth a watch for those who crave vindication for the truth of what happened in Ferguson.

In case you're wondering, the man suspected of shooting the two officers was arrested a few days later, and he reportedly confessed to firing the shots that struck the officers. His name was Jeffrey Williams. He was a twenty-year-old black man.

I wonder how anybody in his right mind can believe that all of the media chatter, political attacks, and the call to arms by protest leaders will avoid the next Michael Brown–type incident. Brown died because he made the decision to use deadly violence against a police officer. What happened next has made that attitude more pervasive, not less pervasive. As a result, more cops than ever are on the receiving end of deadly attacks by young black males. Those attacks have skyrocketed in the St. Louis area. Consequently, more than ever before, cops are being compelled to use deadly force against young black men in order to defend themselves.

The protests in Ferguson and the media and political pontification have only made things worse and ensured that the next Michael Brown is right around the corner on any given day, on any given street. How does that help anyone?

Once I got off the media merry-go-round, I turned my attention to raising money for the two officers who were shot. Along with other members of the Shield of Hope, I visited them and gave them checks to offset medical expenses and loss of income while they were recovering.

I spent a lot of time with the St. Louis county officer who had been shot in the shoulder. He worked for me when I was a police sergeant, and we had always been friends. He was a really good cop.

I didn't know the officer from the nearby Webster Groves Police Department who was shot in the face in front of Ferguson PD. His injuries were far more debilitating, and as I understood it, he was very self-conscious about his disfiguring wounds. As fate would have it, one of the Shield of Hope board members had been shot in the face in the line of duty some years ago. We made it a point to use him as our contact for that officer because we thought it would be reassuring for him to see how well Joe had recovered from being shot in the face.

I wanted to write a story for the *Gendarme* about the shooting from the perspective of the two officers, but it just wouldn't have been appropriate to bother the officer with the facial injury, so I wrote the column based on an interview of the county officer.

As I've said before, there has been a lot of dehumanizing of police officers throughout the post-Ferguson saga. I think the humanity of this officer comes shining through in the story he did with me:

FERGHANISTAN: THE WAR ON POLICE DRAWS BLOOD[3]

"Eerie." That's the word that the St. Louis County police officer shot in the shoulder in Ferguson on March 12 used to describe the shooting and its aftermath. "Just plain eerie."

I sat down with the county officer at his home ten days after the shooting. For obvious security reasons, I won't use his real name here. Instead, I'll call him "Sam." Even though I've opted to use a pseudonym for him, it's important to give him a name. It humanizes him. Over the last seven months, far too many in our community and across America have forgotten that cops are real live people. That dehumanization makes acts of violence like this too easy.

In *The Merchant of Venice*, the Shakespearean character Shylock famously makes the case for the humanity of his kind, exhorting to his critics, "If you prick us, do we not bleed?" To those who've spent the last seven months dehumanizing cops, one might ask, "If you shoot us, do we not bleed?" That rhetorical question got a very literal answer on March 12.

For Sam, it was a life-altering answer. As I spoke to him in his living room, it was obvious he was still in a lot of pain. He and the Webster Groves police officer who was shot in the face by the same gunman, are both lucky to be alive.

The bullet that seared through Sam's shoulder fractured his scapula (shoulder blade) and left bone fragments floating around in the muscle sheath. The doctors think that there may be bullet fragments in there, too, but they are reluctant to do an MRI because the magnetic imaging could tug at the metal shards causing even more damage. The good news, and it's really quite astounding, is that there doesn't seem to be any significant nerve damage. That is quite a stroke of luck, given the number of major nerves that run through that area.

According to his specialists, the road to recovery for Sam will be a long one. Doctors expect him to be in physical therapy and wound care for twelve to sixteen weeks. Still, Sam fared far better than his fellow officer whose injuries from being shot in the face are sure to require additional surgeries and recovery time.

March 11 was a normal day for Sam. He spent most of the day with his family and had to rush around to get to work for his shift that started at 9:00 that evening. He had heard on the news about Chief Tom Jackson's resignation from the Ferguson Police Department and thought that there could be demonstrations. He imagined that those who would gather for such a purpose would probably be celebrating what they saw as a victory. Little did he know that some people consider shooting cops to be a form of celebration.

By the time Sam got to work, a Code 1000 had already been called in Ferguson as a result of threats to overrun and take siege of the Ferguson Police Department. Shortly after roll call, a Code 2000 went out and Sam's sergeant called him and another officer from his platoon back to the precinct. "You're going North, boys," he told them.

This was nothing new. It was the fourth time Sam had been sent to Ferguson in response to civil unrest, and other officers had been sent up there a whole lot more. It was a typical protest. Demonstrators got up as close as they could to the skirmish line and cursed at officers with hate-filled, demeaning language that I can't repeat in these pages.

I've been to Ferguson many times over the last seven months and I've heard the hate-speech that spews forth from these demonstrators. These are not, in my opinion, peaceful protesters. They want blood. They want cop's blood. They proved that on March 12 as the clock struck midnight and shots rang out in the streets of Ferguson.

I don't mean to paint everyone that has marched in the streets of Ferguson with the same brush. Some had peaceful intentions, but those intentions were co-opted by the brutal radicals' bent for violence and chaos. The mob mentality that permeates a volatile situation like the one we've watched in Ferguson over the last seven months endangers everyone there. When you're in a crowd of people who are shooting, looting, burning, and rioting, you either go home or you become part of the problem.

The media and politicians overlooked this undeniable truth as they ignored the violence and mayhem and tried to conjure up a new way to blame the police for the actions of the mob night after night, month after month. Then again, every war needs its propaganda ministry, and what we've seen in Ferguson is undeniably a war.

As Sam and his brothers-in-arms stood sentry over the otherwise defenseless police station, the stage had been set for just the sort of violence that was about to unfold. Sam recalled as we spoke that a protester had yelled, "Just tell us where Darren Wilson is and we'll leave you alone and go take care of it."

Despite what their signs might say, these are not people who want justice or peace. They simply want revenge for this "Hands-up, don't shoot" myth. If we're going to be historically accurate, it's the cops that should be holding up signs that say "don't shoot" because that's what happened next. After months and months of shooting at cops, one cowardly protester lurking in the shadows finally did what all the others failed to do. He hit his target. Then, he did it again.

The scene, as you can imagine, was pandemonium. Sam lay bleeding on the ground, writhing in pain. Unbeknownst to him at the time, the nearby Webster Groves police officer had been struck by gunfire as well. Sam's fellow officers hurriedly picked him up and shuttled him to safety behind a nearby parked car. Sam was a veteran of SWAT and had been shot at on three previous occasions, but he wasn't ready for this. The pain was excruciating. He described it as, "the most intense pain I ever felt."

Sam lost a lot of blood quickly, so he was starting to go into shock. It was a cold night, so as fellow officers stripped his shirt off to examine the wound, he began to shake violently as his body was exposed to the elements. His eyes were clenched in pain, so he was fairly unaware of his surroundings, but there is something Sam remembers vividly . . . something he'll never forget. A black, female police officer from Normandy took his hand, and in what he described as one of the most calm, soothing voices he had ever heard, she assured him that he was going to be alright, that he was going to see his family again. She was, as he put it, "an angel from heaven." Sam said he wasn't able to focus on her face because of the pain and chaos, but he will never, ever forget that voice.

Once it was clear that the shooting had stopped, officers carried Sam closer to the nearby Ferguson Fire House, all the while that angel holding his hand. A paramedic from the Fire Department checked the wound and assured Sam that the shot went through-and-through. Now, the critical thing was controlling the bleeding and getting him to a hospital. It was no longer safe for ambulance crews to be stationed at the Ferguson Fire House, so it took over fifteen minutes for an ambulance to get to the scene. Sam's fellow officers were just about to throw him in the back of a patrol car and convey him to the hospital themselves when the ambulance arrived.

It took a total of five different attempts to start an IV on Sam. As a result, it was difficult for the ambulance crew to administer any pain meds or push any fluids to replace the blood he had lost. His cell phone was still at the shooting scene and Sam couldn't remember any phone numbers for his family. He finally remembered his dad's number and called him from one of the medic's phones to let him know that he was shot. At that late hour of course, he woke his dad from a sound sleep with the call that every parent fears with all their heart. Sam assured his dad that he was okay and asked him to let other family members know what was happening. Sam's mom had been deathly ill with the flu, so he begged his dad to stay home with her.

Think about that for a second. There is not a man or woman among us who wouldn't want their parents by their side in a situation like Sam's but this is what we call "selflessness." This is what cops like Sam are made of despite the undeserved beating they've all taken from so many in the public lately.

Sam was taken to Barnes Hospital where he described the care he got as "incredible." He used similar adjectives to describe the police officers and emergency medical workers who helped him that night. "Every single one of those guys was absolutely amazing," he said, especially the two county police officers that followed him to the ER to make sure that he saw friendly faces while he was receiving treatment. Sam was also praiseful of the investigators that put the man who shot him and his fellow officer behind bars where he belongs. Investigators made sure to let him know what had unfolded as the manhunt progressed, so that he and his family could have some peace of mind.

The acts of compassion didn't stop there. Friends, family, and co-workers have been reaching out to Sam with one gesture of kindness after another since the shooting, making sure that he and his loved ones are well cared for. Sam was visibly moved when he talked about what the FOP did for him. Within twenty-four hours of the shooting, he had checks in hand from the St. Louis County Police Association, FOP Lodge 15, the St. Louis Police Officers Association and the Shield of Hope totaling $2,500.00 to defray expenses.

I was part of the group that delivered those checks to Sam. Although we as members of the law enforcement family take it hard whenever an officer is shot, this one was more personal for me. I've known Sam since he was a rookie cop and we've been friends for nearly twenty years. When I found out he was one of the officers who was shot, my heart sank to the pit of my stomach. It was an indescribable relief to see him up on his feet just twelve hours after being shot, and acting as though nothing happened. And, it was just that, an act. Sam is a tough guy. He didn't want his loved ones or his co-workers to see that he was in physical pain and mental anguish. So, he soldiered through it to give comfort to others. Again, selflessness.

As Sam followed me out to his driveway ten days after the shooting, I put my steno pad away and we just shot the breeze. He recalled a night many years ago when he was a street cop and I was an undercover narcotics detective. I was doing a drug deal in a park and we decided to do a buy-bust once the drugs and money changed hands. In order to conceal my undercover identity, Sam cuffed me and booked me along with the thugs I was buying dope from. We had a good laugh as he recalled the story, but there was something different about him as we stood reminiscing under the cloudless, starry sky. It was something dark, something distant. It wasn't the same guy that I have known for all these years standing there with me. I hope as his recovery progresses, that all of the pain and uncertainty that Sam is enduring now melts away, and that everything goes back to the way it was in his life. Only time will tell.

We hugged and I told him how happy I was that he was doing so well, but it was hard to keep a stiff upper lip as I thought about the horrible way this whole thing could've ended.

As I drove away, I thought to myself about the full quote from Shylock's exhortation to his enemies, "If you prick us, do we not bleed? If you tickle us do we not laugh? If you poison us do we not die? And if you wrong us, shall we not revenge?" Through his admonishment to those who had done him harm, Shylock was warning that his revenge would be far worse than those misdeeds visited upon him.

When the hatred and violence of war go unchecked, revenge begets revenge begets revenge until everyone on the battlefield has been laid to waste. Will the war against police in Ferghanistan wage on, or will it end with this shameless, cowardly attack against two of our fellow police officers? Is this what it's come to, perpetual acts of revenge for the perceived misdeeds of police? Is the urge to cling to this myth of "Hands up; Don't shoot" so overwhelming for those who would turn to violence that we can never get past this? Or, can we all agree that justice was served in the exoneration of Darren Wilson and finally have the peace that was promised in exchange for the justice that was demanded and end the war in Ferghanistan?

17

WE ARE DARREN WILSON

One of the few things that has allowed me to unwind and escape from all the madness of Ferguson and its aftermath has been golf. Almost all of my closest friends—some cops, some not—play golf, so it is a chance for me to hang out with my boys, get some exercise, enjoy the outdoors, drink a couple of beers, and perhaps most important, relax.

I used to stress out over an errant golf shot. I'd throw my club, kick at the turf, drop the F-bomb. Now, I just shrug them off.

A year of dealing with the cops I represent being shot at (and sometimes hit), having bricks thrown at their heads, dodging Molotov cocktails, and being derogated by their critics took its toll on me. So did the eighteen-hour days I've worked, the death threats my family and I have endured, sticking my head in the lion's mouth at the media circus, and for that matter, writing this book.

After a long, long year, enjoying time with my friends makes perfect sense. Getting upset about a golf shot makes none.

There is something liberating about not caring anymore. It has absolved me from the worst parts of the game and freed me to enjoy it for what it is: a game. Consequently, I swing freely, un-impinged by the performance anxiety that plagued me as a golfer before. My game has improved considerably because—and here's the paradox—I don't give a shit. You see, in golf, a free swing is the most effective swing; it yields well-struck balls. The only thing that interferes with me swinging freely at the ball now is the restrictive feeling of having something around my wrists. I can't stand to have something around my wrists when I swing a golf club. I never wear a wristwatch. The little black beaded bracelet that my daughter got me on a trip to Fisherman's Wharf always comes off when I play. The "I Am Darren Wilson" rubber wristband that I have worn for the past year comes off too. But it only comes off then, when I'm playing golf. Otherwise, I sleep in it. I shower in it. I wear it to church.

I started wearing it a couple of weeks after the Michael Brown shooting when the protest chant "I am Michael Brown" took hold. I'm sure that expression means different things to different people, but to me, "I am Michael Brown" is nothing more than glorification of violence toward a cop, carried out by a scared kid whose bad decisions devastated his family and community and got him killed. People should be loath to identify with that given the mounds of evidence that emerged from the crime scene, the autopsies, the grand jury investigation, the DOJ investigation, and the video of Brown behaving like a berserker as he pillaged cigars from the Ferguson Market.

Deciding to don an "I Am Darren Wilson" bracelet was about far more than glorifying Darren. I started wearing it before I had ever even met Darren, so I was in no position at that point to judge him as a man. I am, by the way, in a position to judge him as a man now, after becoming one of his confidants over the past year, and he is indisputably a good man.

But the piece of rubber wrapped around my wrist is not about the man. It is, rather, about the deed.

To me, "I Am Darren Wilson" means that had I been in Darren's shoes, I would have reacted exactly as he reacted, done exactly what he did. Simply put, "I Am Darren Wilson" means, as they say, "There but for the grace of God go I." That's what it means to me, and that's what it means to hundreds and hundreds of police officers I've talked to since August 9, 2014, who see it precisely the same way.

I am fortunate. I never had to fire my weapon in the line of duty. Three times during my seventeen-year police career, I faced off against bad guys flourishing a gun at me. In all three cases, I was able to end the confrontation without firing my weapon, although, for all the critics of the Ohio police officer who shot Tamir Rice, I'll tell you that the closest I came to shooting a guy was when a motorcycle gang prospect stood in the drive-thru of a Jack in the Box, waving a very real-looking BB gun around, no doubt as part of his gang initiation.

Another incident involved a drunk who had fired at his neighbor with a shotgun. He was standing in the middle of the street with the gun when I arrived in my squad car. He threw the gun and took off running when I bailed out of my car, weapon drawn. The third incident happened while I was working undercover narcotics. A guy who had just sold me dope stuck a gun in my face and asked, "Are you a cop?" I talked my way out of that one.

My partner in Narcotics, Doug, and I also had a dicey deal go bad one night when a buy-bust went south. Doug said he'd take the car and I should take the guy on foot because I was quick on my feet. We got made (that's dope cop talk for being recognized by the bad guy) before we could get close, though. My partner ended up getting hit by the car carrying the cocaine, while I chased the guy with the money, who had taken off on foot. Doug got off several shots as the driver tried to run him down, but by that time I was already bearing down on the guy who'd rabbited. I looked back over my shoulder to check on my partner, who was okay; the surveillance team had quickly come to his aid. The only reason that hadn't been me slinging lead at the dope dealer's car was I was faster, way faster, than my partner (sorry, Doug). By the way, I caught my guy as he tried to clear a fence.

I've had other hairy situations that didn't involve gunplay. I was dragged by a car during a traffic stop, but I was able to get the driver to stop when I put my flashlight through the side window of the car. I ended up with two bulging disks in my neck from that one and still have pain from it today, especially when I play golf.

I've also had guys pull knives on me, kick, bite, punch, roll on the ground fighting with me, you name it. That was kind of a normal Saturday night in the town I worked in for most of my police career.

In the entire duration of my police career, which was about three times longer than Darren Wilson's, I never had to go through anything like he did. One of my instructors at the police academy taught us that we should go through our "fight sequence" in our heads every day. He told us to mentally envision a different scenario with a different threat involving different weapons at the beginning of every shift. We were to imagine how we would react to every punch, to each furtive movement, to each new threat that was introduced into the confrontation. Good cops do this even if they don't realize they are doing it. It is innate in a warrior's heart to be mentally prepared for every possible combat scenario, and to survive no matter what it takes.

I have a police friend who had to take a life in the line of duty many years ago, and it ultimately ended his police career even though the shooting was completely justified. Recently, he put up a post on Facebook of him reading "a letter to the man I killed." It was breathtakingly solemn, almost elegiac. In the post, my friend warned those who might cross his path, innocently or otherwise, "I have a plan to kill everyone I meet." It was striking to hear that. I had never thought about it, but I do the same thing. Cops are constantly assessing threats and planning their counter attacks. You do it in every situation and it doesn't stop when you hang up your gun belt. It follows you for the rest of your days.

I've been in a lot of knock-down, drag-out fights as a cop (and a few as a civilian), but I've never had anyone try to take my gun. I can only imagine what that's like. In fact, I have imagined what that's like as part of my fight sequence hundreds of times. It ends in one of two ways: submission by the attacker, or deadly force. When you're fighting someone who is trying to strip you of your weapon, you have to get the situation under control fast. There is no difference between a guy going for his own weapon or him going for your weapon; in both cases he's going for a weapon. It doesn't matter whether or not he's too big to fight (like Brown was); it's all about weapon retention at that point. Once you've managed to retain your weapon, you put some distance between you and the aggressor. Then you draw your weapon so he can't go after the holstered gun again and because he has presented a deadly threat by going for a weapon—yours. After that, it's up to the bad guy what happens next. The prudent criminal will surrender; the guys with a death wish will go after you and your drawn gun.

That's the fight sequence. That's how that scenario plays out in the head of every cop I know and tens of thousands of cops I don't know. That is why "I am Darren Wilson." That is why "We are Darren Wilson"—because all cops would have responded to this threat in the same way.

As I said earlier, whenever I or anyone else called Darren a "hero," he always rebuffed the praise, saying, "Not a hero; just a cop." True. By that logic perhaps he didn't do anything heroic; he only did exactly what any of us would have done in the same circumstances.

Looking at it that way does make the actual kill-or-be-killed situation in which he found himself less special. But I was never talking about the shooting itself; I was talking about the heroic manner in which he handled the aftermath.

There was a certain pride in Darren's bearing, a kind of grace, an abiding stoicism in the aftermath of the shooting. I've said this before, but I was always amazed that he wasn't more jaded by the events he lived through. Maybe there is an unshakable solace in the certainty of knowing you did what you had to do, that there was no choice.

In the aftermath of Ferguson, cops have gotten a very bad name. It is undeserving criticism and cops have held their heads high through it all. I've watched cops on the protest line stand statuesque in the face of furious, hate-filled invectives from those who want to bring down this noble profession, the guardians of our homeland, the keepers of our fragile peace. They shouldered the abuse and did not capitulate to the torment and torrent that rained down on them after Ferguson and Staten Island and Baltimore.

Law enforcement is under a full frontal attack by those who long for chaos and strife. It is reminiscent of the way servicemen returning from combat in Vietnam were treated by the "counterculture" some forty years ago; although, perhaps it's unfair to compare peaceniks who wanted to end a war, to cop-haters who wanted to start one. The contemptuous disrespect is as undeserved now as it was then. The way cops are maligned and attacked today is a blemish on our nation, just as it was when the young heroes that returned from the horrific jungle warfare in Southeast Asia were labeled as "murderers" for defending their own lives in response to the deadly assaults of enemy combatants. Just as soldiers in Vietnam answered the desperate call of an ungrateful nation, so, too, do today's police. But still, the men and women in blue continue to do their jobs with pride, with professionalism, with resolve.

There is nothing to be ashamed of for those who place themselves in harm's way in the service of humankind. Darren Wilson has been absolved of guilt. Police officers who have been wrongly accused of misdeeds all across our country will hopefully be absolved of guilt as well. They will again someday be celebrated as the heroes they are.

Our society celebrates a lot of people as heroes who do not deserve that laurel. We idolize sports figures, Hollywood stars, and music icons whose success might be laudable, but should never be confused with heroism. In this topsy-turvy world gone mad, we even celebrate those souls who dare to be different, people like Caitlyn Jenner and Rachel Dolezal. While perhaps courageous in the sense of exposing oneself to the scolding gaze of a cruel world, they are in no way heroic.

It is time to put this year of unbridled anger and unwarranted attacks against our everyday heroes behind us.

I am proud of my service as a police officer. Everyone who has worn the badge with honor or wears it still should be proud. We are Darren Wilson; we are heroes; we are cops!

If you try to take that away, we'll have no heroes left.

Following is a commentary I wrote about celebrating the real heroes in our society.

IDENTIFYING COP[1]

Former Olympic men's decathlon gold medal winner and current standard-bearer for trans-genderists, Caitlyn Jenner, identifies "female." Spokane, Washington NAACP chapter president, the police oversight board member who was recently outed by her white parents for her eschewed European bloodline, Rachel Dolezal, identifies "black."

Oh . . . and me? I identify "cop."

Let me be clear: I am not judging anyone. It would be impossible to put into words my complete and utter indifference to Jenner and Dolezal's current predicaments. I simply could not care less. In fact, I can't for the life of me understand the national obsession. We live in a country mired in the constant threat of terrorism, fraught with economic woes, saddled with skyrocketing violent crime, and these two, THESE TWO, are the subject of front page news?!

You can't see me right now but I'm scratching my head so hard, I just drew blood.

While I've tried to avoid getting drawn through the tent flaps of the Jenner–Dolezal carnival sideshow, all of the furor has given me pause to explore my own identity. I'm coming out of the closet . . . Mom, Dad: I'm blue.

Identifying cop, or more colloquially "coming out blue" is about more than your shirt color. I was born a civilian, but deep down, in the furthest reaches of my psyche, I always knew there was something different about me. While my male classmates were secretly prancing around in their mother's clothes or wearing droopy-pants and listening to cassette tapes of Run DMC on shouldered boom boxes, I was trying on plastic toy police badges and playing quick-draw in the mirror with my Crosman replica .357 BB gun. I know, I guess I was just a weird kid.

It's not just shirt color though; it's about body type as well. Even if you don't have a natural propensity toward the beer and donut-fueled, pear-shaped figure that "society" says you have to fit into in order to be truly blue, you can still identify as cop. Sure, I've lost some weight and I have a trendy haircut, but don't you dare pigeonhole me with your pop culture stereotypes! What gives you the right?! Just because I've shunned the beer belly and the five-dollar barber cut, it doesn't give you and your judging eyes license to tell me who I should be. I am copper; hear me roar!!!

And, there is a distinction between being commissioned by a law enforcement agency and "identifying cop." There is that handful of souls who are just wearing the blue uniform for all the money and glamour that comes with being a police officer. Posers! Those phonies bask in the glitz and glean of earning just over minimum wage or being shot at from dark corners or having a protester stand two inches from your face and tell you he's going to kill your family and rape your housekeeper's dog. Glory hogs! Geesh, save some of the fun for the rest of us, would ya?

I myself have been out of law enforcement as a profession for over a decade. It's been eleven years since I've arrested anybody. It's been eleven years since I've had a resisting (which, to the best of my recollection, was probably that same arrest). To quote the immortal police philosopher, *The Naked Gun*'s Frank Drebin, "Just think; next time I shoot someone, I could be arrested." You can strip me of my badge and uniform; you can take the lights and siren off my car; you can even force me to stop at traffic lights, but deep down, in that immutable, ineluctable pit of my existence, I know what I was born to be.

Here's why.

I believe that people have a right to feel safe in their homes. I believe that you should be able to go to a baseball game without worrying that you're going to be mugged. I believe that when you leave your house to go to work in the morning, you should find your car parked in your driveway where you left it, not a pile of broken auto glass where it once sat. I believe that our kids should go to school to get an education, not to have someone try to sell them drugs. I believe when a teenage girl or someone's grandmother walks down a dark alley, she should emerge on the other end unscathed. And, I believe that when you put your baby in its crib, even in the worst neighborhood in St. Louis, that you shouldn't have to worry about a stray bullet ending that child's life.

I know, I know, these are not mainstream beliefs anymore in a society that celebrates would-be cop killers, rioters, looters, snipers, and arsonists; but these are my closely-held beliefs despite their dwindling popularity. What can I say? I suppose I was just born this way.

While the minstrel show and drag show that has captured the hearts and minds of America unfolds on the front covers of glossy magazines, I'm just going to quietly embrace who I am. I know what that means. While Caitlyn and Rachel will ultimately be celebrated as courageous heroes for coming to grips with their true identities, I'll continue to be called a police union thug and the apologist-in-chief for law enforcement.

Well, you know what I say to that: "Screw them, and screw you, too, if you don't like it."

I know what another great police philosopher, *The Departed*'s Captain Ellerby, might say about my surly response to critics, "I think you are a cop, my son."

18

PROJECT MAYHEM

When we were young boys, my grandmother used to call my cousins and me "rambunctious." The three of us were very close in age—my cousin Bobby was a year older than me nearly to the day, and my cousin Steve was six months younger. We were like any boys our age really—competitive, energetic, restless, disobedient, fearless—just boys being boys, I suppose.

I guess nowadays, they would label us with some acronym and addle us with prescription drugs, but we were just old enough to have missed the ADHDHDDD diagnostic catchalls that define our modern society. Instead, we were lucky enough to have lived through an era where they dubbed us "hyper" . . . or, you know, "rambunctious." The downside of living through *pre-hysteric* times was, instead of a fistful of magic pills, we got a whuppin' when we were unruly.

Imagine that! How barbaric!

We rarely, if ever, got a spanking from my grandmother though (except for Bobby; he was a little shit). Instead, we got lectures; we got idioms; we got parables; we got nuggets of down-home dime-store wisdom.

Being rambunctious little waifs, we were always in a rush to dash out the basement door and frolic about in the backyard. That meant hurriedly throwing on our sneakers and bolting out into the yard before the others because everything then was a competition . . . for some reason. And if you really wanted to get an edge over your cousins, slipping on your tennies without socks would allow an undeniable advantage.

But that—*that*—was certain to earn you a chiding lecture from Grandma about li'l Calvin Coolidge. The ill-fated scion of the thirtieth president of the United States made for the perfect object lesson for impetuous ragamuffins like my cousins and me. There we stood in a row, shod and sockless in our Keds, being regaled by Grandma Ruthie with another tale of woe . . . in this case, the story of Calvin Coolidge Jr.

President Coolidge's namesake wasn't all that different from my cousins and me. Sure, instead of playing Wiffle ball in his grandma's back alley like me and my kin, the more dignified, princely young Calvin was prone to playing tennis in the south yard of the White House with his brother. His last match—well, let's just say it didn't end well. You see, Calvin Jr. was also rambunctious, and you know what happens to rambunctious boys? They die a horrible, grisly death, that's what (or so my grandma would have had us believe). Geez, I would've rather had the whuppin'!

Grandma Ruth had a way of instilling sheer, unabated fear in us boys. It seemed to circulate around calamitous presidential offspring too. Whenever we went outside in the cold with wet hair, we had to hear how Baby Ruth Cleveland's sore throat turned into a fatal bout of diphtheria. My grandma Ruth was named after Baby Ruth—as was the candy bar—so that story held a special place in her heart. But I digress.

In the case of li'l Calvin, as my grandma referred to him—I suppose to distinguish him in our feeble minds from the president that we had never heard of—playing tennis with his brother John without socks led to a blister on his middle toe, which became infected and turned into a septic case of staph in just over twenty-four hours. This, of course, predated the advent of penicillin and other such antibiotic drugs by just a few years, so the sepsis was ultimately fatal.

The tragic death gripped the nation with sorrowful sympathy for the generally stoic president. Coolidge, who had come into office with a fire in his belly and an ambitious agenda, just sort of dolefully meandered through the rest of his presidency brokenhearted by the tragic loss of his beloved boy. History depicts Coolidge as a hands-off, almost disengaged "spectator president." But that's not the man Coolidge was before tragedy befell his youngest boy.

As governor of Massachusetts, Coolidge gained national prominence for his decisive action in the Boston police strike. He was unflinching before Cal Jr.'s death but inconsolable afterwards. He is remembered kindly by some historians as a small-government conservative, but the truth is most likely that his arms-length approach was less ideological and more psychological. Coolidge was gripped by unrelenting melancholy after his son's senseless death, and he rode out the rest of his presidency unable to rebound from the terrible grief of losing a child. Coolidge's unfortunate legacy is that his laissez-faire approach in his second term led to the near-total deregulation of Wall Street. That, along with his utter inaction in the face of a looming agricultural crisis, set the table for the Dust Bowl and the stock market crash.

It is certainly not unreasonable to suggest that Coolidge's grave depression led to the Great Depression. Just think: the course of history might have been changed by something as simple as a pair of socks.

And to this very day, my grandma's admonishments about li'l Calvin's fate are what rattle around in my brain whenever I throw on my shoes without first slipping on a pair of socks.

More poignantly for the purpose of this book, the story of li'l Calvin is what I am reminded of as I witness the infectious antipolice, anti-American hatred and violence that started like a tiny blister in Ferguson, rapidly spread throughout our nation like a runaway infection.

But to extend the metaphor, if Ferguson was the blister, what was the pair of socks? What was it that really led to this runaway infection? What launched *the war on police*?

✪ ✪ ✪

For a long time, I thought the roots of the war on police traced back to when Trayvon Martin was killed in 2012. That is certainly what launched the so-called Black Lives Matter movement.

But now, I'm not so sure. I've become increasingly convinced that the beginnings of the war on police antecede the "Justice for Trayvon" phenomenon.

Perhaps it was the controversial arrest of Harvard professor Henry Louis Gates Jr. by the Cambridge, Massachusetts, police in 2009.

It's been a while, and the media have been busy since distorting what happened in Cambridge, so let me refresh your memory. Gates lived in swanky, university-paid-for digs in an upscale Cambridge neighborhood. The professor had been traveling abroad, and when he arrived home, his key wouldn't work, so he and his driver decided to break into the house. A neighbor witnessed the two men jimmying the door and didn't recognize the good professor. She called 911 and reported a burglary in progress.

When police arrived, they found Gates inside the house. When the officer asked Gates to step outside the house while he investigated the situation, Gates, according to reports, barked, "Why, because I'm a black man in America?!"

Wow!

The professor had just flown back from China. I've never been to China. I could never afford to go on an honest cop's salary. But PBS (yes, the publicly funded television network) paid for Professor Gates to go there to investigate the ancestry of classical cellist Yo-Yo Ma.

No doubt the professor was weary from his extended globetrotting. I'm certain that the intercontinental flight from China to the United States is long and grueling—even in the steeped comfort of first class—but I am equally confident that simply cooperating with police investigating a crime in progress would've been a better way to go than plucking the race card out of thin air.

The livid professor's behavior became so explosive as he followed the officers out of the house that he was ultimately arrested for disorderly conduct.

Now, understand this: none of this had anything to do with the professor's race.

If someone sees two people breaking into my house, here is what I want them to do: CALL THE POLICE!

If it ends up being me and a friend breaking into my own house because I've locked myself out, I expect the police to hold us at gunpoint—something the police *did not* do in Professor Gates's case but certainly would've been justified in doing if they had—until they verify that I live there. Then, after they've picked us up off the ground and dusted us off, I'm going to thank them profusely for doing their job and apologize that my own blunder, locking myself out of my house, took them away from more important duties.

I most certainly would not accuse the officers of accosting me because of my skin color.

"Now, just hold it right there!" some might shout. "You're white!"

That's right. I'm white. But there would be no so-called white privilege in the situation I'm describing. Any cop responding to a burglary in progress should do so with a great degree of caution. Officers should err on the side of caution. If they play that situation cheap, lives can be lost: the homeowner's; the cops'; even the burglar's. If they play it cautiously, the worst that can happen is they owe a keyless, clueless homeowner an apology.

That's what Professor Gates got—an apology—but it wasn't good enough for him. He wanted to make a spectacle of himself, so much so that the officers were left with little choice but to lock him up for the disturbance he created. But what he really wanted to make was a point. He wanted to make sure those officers would second-guess themselves the next time they were engaged in a similar encounter with a person of color, an encounter that could have just as easily been a crime in progress as it could an innocent indiscretion.

Professor Gates wasn't treated differently because of his skin color, but he wanted to be. In my opinion, he wanted the officers involved to be afraid of making the same "mistake" again because of skin color. He wanted cops everywhere to be tentative and irresolute when responding to calls for police involving a person of color. He wanted every police officer in America to err, not on the side of caution, but on the side of imprudence. Better a cop die than an Ivy League professor be inconvenienced because of his own mistake, I guess.

Do you see the similarity between the Gates incident and the "Justice for Trayvon" movement and the "Hands up, don't shoot" protests in Ferguson and beyond? They all seem designed to instill fear in cops and the public, fear of being labeled a racist even in circumstances where race played no role. The evolution of this movement seems to be crafted in particular to create indecision among law enforcement, to make cops diffident in encounters with persons of color and wary of the second-guessing that might follow.

It is more than just the Ferguson effect. This is the cumulative effect of all of these race-infused incidents in Cambridge, Sanford, Ferguson, Staten Island, Cleveland, Baltimore, and parts unknown. This is the thread that seams these encounters together, not the fact that the authority figure (a term I use to include George Zimmerman) was white and the person on the other side of the confrontation was black. In all of these instances, the participants' race was of dubious consequence to the outcome; it was their bad decisions that sparked a showdown.

The injection of race into a situation that just as easily could've involved a white citizen and a white police officer is purposeful fear mongering and race-baiting. It is meant to intimidate cops from doing their jobs and to dilute public support for law and order.

And it's working.

But even though Cambridge is part of the lineage that spawned the Ferguson effect, it is not the origin. Not in my opinion.

✪ ✪ ✪

I harkened all the way back to March 3, 1991, for the first clamor of revolution that composed the Ferguson effect we now experience. It was the night we crowned a new king—Rodney King—the sire of the real "Project Mayhem."

Rodney King was a dangerous man. He was on parole for robbery and under the influence of alcohol and other unknown substances when he led police on an eight-mile pursuit at speeds over one hundred miles per hour. The DWI arrest would have likely sent King back to prison, so eluding capture through flight or through fight was the only thing he cared about—not his own safety, not his passengers' safety, not his fellow motorists' safety, and certainly not police safety. His *only* concern was escape at all costs.

After the culmination of a long, dicey chase, King decided that resisting the California Highway Patrol and LAPD officers who had pursued him was preferable to simply complying. It is worth pointing out once again that, just like the Michael Brown confrontation and all the others, the Rodney King incident started with King's *own* illegal acts, not the cops'. Cops merely react to the actions of their adversaries in these situations. They are not responsible for the situation the bad guy creates. The bad guy is responsible for that. Cops are only responsible for one thing—ending the situation.

Rodney King was a big fella. He was six foot three and probably weighed close to 250 pounds. More important, he was amped up on something on the night of March 3, 1991. When cops tased King as he first emerged from the car, he just laughed. He was exhibiting all of the classic signs of phencyclidine (PCP) intoxication: no response to pain, hyperaggressive behavior, and superhuman strength. Although King's tox screen came back negative for PCP, there were more than a dozen varieties of angel dust floating around the streets of Los Angeles at the time, and the drug screen only tested for the most common formulary. King was, by his own admission, a lifelong PCP abuser. He even used it, according to an autopsy, on the last day of his life, when police found him dead at the bottom of his swimming pool.

Every cop at the scene at the pursuit concluded that King was high on angel dust, and they responded accordingly. One of King's passengers even testified at the trial of the LAPD officers that he also believed King was on PCP. The other passenger was killed in a car accident before the trial, so we'll never know what he thought.

Both of King's passengers, by the way, surrendered immediately when police stopped the car, and neither suffered any significant injuries. They were both black. Odd that the "racist cops" would have missed the opportunity to beat the other two—unless, of course, the force used on King was unrelated to his skin color.

Clearly, the force needed to subdue King was not about his race but instead about his resistance.

So why, then, did the cops have to beat him repeatedly, almost incessantly, with their batons?

I'm glad you asked.

Something new was happening in law enforcement during the late 1980s and early 1990s when I was attending the police academy. Gutless police chiefs, fearful of lawsuits against their agencies, decided cops could incapacitate somebody who was physically resisting arrest without injuring him. It was one of the worst things that's ever happened to law enforcement, and it directly explains the Rodney King video.

I am very keen to this because the idea of "pressure point control tactics" (PPCT) was brand-new and all the rage when I was in the police academy. Problem was, it didn't work. The tactic was based on the Japanese martial art of *kyūsho jitsu*, a cousin to the more popular jujitsu. It was somewhat effective on gym mats but useless in a street fight.

Here's how it worked. The police officer was trained to use his knees, elbows, baton, or some other impact weapon to strike large nerve bundles or muscle groups, which would, in turn, instantly disable his aggressor. A knee strike to the common peroneal nerve in the thigh or a baton strike to the radial nerve in the forearm or an open hand chop to the brachial plexus in the shoulder was supposed to drop an attacker to the ground.

Now, it hurt, mind you; it hurt like the dickens. The first time I got a good shot to the peroneal in defensive tactics class, it really stung and it *really* pissed me off.

That was the trouble with PPCT: it didn't take the fight out of people. It only made them madder.

I had some incredible mentors as a young police officer once I got out of the academy and hit the streets in the real world. I learned a lot from them about being a cop. They all taught me the same thing, "Hit a guy once as hard as you can and the fight's over." Fact is, I learned that at about eleven years old in the school yard, so it didn't really have to be taught, only reinforced.

A lot of people don't know this because the vast majority of Americans have never been in a fistfight, much less a fight for their lives. After all, "how much can you really know about yourself if you've never been in a fight?" You might recognize that last snippet as a quote from the movie *Fight Club*.[1]

As I think about how little most people know about being in a fight, I'm also reminded of a scene in the movie where the narrator's alter ego, Tyler Durden, gives the fight club members a "homework assignment" to go out and start a fight with a random stranger. The narrator observes, "Not as easy as it sounds. People'll do just about anything to avoid a fight."

If you want to understand the world, you needn't take a philosophy class; just watch David Fincher's gritty cinematic opus. *Fight Club* is one of my favorite movies, if not my absolute fave. I even quoted it once on national TV during a guest appearance on *CNN Tonight* about a racially motivated beating of a white man on a St. Louis light rail train: "The first rule of fight club is—you do not talk about fight club."

In the movie, which at its core is really about anarchy and chaos, the fight club morphs into something larger and more insidious, a social experiment that Tyler Durden dubs "Project Mayhem."

Hence the title of this chapter, because that's what Rodney King launched that night in Los Angeles, the *real* Project Mayhem, which has evolved into the current war on police.

The cops who arrested King weren't beating him mercilessly because he was black, as the media portrayed. They were following their mis-guided training to try to take a big, strong, yoked-up felon into custody without injuring him. All the baton strikes you see the LAPD officers deliver as King struggles to try to get back on his feet are pressure point strikes. A couple of them miss or glance off the brachial plexus and hit King in the head, which is another problem with PPCT. But this was not some racially motivated revenge beating by the police. It was the culmination of a colossal training failure for American law enforcement that got a lot of cops hurt or killed.

Some people will find this unsettlingly frank to read, but give me an old hickory nightstick—not some plastic toy baton, like the LA cops were issued—and I'll end the fight with one hit, maybe two in a case like King's, since he was so big and so high. The aggressor will most likely get hurt too, but nothing life threatening. This is another little chestnut that people who have never been in a real fight don't know: it is really hard to kill a guy with a blunt instrument. I mean, really, really hard even when you hit him in the head. And the best part is, when you knock a guy out with the first hit, the fight's over, cops and bystanders are unharmed, and no one has time to get out a video camera.

We went the other direction in this country, though. After Rodney King, using an impact weapon of any sort became so taboo in law enforcement that batons now are essentially little more than a uniform accoutrement.

When we took the nightstick out of police hands, the world became a lot more dangerous. Spare the rod and spoil the vile, if I may be so politically incorrect.

When I was a young cop, the crusty old veterans would show up on sketchy calls pounding their battle-worn wooden cudgels into the palms of their hands. The bullshit would stop almost instantaneously without a drop of blood being spilled.

The advent of less-than-lethal weapons has also contributed to removing the billy club from the police arsenal. Pepper spray and Tasers certainly have their place, but you can't use either in hand-to-hand or close-quarter combat. You probably shouldn't use Tasers when you and your aggressor are standing on a wet surface. And holy cow! How many times have I seen cops get maced worse than the bad guy because of close quarters, the wind, or overspray?

I still remember the first time I maced a guy after pursuing him on foot, kicking his door down, and chasing him into his tiny kitchen. I was in the narcotics unit at the time, and we were working a prostitution case where a guy was making his girlfriend turn tricks to get money to buy heroin. Between the indiscriminate hypodermic use and the unprotected sex for profit, I didn't want to put hands on the noncompliant needle junkie so I pulled out my newly issued can of pepper spray and doused him with a generous capsicum soaking. I was ill prepared for the way the spray would fill up the entire room. Imagine my partner's surprise when he came charging in the house a few seconds later to find me gasping for air. He seriously thought I was having a heart attack.

So cops are understandably selective about deploying less-than-lethal weapons, but because impact weapons are so verboten, police are left without any viable transitional option between less-than-lethal weapons and deadly force.

The most recognizable manifestation of the Rodney King incident is the injection of race into every situation where a white police officer interacts with a black suspect, but perhaps the true legacy of Rodney King is this: after the LA riots, it simply became easier for a cop to shoot an aggressor than to deploy the appropriate impact weapon. A whole lot of modern-day police officers have never hit a guy with a baton, but because we folded to media pressure and took that option off the table, many young black men—and young white men—have been shot by police when another weapon would have been more appropriate.

That's the truth.

✪ ✪ ✪

So this is the battle sequence that led to *the war on police* as I see it: Rodney King to Henry Louis Gates to Trayvon Martin to Michael Brown and beyond.

By the time Michael Brown happened, the incidents that preceded it had borne a new civil rights movement. No, that's not the right thing to call it. There was nothing civil or right about the movement. Let's call it the *uncivil wrong movement,* aka Black Lives Matter.

Now, I do not mean to deride the real civil rights movement in this country that culminated with the passage of the Civil Rights Act of 1964. Those folks did some heroic, important work to address racial disparities and injustices in this country. The real civil rights movement made great strides toward bringing our nation together and achieving the dream that America was meant to be.

The Black Lives Matter revolution is not a civil rights movement. It is a crusade to overthrow our American way of life. It has nothing to do with righting racially motivated injustices. It is, as I've said before, a proxy war against our government aimed at its most visible agents: law enforcement.

BLM and other radical groups have engaged in a campaign of fear, disinformation, and violence. We saw it play out in the streets of Ferguson and we continue to see it play out in the streets of countless other American cities. This is not some righteous cause; it is opportunism by a small, radicalized element of our society that represents the viewpoint of relatively few African-Americans.

When Michael Brown died, these chaos lovers saw an opportunity for more anarchy and discontent. These are angry, irrational people who were mad about King and Gates and Trayvon and didn't need to hear the facts of what happened in Ferguson. This was their big moment. They wanted to bundle these perceived racial atrocities together and ignite a revolution.

To bring these unrelated events together in the American psyche, they needed a catalyst. Barack Obama's presidency provided the perfect conditions. After all, Obama's presidency was a direct result of the Rodney King incident.

I know what some of you are thinking: *That's an absurd thing to say!* I didn't say it. Rodney King did.

In an interview right before his death in 2012, Rodney King was asked about the president. "Obama," he said, "he wouldn't have been in office without what happened to me."[2]

Thanks a lot, Rodney!

He was right though. The Obama presidency in many ways was the product of white liberal guilt. And a lot of that guilt came from the Rodney King incident.

Obama has made no secret about his disdain for law enforcement. It reverberated in his comments about all of these high-profile incidents. When someone observed that the Freddie Gray riots in Baltimore fell on the twenty-third anniversary of the Rodney King riots in LA, the president snarked, "This is not new and we shouldn't pretend it's new."[3]

He's right. Violent, fiery riots started by people who demand revenge instead of justice are not new, although I doubt that's what he meant.

Of course, the president made so many comments of this variety during Ferguson that they are too numerous to repeat. By that time, he was highly experienced at making the most divisive statements possible in circumstances such as these.

Before any facts were really known about the Henry Louis Gates incident, which occurred just six months into Obama's presidency, Obama instantly declared:

> I don't know, not having been there and not seeing all the facts, what role race played in that [Gates case]. But I think it's fair to say, number one, any of us would be pretty angry; number two, that the Cambridge police acted stupidly in arresting somebody when there was already proof that they were in their own home, and, number three, what I think we know separate and apart from this incident is that there's a long history in this country of African-Americans and Latinos being stopped by law enforcement disproportionately.[4]

As more facts emerged, the president had to eat those words. But he washed them down with a cold, frosty beverage at the so-called beer summit to which he invited both Gates and his arresting officer at the White House.

Of course, that experience didn't keep President Obama from making outlandish remarks in the wake of Trayvon Martin's death. He famously said, "If I had a son, he'd look like Trayvon."[5] He probably would, Mr. President, but how do comments like that help bring the nation together?

It would be easy for me to say, "If I had a brother, he'd look like all the cops that President Obama has publicly convicted as guilty before they even had a trial." Wait a second: every one of those cops—black or white—was my brother. But reminding people of our glaring differences only etches the battle lines deeper into the ground. A president is supposed to be a uniter, not a divider. When it comes to race and policing in this country, President Obama is always driving wedges between Americans. We've got way too many political wedge issues in this country. Making policing a wedge issue for political gain is really quite unforgiveable.

19

CASUALTY OF HISTORY

The central reason I wrote this book was an unshakable fear that if I didn't chronicle the events in Ferguson as I witnessed them, the truth of what happened there and how it led to an antipolice revolution elsewhere would be lost to history. That idea really did bother me greatly. A friend of mine who is a newspaper reporter said to me during all of the acrimony in Ferguson, "You know, history is written by newspapers, right?" That insight scared the living shit out of me. Newspapers and other media hadn't done justice to the truth in Ferguson and the other battle fronts in the war on police.

She was right, after all. When you think about it, newspapers have often been the lone surviving vestiges of past generations in the post-Gutenberg era. They are, in fact, where historians routinely turn to research times past. In the electronic age, I'm sure CNN online transcripts, news blogs, and tweets from famous twits will contribute to the body of knowledge future generations will use to glean answers about our times. But the one constant that goes back as far as the written word are books.

Books are a permanent record. They have the staying power to survive wars, disasters, and time itself. I've done a lot of good things in my life that I'm very proud of. I've served my community in many aspects, I've touched the lives of others in meaningful ways, I've raised a wonderful family, and I've lived a good, respectable life. But none of that is as enduring as contributing to the permanent record of history and documenting for the ages what *really* happened in Ferguson and beyond.

I used the term "casualty of history" a lot in the aftermath of Ferguson to describe the way Darren Wilson was being cast as the villain in the rewriting of the events that occurred that fateful August day.

Ultimately, the real casualty of history was the truth.

And it wasn't just the truth about what happened in Ferguson. Ferguson was simply the Fort Sumter of the war on police. As the war spread, so did the lies. So did the casualties of history.

I've become a student of critical police incidents in the United States since August 9, 2014. It is an obsession born of necessity. You can't defend what Darren did to a hostile adversary without that person saying, "Oh yeah? Well, what about the [fill in the name] shooting in [fill in the city]?" As a consequence, I read every article I come across about high-profile police shooting or other fatal encounters from across the nation. When I travel, I talk to cops from other jurisdictions to get the real story of what's happening in their towns. And when the next big police story breaks, I pick up the phone and call my counterpart at the police union there and offer my assistance and share my experiences. They very often reciprocate with intimate details about the front-page drama they are struggling through.

I've also been tapped by national media outlets to discuss unfolding stories involving deadly force incidents on their programs. In addition to the dozens of TV appearances I've done to push back against the Ferguson diatribe, I've also weighed in on fatal police-suspect confrontations in Staten Island, Chicago, Baltimore, North Charleston, and other cities.

I think—I hope—I've done a good job of setting the record straight about what happened in Ferguson. Some minds are unchangeable, intractable. But for people who are open to the truth and just want to understand what really happened, I've at least given them something to think about even if I haven't persuaded them fully.

So let's turn, just for a moment, to these other places where police were attacked, lives were lost, and history was obfuscated.

Despite the way the Michael Brown shooting became an overnight sensation in the media, there were three in-custody deaths that happened before Brown's but didn't really get much media attention until the hype-filled post-Ferguson environment created the perfect storm for reporting on all things police related, you know, as long as there was a white cop and a dead black kid involved.

First, understand that the coverage of the deadly police encounters was a ratings bonanza for everyone: print, radio, cable, network, everyone. I can't tell you how many editors and producers I literally saw high-fiving each other when their readership or viewing numbers came in. I'm not just talking about the outlets that were reporting with an antipolice slant; these were BIG numbers with the prime demo whether you were bashing cops or running to their defense. Hell, maybe I'm guilty of it myself between mugging for the cameras and penning this manuscript, I've certainly raised my own profile. I'd like to think my motives have been more altruistic. Frankly, reaching a broad pro-police audience with this book won't be easy in these times where sticking up for cops is about as popular as burlap toilet paper. I'll be happy if I make enough money to pay for the electricity I used to run my laptop.

The three big pre-Brown police incidents that contributed to the start of the war on police involved Dontre Hamilton, Eric Garner, and John Crawford.

I'll start with Garner since his became the biggest story among the pre-Ferguson fatalities. You'll recall that Garner's death spawned the expression "I can't breathe." "Hands up, don't shoot"; "I can't breathe" . . . it seems like every in-custody death has to have a tagline, some quippy, hashtaggable slogan that serves as a battle cry and a call to arms for the easily outraged.

Garner was selling black-market cigarettes in a Staten Island neighborhood plagued with unbridled lawlessness. This had become such a big deal that NYPD had assigned a task force to deal with these problematic street crimes. Garner had been in trouble for similar excise violations and had had numerous other run-ins with the law in the past.

The NYPD officers approached Garner and confronted him about his illegal activity. He immediately became animated and argumentative. You can watch it for yourself. The video is all over the Internet. When you watch, take note of how Garner towers over the officers that confront him. By all appearances, you could fit two of New York's finest in the ample shorts Garner was wearing.

So here is what I ask people who criticize the cops in the Garner case in my presence: "What would you have done, tough guy?" Garner was a mammoth man. The easy answer is "Call for backup." The people who give that answer are the same ones who criticize the police for "harassing" Garner over a petty crime in the first place. So how many additional cops is NYPD supposed to devote to every arrest of a petty street criminal that they make? I don't know what police manpower levels are like in New York, but in St. Louis, we are almost 10 percent below full staffing, and every police department I talk to everywhere seems to be in the same boat.

You'd get laughed off the radio if you called for ten more cops every time you tried to conduct a misdemeanor arrest. I say ten more because it seems to me after watching that video umpteen times that it would have taking ten cops to bring down that big galoot without him hurting himself.

Yes, I said hurting himself. Much ado has been made about Officer Daniel Pantaleo using the department-prohibited angular neck restraint (or "chokehold," as media and protestors incorrectly refer to it[1]). Ask yourself why Pantaleo opted for the neck restraint. It certainly wasn't to hurt him or to kill him. It was to try to bring him under control without resorting to a higher level of force. It didn't work out so well that time, but it has worked to end confrontations between cops and resistant suspects thousands and thousands of times before. Isn't it just a little bit possible that it didn't have the desired outcome because of some underlying health problem that Garner had? After all, the 350-pound Garner suffered from asthma, heart disease, and other medical conditions.[2]

When I said on TV that Eric Garner would still be alive if he had complied with police, the host gasped aloud. But maybe if you're morbidly obese and plagued by cardiopulmonary conditions, you should just surrender to arrest, even if it's your thirtieth arrest.

Months before Garner's death, Dontre Hamilton was shot and killed by police officer Christopher Manney in Milwaukee. Hamilton's death prompted numerous protests at Red Arrow Park, where he was shot. While the protests weren't as violent as those in Ferguson and Staten Island, dozens were arrested for blocking freeways and causing other civil disturbances. The protesters lauded Hamilton as an innocent victim.

One small problem there. Hamilton, who was a diagnosed schizophrenic, had disarmed Officer Manney of his baton and had beat him over the head with it before Manney finally defended himself and fired on Hamilton. At least, that was the finding of the investigation—an investigation that resulted in Manney's termination even though he was exonerated of any criminal wrongdoing. Is this where I'm supposed to say, "No justice, no peace"?

John Crawford is another name that is frequently mentioned on the list of "unarmed black men murdered by the police." Um, one minor issue: he was armed.

Like Tamir Rice a few months later and a few miles away, Crawford had the brilliant idea of flourishing a fake rifle inside a crowded Dayton-area Walmart. When responding officers arrived at the call for a man waving a gun around, Crawford refused to drop the weapon and one of the officers fired two shots at him. The weapon turned out to be a pellet gun that looked so much like a .22-caliber rifle that one of the officers felt he had no choice but to deploy deadly force. This represents a huge error in judgment. No, not by the officers. By Crawford.

You don't bring a knife to a gunfight, and you certainly don't bring a BB gun to a gunfight. Especially not one you started . . . for no reason . . . in a crowded store . . . in a country that has experienced one tragic active shooting incident after another in places where the public gathers.

Just two days after Michael Brown met his Maker, Ezell Ford was shot and killed by Los Angeles police officers Sharlton Wampler and Antonio Villegas. Like Dontre Hamilton, Ford was mentally ill, and as in the Michael Brown case, witnesses claimed Ford put his hands up in an attempt to surrender. But unlike any of these other cases, Ford was shot by police—are you ready for this—in the back! Gasp!

Stop your infernal gasping, protesters. Though you wanted this to be that smoking-gun case where officers acted out the lyrics of the Rolling Stones' "Heartbreaker," the reason the officer shot Ford in the back was because Ford had the officer on the ground on his back and had his hands on the officer's gun. He was trying to pull it out of the officer's holster. The officer pleaded for his partner to shoot the man. The officer even got off a shot with his backup weapon as his partner shot Ford twice.

Now, I don't plan on going back out on the street again. I loved being a cop, but I love being the head of a police union that stands up for cops even more. But if I do end up going back on the beat again someday, I want every cop reading this book to know that if you get stuck with me as a partner—I'm a miserable prick to spend eight hours in a police car with—you will never, ever have to wonder what I'm going to do if a guy is on top of you, trying to strip you of your sidearm. I'm going to shoot him until you tell me to stop shooting him. They can call me a racist assassin. They can protest me. They can even send me to prison. But when you yell, "Shoot this guy!" I'm shootin' him. I hope you'll do the same for me.

Just two days before the grand jury decision came down in Ferguson, Tamir Rice was shot by Cleveland police officer Timothy Loehmann. This one is tough because Tamir Rice was so young, just twelve. You know who else was young? Rookie police officer Timothy Loehman, who had been on the Cleveland Police Department about eight months. Still, I look at pictures of the baby-faced Tamir and I think about how I might have handled the situation differently and averted the youth's tragic death.

But guess what: I don't get to have those thoughts. Neither do you. Loehmann was responding to a call for a person pointing a gun at people in a park. When he got there, Tamir was still brandishing the firearm. Just like John Crawford's, Tamir's weapon turned out to be a very real-looking replica BB gun. When authorities in Cleveland finally released a picture of Tamir Rice's gun, I posted it on my Facebook page next to a photo of an actual semiautomatic pistol, and I was stunned by the number of people who thought the fake gun was the real gun. I could actually tell which one was the fake gun, but not at night, not from a distance, and not with adrenaline coursing through my veins.

This one is personal for me because, although I've been in a lot of harried situations as a police officer, the closest I ever came to shooting someone, as I said earlier, was a guy who was pointing a replica BB gun at people and then refused to drop the gun when I approached him with my gun drawn. It never occurred to me that the gun was fake. Cops can't afford to think that way. If they do, we're going to have to buy a hell of a lot more bagpipes. The gun *looked* real, so it *was* real. That's the way it's got to be.

Now for the hardest one of all, Walter Scott. Scott actually was shot in the back by North Charleston, South Carolina, police officer Michael Slager. Slager stopped Scott for an equipment violation. A few moments into the stop, Scott bolted from the car and Slager gave chase. It was later learned that Scott had a bench warrant out for his arrest for back child support that would have certainly landed him in jail. When Slager initially caught up to Scott, an altercation took place and Slager tried to subdue Scott with his Taser, to no avail. Scott then got up and continued to flee. Slager fired at him, striking him in the back several times.

The video of the incident is one of the hardest things I've ever had to watch. Anderson Cooper's show called me moments after the video was released and I declined to comment. All I could have said about the video is that nothing on it justified what I saw. Even now that I know the whole turn of events in the stop, still nothing justifies Slager's deadly force in my mind. One thing does explain it though: panic.

Cops are human. They do make mistakes. Usually, they err on the side of caution, and if that error results in death, it is usually their own. Michael Slager is guilty of blind, unadulterated panic, of terrible judgment. But that doesn't mean he's guilty of a crime. Only a jury can decide that, and they will. That's the way the system is supposed to work.

Let's remember though: Walter Scott could have done things differently, and if he had, he'd be alive today. He could have been a good father and paid his child support. He could have been a good citizen and remained in his car even though he faced certain arrest. And he could have been a good man and surrendered when Officer Slager caught up to him.

I'm not saying that any of this absolves Slager of his guilt. I am saying that Scott and Slager were standing on the same ledge. When one of them decided to jump, the other fell with him.

While the Laquon McDonald shooting happened before many of these other police shootings, we didn't hear about it until well after the rest of them when the Chicago DA released a dramatic video of his death. Chicago officer Jason Van Dyke shot McDonald sixteen times.

That seems excessive, but McDonald was armed with a knife as he came stomping toward officers, ignoring their commands. There is some dispute as to whether or not the blade of the knife was opened, but if you'd like to come by sometime, I'll show you how quickly I can open the blade of a knife with one hand and close the ten feet of distance between Van Dyke and McDonald. I'll just stab you once in the arm, and I'll try to stick it in the meaty part so you don't suffer any permanent damage, but I think you'll get the idea. You'll probably need to buy a new shirt because you're gonna bleed like a muthah.

A lot of cops have died from knifings. It must be a horrible, horrible way to die. If you want to second-guess Officer Van Dyke, go ahead. But I'm not going to. Not now. Not ever. In fact, I defended him on national TV, and I'm damn proud to have done so. I've actually talked to Jason on the phone—not about the shooting, just about his general well-being. He seems like a good kid. I'm guessing that all of these cops would if you got a chance to talk to them. They are not the monsters that the media wants them to be.

I will talk at length about Freddie Gray in a later chapter contrasting Ferguson and Baltimore, so I don't want to give away the surprise, but I'll give you a hint: a young African-American perpetrating a crime who resists arrest dies in custody with no evidence of any criminal wrongdoing by the officers, and all six of them—Brian Rice, Alicia White, Garrett Miller, Caesar Goodson, William Porter, and Edward Nero—are promptly charged with crimes stemming from the arrest. Sound familiar?

There is a lot that is familiar about all of these shootings. In each case, the bad outcomes were precipitated by the suspects' actions, not the officers'. The suspect was either noncompliant or resistant to orders by the police. In each case, the suspect turned violence against the police officer; in many of them, deadly violence. Then there were protests, usually violent, demanding the officer's arrest. In almost every case the public pressure resulted in the officer either being charged criminally or subject to discipline by his department. In virtually every case, family members of the deceased got a big, fat check from a city that couldn't afford to pay its police officers a competitive salary.

And in every single solitary case, the officers involved had to carry—and will always carry—the heavy, heavy burden of having taken another human being's life. That burden was compounded greatly by the mischaracterization of the officer's actions and the sanctification of the criminal who literally forced their hand.

As we ponder the unthinkable nightmare that Darren Wilson has had to endure, let's not forget the other casualties of history: police officers Daniel Pantaleo, Christopher Manney, Sharlton Wampler,

Antonio Villegas, Timothy Loehman, Michael Slager, Brian Rice, Alicia White, Garrett Miller, Caesar Goodson, William Porter, Edward Nero, the two unnamed police officers in Beaver Creek, Ohio, and all of the other police officers who have been or will be the victim of maligning character assaults as a result of skirmishes in the war on police.

20

A TALE OF TWO CITIES

After the exploits of 2014 and 2015, the cities of Ferguson, Missouri, and Baltimore, Maryland, will forever hold a shared place in the history of human events. Much like Lexington and Concord, they will be remembered almost synonymously as the places where a revolution started, irrespective of your view of this as a commendable revolution or a calamitous one.

That is a vague, superficial way to look at the tale of these two cities, though. The differences really are quite noteworthy and should be taken stock of before the truth dissolves into the sands of time.

At first glance, it's easy to lump these two towns together. Each famously became the backdrop for social upheaval in response to the death of a young, black, "unarmed" man who died in conjunction with some interaction with the police. Both towns faced nearly unprecedented riots and mayhem, and both experienced runaway increases in violent crime. Both Ferguson and Baltimore witnessed demands for police reform. And they both underwent social change that made things worse, not better, for young men who shared the ill-fated demise of Michael Brown and Freddie Gray.

Perhaps though, the coalescing of these two stories into one con-glomerated idea of bad policing or violent civil disturbances, depending on your perspective, is too convenient; too perfunctory.

From my vista, these are two very different cities and two very different tales.

Let's take Ferguson first. The narrative we heard was that this majority African-American city was under the lug-soled oppression of an almost all-white police force, complete with a racist city regime made up of white elected officials, a white police chief, and profiteering municipal courts. The downtrodden black population was subject to unbridled abuses based on their skin color. There were no body cameras, no civilian review boards, no special prosecutors, no requirement to release the names of officers involved in shootings, nothing at all in place to protect the masses from the unwieldy might of a power-drunk police state.

A young, unarmed, baby-faced, black teen—a good, gentle boy with a bright future before him—was cold-bloodedly executed by a callous white police officer as he tried to peacefully surrender with his hands up and his back to the officer.

When the townspeople—local residents every last one—took to the street to solemnly ask for answers, hyper-militarized storm troopers were turned on them with the vicious fury of the *Sturmabteilung*, gassing, beating, and illegally imprisoning the peaceful protesters and silencing their halcyon chorus for positive change.

Oh, stop yelling at the book; I said this was the narrative, not the reality.

Although almost every detail of this Ferguson narrative has been debunked, or at least recognized as hyperbole by the ever-dwindling audience of rational-minded observers among us, the story took on a life of its own among the denizens of the antipolice, antigovernment, anti-everything movement.

So, what about the Baltimore narrative? The stories are pretty similar prima facie. Freddie Gray, like Michael Brown, died after a confrontation with police. Some people say that Gray was unarmed, just as they did with Brown. Brown, by the way, had two big, strong arms, and he used them to beat and attempt to disarm a police officer. Gray, by the way, was armed with a spring knife that I would have arrested him for had I been a police officer in Baltimore, despite the prosecutor's protests. In the sense that neither of them brought his own gun to use against the police, we'll call them both "unarmed" (picture me sardonically using air quotes right now).

In Baltimore, in contrast to Ferguson, the mayor was black, the chairman and most members of the city council were black, and the police chief was black. The city prosecutor was also black, so there were no cries for a special prosecutor. There were no accusations in Baltimore that the courts were engaged in profiteering to the detriment of its black citizens. There was a long-standing police Civilian Review Board in place that had been around for about fifteen years. The city did not have police body cameras, but not because the police had opposed them. Instead, Mayor Stephanie Rawlings-Blake had vetoed a measure to equip the department with them. Virtually every officer who had come in contact with Gray in any way was immediately named and charged criminally. Rather than gear up with "militarized" police equipment, Baltimore's cops showed up at the civil unrest in shirtsleeves, with nothing more than the bulletproof vests they wore every day to protect them.

In every way, if you look at these two cities closely, their pre-shooting histories and post-shooting responses were different. Everything that the protesters in Ferguson blamed the riots on there was different in Baltimore: the racial makeup of the government, the racial makeup of the police department, the practices of the courts, the impartiality of the prosecutor, the existence of a civilian review board, the speed with which officers' names were released, and the leveling of criminal charges against the officers allegedly involved.

Despite those glaring differences, the same civil disobedience that happened in Ferguson happened in Baltimore: riots, looting, arson, barrages of bricks and bottles thrown at police, salvos of gunfire, and bedlam in the streets. Even though Baltimore had done practically everything that the agitators had demanded in Ferguson, the outcomes were worse there, with looting and rioting more widespread, and about one hundred more police officers injured there than there had been in Ferguson.

It's the big lie, isn't it? The grand distraction? The sleight of hand? The intentionally moving target?

These protests aren't about problems or solutions; they're about dissonance and disequilibrium. They're about demanding faux police reforms rather than talking about what really happened or what really caused it. They have never been about getting to the truth of what is happening in our urban neighborhoods, or how we get past it. They ensure, rather than avert, the next Michael Brown or Freddie Gray. There is the real injustice, the real missed opportunity.

I don't know what happened in Baltimore. I do know what happened in Ferguson. We all do now. Darren Wilson was free of wrongdoing. Maybe some or all of the Baltimore police officers are guilty of wrongdoing. I don't believe any of them are. From what I know, and I have the benefit of knowing more than we've seen in the news, I expect that ultimately, all six of the Baltimore police officers will be acquitted and people will come to understand that Freddie Gray's injuries were the results of his own actions, not the actions of the police. We'll see. I asked people to keep an open mind through the investigation of Darren Wilson, so I'll do the same with regard to the Baltimore Six.

Regardless of what happened in Baltimore, the all-too-often deadly outcomes of interactions between police and inner-city black youths are, with very few exceptions, not the result of bad acts by cops. All of the noise and effort about fixing law enforcement doesn't help us avoid the next deadly showdown in the streets of Anytown, USA.

I'll talk in the next chapter about the real root of the problems in our society that lead to the hopeless, hapless lives of inner-city youths and place both them and the police officers with whom they come in contact in mortal danger. I'll also talk about real solutions. In the meantime, I'll leave you with this:

At the height of the antipolice movement in and around Ferguson, the St. Louis City Board of Aldermen pushed through legislation creating a form of police civilian review that they dubbed the "Civilian Oversight Board" or the "C-O-B." I took that premise to task in my December column in the *Gendarme*. Enjoy.

SCORN ON THE COB[1]

Whether you call it the COB, or the Civilian Oversight Board, or the Civilian Review Board, or what it really is—a drumhead court-martial without the benefit of due process—a rose by any other name is still a rose. And, so, too, is the manure that fertilizes a rose.

What we have here is a big steaming pile of it.

The reason for this name game is clear. Missouri state statutes allow municipalities to create "Civilian Review Boards" for the purpose of making recommendations in the case of alleged police misconduct. In fact, the Board of Aldermen already adopted the police manual by ordinance, which includes provisions for a Civilian Review Board that complies with the framework established by state statute. But, that's not enough for a handful of tragically misguided souls on the Board of Aldermen who have cowed their colleagues into support for Board Bill 208. That Board Bill creates a COB that greatly overreaches the city's statutory authority, and is sure to be struck down in court. Calling it something else won't avert that certain fate.

The St. Louis Police Officers Association told the sponsors and the city attorneys as much, and instead of incorporating our feedback in the Board Bill, they went even further beyond what state statutes allow for.

You might ask "why," and you'd be wise to do so.

It is undeniable that we have a problem in this city and in this region. Violent crime is on the rise in this post-Ferguson era. Criminals are emboldened, and police officers are reluctant to do their jobs . . . reluctant to be the next Darren Wilson hanged in effigy in the town square.

Criminals and would-be criminals are keen to this. They hear the political attacks on police, the demagoguery, the distant drumbeat of a call-to-arms by those more interested in giving life to a grand distraction than actually dealing with the systemic issues that have resulted in this new age of lawlessness. And, those who are on a crash course with a life of crime, are delivered to that fate prematurely by the self-righteous piety of the very same politicians who have failed them time and time again.

Let's face the ugly truth. On almost every street corner in North St. Louis, there stands a young black man who is so desperately mired in hopelessness for what he sees as a future of joblessness, violence, incarceration, or death, that he reaches the inconceivable conclusion that, when confronted by a police officer, the only rational response is to direct deadly violence toward that police officer. This apocalyptic world view is what led to the fatal shooting by police of Vonderrit Myers and Kajieme Powell and Isaac Holmes and, yes, even Michael Brown.

The very politicians whose failures landed these kids on that street corner aim to leave them standing there for another generation, by failing to address the true problems we now face.

We have a golden opportunity here. It is undeniable that a century and a half of post-reconstruction policies of economic segregation has cordoned off countless people of color into communities of hopelessness and despair. The consequence of economic plight, broken homes, and failing schools is an almost certain future of under-employment and perpetual struggle even for the many, many law-abiding citizens trapped in this cycle. And, for those who turn to crime, they are bound—if they live long enough—for a penal system that does little, if anything, to rehabilitate those that land behind its walls. In fact, in the vast majority of cases, inmates come out as hardened criminals with more potential to offend than they had when they entered the prison system.

Let's work together to fix that, Alderman Kennedy, Alderman French, Alderwoman Tyus. Here is the unavoidable reality; the one thing that is working well in your neighborhoods is law enforcement. The police have a simple job: to stem violence and crime so that conditions in the given community get better, not worse. They do a damned good job of it, too, and they don't deserve your wrath, your crushing scorn. They can't fix the systemic societal problems that have locked us into this desperate cycle, but you can. And, Americans are ready to address these problems head on to avoid the next Michael Brown.

We get it. You don't want another kid to end up like Michael Brown. Well, guess what? We don't want another cop to end up like Darren Wilson, or worse, like Daryl Hall or Norvelle Brown, the last two St. Louis Police Officers killed by gunfire, both of whom were African American. We have the same goals here. So, why aren't we working together?

Don't turn your back on this chance to reform a failed social system by distracting yourself and those you serve with superficial police reforms that do nothing to address the root problems that have led so many young men of color to make desperate decisions that imperil themselves, the police, and everyone around them. Perform your sacred duty to these kids. And, in the meantime, we'll continue to perform ours.

21

IN LOCO PARENTIS

The *Missouri Times* is the premier statewide newspaper for elected officials and political wonks in the Show Me State. The publisher, Scott Faughn, is an unabashed Republican, and the paper is clearly center-right, but not to the extent that it reads like a partisan rag. Faughn is an affable, pragmatic, political operative and is well liked by people on both sides of the aisle. So much so, that the paper spun off a weekly political talk show hosted by Faughn, which airs on the ABC affiliate in St. Louis.

The show, dubbed *This Week in Missouri Politics*, has a round-table format, à la *The McLaughlin Group*, with Faughn moderating a rotating panel of four commentators—generally, two Democrats and two Republicans—who provide commentary on the important political and policy issues of the day.

Faughn, who I consider a friend, invited me onto the show the week the Missouri legislature passed a bill that capped municipal court revenue in response to the DOJ report on Ferguson's traffic court. The bill cracked down hard on St. Louis County cities, lowering the traffic revenue cap from 30 percent of a city's revenue to 12 percent. The cap for the rest of the state was lowered to 20 percent.

That same week, the legislature passed the so-called student transfer bill. The bill was quite controversial. It allowed students in unaccredited school districts to transfer to nearby, higher-performing school districts. By and large, both transferring districts and receiving districts were opposed to the bill because one was losing state tuition funds, and the other was gaining underachieving students with challenging needs that the receiving schools were ill equipped to address. But, the self-anointed "school reformers" liked the concept, and they were backed by a lot of money and political influence, so it ultimately passed.

Faughn went around the panel, asking about the student transfer bill, but when he got to me, he pivoted to a question about municipal court reform, no doubt thinking that a "police union boss" would have a lot more to say about the court reform bill than a piece of education legislation.

He was dead wrong. The link between failed education policies and the hopelessness that leads to violent police-suspect interactions was exactly what I wanted to talk about. I pivoted right back to the ill-conceived student transfer bill.

ME: Well, let me take a step back first and weigh in just for a second on the school transfer bill. We're not kicking the can down the road [as one of the other panelists had described past policies]; we're putting the can on a bus for an hour ride both ways, and that doesn't solve the underlying societal problems that we have; that leads to the next Michael Brown, or the next Vonderrit Myers. Schools are failing these kids, and we're not fixing the schools; we're just spreading the problem without addressing the central issues . . .

FAUGHN: What could you do to fix the schools? I asked this earlier . . .

ME: Well, we could have schools that sort of fill in for the failures of parents in these urban neighborhoods, where kids would go year-round in these urban school districts; where they're there for breakfast, lunch, and dinner; and they have a support structure, instead of having to struggle coming from, in many cases, either a broken home or a home where you wrestle with poverty and crime and violence in your neighborhood and even in your home. Those sort of structural issues, I think, are what's leading to these deadly confrontations between cops and kids. Not just Michael Brown, eight young black men killed by police when they turned deadly violence towards the police, in St. Louis City and St. Louis County since Michael Brown's death.

FAUGHN: Patrick Lynn, you're one of the brightest policy minds in this state. People don't say stuff like he just said. Is the approach to fill in some of the gaps in some of these schools?

LYNN: Exactly. I've been saying this forever. I echo what Jeff says. It's the most important thing, and you see this in the Harlem Project what they've done with schools there.

Patrick Lynn, a former Jay Nixon staffer, who is a longtime denizen of the state capitol, went on to describe the Harlem Project and how well what I'll call the "in loco parentis approach" worked in that famously challenged urban neighborhood's schools.

Faughn went back around the panel, seizing on the opportunity that the candid conversation provided, to burrow down further into a policy issue that has been so drastically politicized by the push-pull between the status quo advocates protecting their turf and school reformers pushing their own agenda. Nobody seems to have the gumption to talk about education unless they are parroting one of those interest groups or the other. It was a rare opportunity to have an honest conversation, and the frankness of the dialogue seemed to be liberating. We need more of that.

Here's why.

Education is the ultimate equalizer. It can provide people, regardless of their economic status, with the opportunity to better themselves and improve their lot in life. Of course, they have to be willing to do something with that opportunity.

Boosting educational outcomes is absolutely our best chance as a society to break the cycle of poverty, crime, and violence in the urban core. That's how we begin to address the underlying problems that result in the hopelessness and desperation that lead inner-city youths to turn interactions with police into deadly confrontations. I personally don't think we make urban neighborhoods better by clinging to the status quo, or by buying into the faux education reforms of well-healed groups with ulterior motives.

Moving the pieces around on the game board makes no real difference for the kids mired in this cycle of hopelessness. The student transfer approach relies on the theory that it is *where* troubled youth get their education that is important, not *how* they get their education.

Putting a kid on a bus for an extra hour each way to go to a school that is no better prepared to serve the needs of a student who lacks parental involvement, is immersed in an environment where his or her life is in constant jeopardy, and goes to bed hungry far too many nights is no solution at all.

In fact, it's what got us in this messy downward spiral in urban school districts in the first place.

Let me explain.

One of my most vivid early memories was my fourth grade teacher, Mrs. Mitchell, taking me to the principal's office, where I found my parents awaiting my arrival. I nearly wet my pants. I thought, *What did I do to get called in front of my teacher, the principal,* and *my parents?!*

As it turned out, they told me that I had scored extraordinarily well on the Iowa Test, an aptitude test that elementary students took in those long-ago, bygone days. They revealed to me that St. Louis Public Schools at the time segregated nerdy Poindexters (my words, not theirs) like me into special schools for the "gifted." They said that I didn't have to switch schools if I didn't want to, but my parents and the faculty strongly encouraged me to consider it. They told me that one of the kids I was in Cub Scouts with at my elementary school had also scored high and had agreed to transfer. That put me at ease somewhat, so I reluctantly agreed to the move.

Now, this kind of student transfer made sense. The school wasn't that far away, and gifted students present unique challenges for teachers. Tailoring a program to those unique challenges was a very progressive approach at the time. It was a very different tack from the one-size-fits-all approach that is so endemic to public education across the country now. No one can seem to understand that just because it works well in suburban schools doesn't mean it will work well in urban schools.

Because I lived in an all-white neighborhood, the specialized gifted school also had another function. I was now in a highly integrated education environment where I felt more at home because I was in a classroom setting with people who had the same advanced level of intellectual development—and the accompanying lack of social skills—that I did. Like I said, nerds.

They were nerds of all colors and creeds, though. I never really knew a person of a different race before then, and now I had black, Hispanic, and Asian classmates. One of my favorite teachers at my new school was African-American, Mrs. Proctor. The most delightful part was because I had more in common with my geeky compatriots than I did with fellow students at my old school, the differences in race didn't seem to matter at all. Quite the opposite, we were alike in the most important intellectual and social ways, so differences in something as superficial as skin color were of no consequence. Phillip Washington, a black kid in my grade, and I became fast friends.

Then, in the fall of a gavel, that was all taken away by two guys named Jim and Bill. James H. Meredith was a federal district court judge in St. Louis. He approved a consent decree to desegregate the St. Louis public schools in response to a lawsuit filed by Minnie Liddell, the mother of a black student enrolled in the city school system. That action came at just about the same time that a federal court order mandating forced busing in Boston led to riots and deadly violence there (by the way, despite all the hubbub about the riots in Ferguson, nobody died at the hands of police or rioters there as they did in Boston, but then again, no one had invented twenty-four-hour cable TV news networks yet in 1977. So, no big deal, I guess).

My family moved from St. Louis City to the far suburb of Arnold in 1977, the same year as the Boston busing riots. Five years later, the new judge in the St. Louis desegregation case, William L. Hungate, used the threat of forced busing to get St. Louis Public Schools and the surrounding school districts to "voluntarily" participate in a scaled-back busing plan.

Talk about your all-time, unintended consequences! The white flight that resulted from the desegregation of St. Louis city schools left that district in a tailspin, and it has been circling the drain ever since. Here's the dirty little secret: it wasn't just white flight; it was *black flight* too.

Black families of means saw what was coming just like white parents—the depletion of school resources, the brain drain, the long bus rides, the racial tensions in the school hallways—they didn't want that for their kids either. There were several major corporations in the north St. Louis County suburbs that employed a lot of African-Americans, companies like Emerson Electric, Ford Motor Company, and McDonnell Douglas. Black parents who made a good living and wanted to get their kids out of the mess of "voluntary" busing decided to move north, where they had good schools and parents could be closer to their jobs. They clambered to find houses in what was, at the time, considered the best school district in the northern suburbs. That's right; you guessed it . . . the Ferguson-Florissant School District. I'll let you simmer in the juices of irony stew for just a moment.

Ding! Time's up.

The Hungate plan was a stunning failure. Both white and black families who had the requisite financial resources and the parental concern to relocate, headed for the county line like matinee goers rushing toward the exits of a burning theater.

Now, think about the logic of that. St. Louis schools were segregated, but not because of anything the school district did, but rather because of economic policies of the federal government that led to economic segregation largely along racial lines. Federal judges punished city schools, not for the misdeeds of local school leaders, but for the misguided policies of federal lawmakers. Up until the year before he inherited the desegregation lawsuit, William Hungate was a U.S. Congressman. The irony stew is still simmering on the stove if you'd like a scoop.

Now that you've thought about the logic, think about the consequences. Virtually all of the best parents and the highest-performing students, black and white, pulled out of St. Louis City schools. Those folks were also the highest wage earners and the biggest taxpayers. Their departure left the district reeling, and left the city of St. Louis with no black middle-class neighborhoods, which were once prevalent on the north side. The shrinking student body left the district with too many buildings, an oversized faculty, and a bloated, unsustainable budget. The city schools are still selling off buildings to this day. City schools had their challenges before busing, but they were high-performing then compared to what they are now. The destabilizing effect of losing your best students—the ones who have parents that make sure they are school-ready when they enroll, the ones who get a breakfast in the morning and go home to a dinner at night, the ones whose parents sit with them on the couch, helping them with homework—those losses are devastating to a school district. St. Louis Public Schools were not immune.

How is all that different from proposals like the student transfer bill, or charter schools, or private school vouchers?

It's not. These are all wrong-headed ideas that don't improve a system that's broken, not as a function of what goes on inside the four walls of urban school buildings, but rather as a function of what goes on *outside* those walls. Until Ferguson, the consequences were somewhat intangible: high dropout rates, low ACT scores, reading below grade level. That didn't mean anything to people living outside the urban core who have kids that attend high-achieving schools graduating college-ready students. What did they care? It wasn't their problem.

Once you see burning buildings, rioting, and looting just miles from where you live, it places the urban education crisis in the limelight. Then, when you see armed warfare on the streets of your major U.S.

cities—not just St. Louis and Baltimore, but all over the country—where the young men produced by a dysfunctional approach to education in inner cities are turning deadly violence against police officers every day, it brings some clarity to the problem. Don't forget: the only reason that violence isn't being directed at you, John Q. Citizen, is that police officers stand between you and these angry, hopeless, well-armed kids that a broken approach to urban education is churning out by the thousands every year.

The problem is only compounded when we pluck out the handful of kids who have something going for them and send them off to charter schools or transfer them to distant, more affluent school districts. When you condemn the rest of those inner-city kids to an education at "Lord of the Flies" High, the outcomes become self-perpetuating.

This gets to the heart of one of the main points I wanted to make in this book. The tragic outcomes of police interactions with black youths in urban settings that we're experiencing in this country are not the result of the way police approach those interactions. They are the result, and this is nearly an absolute, of the way inner-city youths approach these interactions. I'll say it again, with emphasis, because it is central to the question of how we avoid these deadly confrontations going forward: *The tragic outcomes of police interactions with black youths in urban settings that we're experiencing in this country are not the result of the way police approach those interactions; they are the result of the way inner-city youths approach these interactions.*

While incidents involving black kids and white cops get all of the media hype, there are plenty of inner-city white and Hispanic kids locked in the same cycle of hopelessness and desperation who are making the same sort of bad decisions when confronted with a police encounter.

None of these inner-city kids start out bad. They are born into a generational cycle of poverty and broken homes that is impervious to every remedy save one: hope. If these kids only believed they had a fighting chance for a future better than the one they've seen their parents, siblings, friends, and neighbors inherit as a cursed birthright, how they approach interactions with the police and the entire outside world could be greatly altered.

How do we accomplish such a daunting task? Wouldn't it be easier to just blame the way the police approach these interactions? Wouldn't a spattering of cosmetic police reforms and superficial education reforms be easier than tackling big problems on the scale of education failures, economic segregation, broken homes, and the like?

Sure, if you don't mind repeating this cycle over and over and over again. The only way to avoid the next Michael Brown is to fix the problems that led him to the confrontation he had with Darren Wilson. If you try to address what happened that specific day in that specific confrontation, you're already too late.

I mentioned *in loco parentis* earlier. It is a Latin term that means "in the place of the parent." It is generally used to describe the role of public schools in educating kids, but I want to apply it more broadly here to describe government's role in intervening in the lives of inner-city kids trapped in a cycle of broken, parentless homes, and the attendant challenges that come with that.

I know, I know. To some, that is going to seem like a "nanny state" approach. There is a reflexive repulsion to the idea of an overreaching government intruding into the lives of its citizens.

Guess what? We are already feeding, clothing, providing free health care, and housing the products of our societal failures in the urban core. We call them prisons. No country in history has had more. They are the most financially inefficient way to address the plight of inner-city youths, and they have the costliest consequences for society at-large because we don't do much to intervene in the lives of inner-city youths until they have committed a crime and taken a victim.

Think about this: according to CBS News, the cost per prisoner per year in America was $31,307 as of 2010. Some states, according to the report, spend upwards of $60,000 per year.[1] According to *US News & World Report*, in the 2010 school year, we spent $10,975 per student per year in America.[2]

THE WAR ON POLICE

Does that seem wrong to you? It does to me.

Why don't we take some of that $20,000 a year more that we spend on prisoners over pupils and fix our inner-city schools? Let's start by making them safe and gun-free. A smattering of security guards at urban public schools has done little to make them safer. Let's put police officers there. When cops and kids interact in an amicable setting, particularly white cops and black kids, it breaks down some of the barriers that lead to violent altercations later. It provides each with a better understanding of the other. Cops working in the inner city don't get to see black kids at their best—studying and playing in the school yard with friends—they only get to see them at their worst, when society and public schools have failed them and they've turned to violent crime. Likewise, black kids don't get to see white cops in nonconfrontational situations. Both sides of the equation could benefit from seeing the humanity of one another.

Don't stop with safe schools for seven hours a day, nine months a year. Let's expand them to year-round, sunup to sundown oases of safety for urban dwellers who are in constant jeopardy when they are outside of the school walls, being raised and ruined by the streets.

I know everyone wants a one-size-fits-all model for public schools, but the challenges of educating kids in the inner city are profoundly different from educating kids in the suburbs and rural areas. Jettison the monolith, and recognize the overwhelming needs of inner-city kids, and then do things for them that aren't necessary elsewhere.

Go even farther than longer school days and year-round classes. Let's feed these kids and make sure they are healthy and ready to learn. Provide breakfast, lunch, and dinner so they are thinking about their studies, not where their next meal is coming from. Reinstate shrinking school nurse and school counselor programs, and expand them even more so these kids are physically and emotionally healthy and can better perform academically. And don't just provide for them academically. Help prepare them for success in other ways with practical, life-skills training.

For the kids who can demonstrate that they don't have a safe place to go home to at night, build dorms on public school campuses so the gains we make for these kids during school days aren't erased at night when they are potentially exposed to crime, violence, drugs, and abuse.

This will sound to some like another spend-spend-spend liberal advocating for social programs. Far from it. This is fiscal conservatism. We've wasted billions of dollars on incarceration rather than spending pennies on the dollar by intervening before these kids turn to a life of crime. Would you rather pay to build dorms on school campuses or dorms on prison grounds?

I not only want to trade relatively low-cost education reforms for high-savings prison depopulation, I want to reform welfare too. The money we put into the hands of parents in urban settings has clearly done nothing to improve the lives of kids in the inner city, or to change the inevitability of the bad outcomes visited upon them. Cut off that money and divert it to the education system to help pay for some of the reforms I've suggested. Instead of buying illicit drugs for absentee parents with public assistance dollars, let's buy textbooks for their kids.

Let's do something about guns too.

Before you sic the NRA on me for speaking blasphemy, you should know that I'm a gun owner and NRA member myself. I don't think we should ever do anything to interfere with the rights of law-abiding citizens to own guns and to use them in their defense when necessary. But we can protect the gun rights of responsible gun owners and at the same time do something to make things safer in the urban core, where gun violence is spiraling out of control.

In Missouri, it is legal to carry a gun in your car without a carry-conceal permit as long as you're not a convicted felon. Most folks in the suburbs and rural Missouri don't know this. They generally go out and get CCW permits because they are law-abiding citizens. Inner-city youths know about this law, though. They make sure to always have one guy in the car who has never been *convicted* of a felony, and when they get stopped, he claims ownership of the guns in the car. It doesn't matter what awful crimes the other three or four guys in the car have committed. The cops can't do anything to take the weapons out of the dangerous hands they're in unless the guns are reported stolen (by the way, a lot of those guns *are* stolen, but haven't been reported).

Since this law passed in Missouri, there are more than twice as many guns on the streets in the inner city, and less than half as many gun arrests as there were before the law was passed.

Let's get the guns out of these neighborhoods and require CCW permits to carry guns in your car. If you don't want to do that statewide, let's at least allow local jurisdictions to establish gun-free zones where you have to have a CCW permit to carry a gun in your car. That'll immediately suppress the spread of illegal firearms in the inner city. While we're at it, let's make it a requirement that people report their guns stolen within twenty-four hours of discovering the theft. If your gun is out there on the streets in the hands of the criminal who stole it, or in the hands of the criminal he sold it to, the police really, really need to know that. Hopefully, the police will recover it and you'll get your gun back before someone gets killed with it.

We also need sentencing reform. You can't depopulate prisons and reinvest that money in inner-city schools without changing the way we handle offenders. Nonviolent criminals needn't take up space in our prisons. I want to offer a caution here. Some folks believe that all drug crimes are nonviolent offenses. That is a bunch of malarkey. A guy who is selling heroin or manufacturing methamphetamine is engaged in a deadly criminal enterprise and should be locked up for a long, long time. A junkie who can't kick crack or prescription meds is better served with treatment than incarceration. Society is better served, too, because, just like education, addiction treatment is far less expensive than confinement. In-custody shock time followed by court-ordered treatment has worked really well with drug and alcohol offenders and should be our first option.

There's also this: I have been a hardliner against marijuana decriminalization my whole life, but it's time to take a step back and rethink that policy. I've arrested a lot of really bad men who have been in the business of marijuana distribution, and we should keep putting pot dealers in jail; but compared to almost any other crime on the books, marijuana possession is probably one of the least harmful offenses that anyone can commit. Damn, I never thought I'd say that.

Arrests for petty marijuana possession, by the way, disproportionately affect inner-city blacks. No one should ever go to jail for possessing anything less than a quarter pound of marijuana. We just don't have the space for them. It was a real epiphany for me when I stood on the floor of the Missouri House of Representatives in 2014 and argued in favor of passage of a medicinal marijuana bill that legalized the use of CBD (cannabidiol) oil for treatments of some chronic conditions in Missouri. It was a small step toward recognizing that we really need to reevaluate our priorities.

While we're closing prisons, let's open some mental health facilities. We have disinvested in state-provided mental health services for the last couple of decades or longer, and the people who need those services end up either in prison or on the streets. The ones on the street often engage in acts that endanger themselves or others. That's a high price to pay for the relatively modest savings we've realized from defunding mental health services. Remember, at least three of the young black men killed by St. Louis–area law enforcement since Michael Brown's death had either clearly evident or previously diagnosed mental health conditions so profound they led to their deaths.

There are no easy fixes, but I've laid out a road map for real, meaningful reforms that would sharply reduce the number of deadly confrontations between police and inner-city youths who are almost exclusively people of color.

I say *meaningful* reforms because all we've heard about with the exception of municipal court reform in the year after Michael Brown's death have been faux police reforms that will do nothing to avoid the next Michael Brown. In fact, they will only hasten the next Brown-type confrontation. Yes, we needed to reform our municipal courts in Missouri because their profiteering was creating a modern debtors' prison system that would have been repugnant to our Founding Fathers, but it was not—I repeat, *was not*—a racially motivated system. It was a system that preyed on economically disadvantaged blacks and whites alike. The reason it disproportionately affected blacks is that blacks disproportionately live in poverty in this country. That is a problem that's way over the pay grades of city judges and municipal prosecutors.

The other faux police reforms, like body cameras, civilian review boards, special prosecutors, and so forth have big price tags affixed to them. We're talking about tens of millions of dollars that could be spent on inner-city public school reform, or summer job programs, or for that matter, on increasing police salaries so that we maintain well-trained, experienced law enforcement agencies. Novel idea, huh?

I know my critics will say I don't care about black kids in the inner city, and that this is all a diversion meant to push back against proposed police reforms. I do care about those kids, and I don't want to ever see another Michael Brown incident. Believe that, and believe this also: I care even more about the cops on the other side of those deadly confrontations. I care that these shootings can leave their careers in ruin. I care about the heavy burden they carry around with them when they have to take a life. And I care that sometimes it is the cop, not the kid, who dies in these deadly, unnecessary confrontations.

I've said it before: these confrontations result almost exclusively from bad decisions made by the person being stopped by the police. Even in cases like the shootings of Walter Scott in North Charleston, or Eric Courtney Harris in Tulsa County, where I can't justify or explain the actions of the officers, those confrontations started with some sort of physical aggression on the part of the men that ultimately died.

We need to do something to help the folks who are dying at the hands of police learn to make better decisions, to find their way to better outcomes. It is expensive, to be sure, but as we watch both cops and young black men dying, as we see American cities burning, it is time we realize that the cost of doing nothing—or the cost of doing the same old thing—is too high.

We live in a country where economic segregation based on skin color is a very real phenomenon. It is not the America we were supposed to inherit. I use the term *black* rather than *African-American* throughout this book intentionally with clarity of purpose. People aren't treated differently by our society because of their continental origin; they are treated differently because of the darkness of their skin. They are disproportionately born into poverty because of an economic system that provides them with a tough start in life and little opportunity to change that. I'm not for expanding the welfare state. Quite the contrary. Government aid has to stop coming in the form of free money, and instead, take the form of greater opportunities—opportunities that you must seize upon in order to enjoy a benefit.

This great Commonwealth was founded on a divine covenant between its architects and its people. The wealth we hold in common isn't financial; it lays in the providence of a land of limitless bounty where a man can choose to master his own fate. It is not meant to be a place where wealth is re-distributed to those who would squander it; it is meant to be a land of boundless opportunity where everyone has a chance to seize on a brighter future. That is the social contract we have inked in the blood of our forbearers. It is a contract we should breach no more.

MAMA DORIS

Norman Lear, the creative genius behind a critically acclaimed gallery of classic television sitcoms that included *Sanford and Son; Good Times; One Day at a Time; Mary Hartman, Mary Hartman; Different Strokes*; and *What's Happening!!*, just to name a few, was best known for his celebrated masterpiece *All in the Family*.

Lear loved to pepper *All in the Family* episodes with antagonists to the show's crass, insensitive central character, Archie Bunker.

While we best remember George Jefferson and Maude Findlay—two Archie nemeses whose popularity led to a pair of hit spinoff series, *The Jeffersons* and *Maude*—two of my favorite characters were Bunker neighbors Frank and Irene Lorenzo.

The Lorenzos were proof positive that Archie's prejudices weren't confined to skin color. The ultraliberal, nontraditional, devoutly Catholic couple represented everything Archie despised. Frank was a flamboyant, hyper-ethnic Italian, stay-at-home husband while Irene was an unapologetic, liberated woman of Irish descent who worked on a loading dock. *What is the world coming to?* Archie must have wondered when the unconventional couple moved in next door.

The episode featuring the Lorenzos that I most remember was a season four offering titled "Archie and the Kiss," written by John Rappaport. It was an uproarious, nonstop roller coaster of laughter and social commentary, as were so many of the show's episodes. This one, though, gave viewers their first glimpse into the Lorenzo household. In the scene, Frank and Irene ended up in a heated argument over Irene giving away Frank's favorite statue to Archie's daughter, Gloria.

As the argument boils over, Irene, in her frustration, blames Frank's Italian heritage for his irrational reaction. This elicits a seething response from Frank, who rants: "There it is; it all comes out in the open after all these years . . . Oh, they told me, they told me before we got married. They said, 'You marry somebody who's Irish and someday you're going to get into an argument with her and she's gonna say, aha, Wop'!"

Of course, Irene never called Frank a "Wop" or any other ethnic slur, but the scene perfectly illustrates a dynamic that pervades so very many interactions in our society between people of different races, ethnicities, or skin colors. It is the dilemma of majority-minority relations, the overwhelming sense on both sides of a conversation, that, while the differences between the two participants are never verbalized, they are right there, just below the surface, in constant danger of bubbling up through some Freudian slip of the tongue. The person of color in the conversation is often left with the impression that the white participant is trying too hard not to insert race into the dialogue, while the white conversant is selecting each word with such painstaking care so as not to offend, that their syntax seems forced and unnatural.

I'm not quite sure what the white person is afraid of saying, or the person of color is afraid of hearing, but it is entertainingly awkward to watch at times. It's more amusing yet to watch these interactions when they are between people who are from somewhat isolated segments of society and have little experience with people from one another's walk of life. I simply delighted in watching urban black Democrats talking to rural white Republicans when I was a Missouri state representative.

It was like watching two people with low pain thresholds stopping to chat about the weather while walking barefoot across a bed of hot coals. Observing those painful interplays never stopped being humorous to me.

It's not the way I approached a conversation with someone who was different from me. In my experience, acknowledging and celebrating our differences is far preferable to engaging in some charade where we pretend our diverse characteristics don't exist.

Maybe some people would say that inserting such things into small talk reflects some sort of inappropriate hyperawareness to our dissimilarities. Maybe so, but isn't that preferential to sterilizing a conversation so much that you aren't really even talking? In my experience, people of both minority and majority status appreciate respectful acknowledgements of each other's differences. But here's the key: the differences don't matter and they shouldn't matter, but that doesn't mean they don't exist, so why go through all the clumsy verbal calisthenics?

The interaction is quite different, however, when it is between a police officer and a person of color.

It is a sort of an "Aha, Wop!" situation for police. Anything the cop might say or do that is even the slightest bit suggestive of racial awareness, no matter how innocent, is almost certainly going to be greeted with indignation by the recipient of the perceived offensive language or act.

I think there is a popular belief among many in our culture that cops are more likely than other segments of our society to be racists, a belief that racially charged language is something they use with reckless abandon, a belief that the "N-word" is always on the tips of their tongues and that it might slip out at any given moment. There is no truth to such notions, from my experience. Cops, and I've been around a lot of them, are less likely than the general public to use racial epithets. Far less likely. This is particularly true of this current generation of police officers, who, like their fellow Millennials, seem to not be intolerant of anything—anything, that is, except *intolerance*. The image of racist, thuggish cops is a pervasive one, though. It is one that is hard for law enforcement to shun.

Just as it was for Irene Lorenzo, who never actually called her beloved husband a "Wop," a police officer is just as vulnerable to doing or saying something that is destined to elicit a brusque "Aha! N-word!" from a person who has embraced the idea that all cops are racists. Conversely, when the righteous indignation comes pouring out, it is a self-proving theorem for cops who have the expectation that all people of color are just waiting to play the race card. The inevitable "Aha! Race-baiter!" reaction by cops is undeniable evidence that racial tensions are alive and well in our culture.

Police officers are acutely aware of all of this. These tête-*à*-têtes between police and people of color are always potentially charged with matters of race. A police officer—and, in fact, the entire criminal justice system—is supposed to be color-blind. They are supposed to be that way for good reason. Race shouldn't matter. It *can't* matter in the eyes of the law, otherwise our whole system unravels.

I know there are many who think our justice system has already untwined in light of allegations of racial profiling, disparate sentencing, and so-called police murder motivated by skin color. I'm here to tell you, I think people who believe that are dead wrong.

There is no denying that relative to their proportion of the population, people of color, particularly black people, get stopped more, go to jail more, and are killed more by police than whites. By and large, and overwhelmingly so, this is not—I repeat *not*—about the way police officers see skin color.

Here are the plain, unadulterated facts: police officers come into contact with blacks more often because there are more police officers in black neighborhoods because there is more serious crime in black neighborhoods. Blacks are statistically more likely to commit traffic violations.[1] Blacks are more likely to commit serious crimes.[2] And blacks are more likely to turn deadly violence against police.[3] It's not because of their skin color. Well, not directly anyway. There is a different explanation for these propensities.

In the city of St. Louis, nearly 70 percent of homicides, where a witness identifies the race of the perpetrator, are committed by blacks, almost exclusively, black males. For burglary, the numbers are over 70 percent, and for robbery they are a staggering 80 percent or higher. These are not numbers based on the results of a police investigation leading to a suspect of a certain race. They are cases where a victim or witness—the vast majority of whom are black themselves—identify the perpetrator's skin color as black.

As a nation, Americans are in utter denial of these inescapable statistics. We have to call it racial profiling; otherwise, we've got to answer some very tough questions about ourselves as a society.

Let me answer one of the tough questions: it is about economics, not skin color, or, better said, it's about the economics of skin color.

Blacks are disproportionately born into poverty in America. Call it economic segregation. Call it the legacy of slavery and the failure of post–Civil War reconstruction. Call it the product of the welfare state. Call it whatever you please; just don't deny its existence.

The dirty truth is that people who live in poverty are more likely to be the victims of crime and violence, *and* are more likely to be the perpetrators of crime and violence. Both their own financial struggles and their proximity to those with a shared economic plight result in a self-perpetuating cycle of poverty, crime, and violence. Our government's welfare state response to that cyclical predicament over multiple generations has made that plight worse rather than better.

There are no easy solutions to this generational cycle of disproportionate poverty based on race. There is an easy political strategy, however, and that is the time-tested strategy of blame. For many years, the blame has been leveled squarely at blacks themselves for their inability to rise up from poverty in this "land of opportunity." Today's convenient scapegoats are police officers.

Somehow, the decades-long failure of politicians to do anything to address this social reality is suddenly our fault as cops. What the . . . ?!

Let me lay it down for you one more time. The reason we have these deadly confrontations between cops and black kids is the bad decisions made by kids who grow up in desolation and hopelessness. The reason for that hopelessness is the virtually inescapable trap of poverty, crime, and violence that blacks are disproportionately born into. The reason for this unbreakable cycle of economic segregation is the failed policies of lawmakers on both sides of the aisle who have forsaken these communities. Those very same lawmakers who used to blame blacks for the very same deadly outcomes, now blame cops. Buy a mirror, jackasses!

Some smart aleck is bound to point out that, I, too, was once a lawmaker. That's right; I was. I actually tried to do something to change the plight of inner-city dwellers. I fought for increases in the minimum-wage (a sensible $8.25 hourly wage, not a Marxist-inspired $15-an-hour, backdoor hamburger tax). I fought for increased funding for public education, particularly for urban schools. I supported medicinal marijuana legislation that opened the way for marijuana decriminalization. I sponsored a death penalty moratorium that would have ceased executions until we got a handle on racial disparities in capital punishment. I supported tax credits for inner-city neighborhood regeneration. I supported sweeping sentencing reform, and the list goes on and on and on. Most important, I did all of this while maintaining my law enforcement credentials, which gave me more credibility when arguing for criminal justice reform.

The record is there for anyone to see. Type http://www.house .mo.gov/member.aspx?district=113&year=2014 into your browser and look for yourself. I put my money where my mouth was, while other politicians were putting their thumbs where their asses were.

★ ★ ★

It was wrong of Darren Wilson to compare Brown to a "demon" in the now-famous George Stephanopoulos interview.[4] I've told Darren and his lawyers so. I don't think he meant it to sound like it did. But it dehumanized Brown. It's okay to set the record straight on the very bad, deadly decisions that Brown made that led to his death, but he is still a human being . . . a person, not a devil.

In fact, I'm going to call him Michael from here on out because calling him by the name his loved ones called him humanizes him. His humanity doesn't excuse his theft, or his violence, or his effort to disarm and harm another human being, Darren Wilson, who himself has been demonized plenty. Yet, it is so very important that we remember that Michael was a young man who once had hopes and dreams just like the rest of us. If we forget that, it makes all this too easy to happen again to someone else's Michael.

I mentioned at the outset of this book that I feel a deep sympathy for Michael's parents. My parents suffered the loss of a son, and it is a terrible suffering to witness. I feel a concord with the Brown family because of what my family went through. Despite my anger over the riots and the violent protests, regardless of my disdain for Michael's act of violence against a police officer, without regard for the undeniable differences between the Brown family and mine, I still, through it all, feel a connection that I cannot ignore.

Just like Michael, my little brother, Timothy Michael, died at the tender age of eighteen. Like Michael, Tim had just graduated high school and should have had his whole life ahead of him, but also like Michael, Tim made a terrible mistake that endangered himself and others: he got behind the wheel when he shouldn't have. Tim died violently, scared, without his loved ones by his side—just like Michael.

When I think of the painful image of Michael's family seeing his body lying motionless in the bloody streets of Canfield, it takes me back to the night we lost Tim. I was working part-time as a police officer then and full-time as a 911 dispatcher. I received a grim phone call from one of my fellow dispatchers telling me that there had been an accident and that I should get to the hospital right away. As I met my parents at the hospital, I got a glimpse of the two paramedics that had brought my brother into the ER. Their bleak expressions made my heart sink to the floor.

The ER staff knew I was a police officer, so they pulled me aside and asked me to come with them. I was hoping against hope for good news, but what they asked of me was something that no twenty-four-year-old should ever be asked to do, identify his brother's body. The slow, almost interminable march to the trauma ward was unbearable. Not as unbearable as what I saw on the other side of the door, though. I felt all of the air leave my body as I gasped in horror at the sight of my baby brother on the gurney. I howled in unspeakable pain as I rushed down the hall and broke the almost unutterable news to my parents. It is a moment that I relive every day.

I can't look at the faces of Michael Brown's parents without seeing the faces of my own parents. I just can't. Even now, tears stream down my face as I write these words and picture the faces of these two families, mine and Michael's.

I've been called a racist a hundred times over by the haters that marched in the streets of Ferguson. In many ways, it would be easier if I was a racist. If I believed that people of color were somehow inferior to me, it would make it easy for me to put aside these feelings of empathy I have for Michael's parents. It would be easy to convince myself that their love for Michael was somehow lesser than the love my parents had for Tim. It would be easy to think that Michael's life didn't have as much value as Tim's. It would be easy to conclude that white lives matter more than black lives matter.

But I don't see the world that way.

When I look at Michael's parents, I don't see the color of their skin; I see the pain in their eyes, the dark stain on their hearts. I see only that unmistakable look, that expression of immeasurable grief, and it looks just the same on the Browns' faces as it did on my parents' faces, as it would on the face of any parent who endured that loss. How could something as insignificant as skin color matter when you look upon the sorrowful faces of mourning parents?

How indeed?

Some people are ruffled by the Black Lives Matter movement. It doesn't bother me, because I agree. Black lives do matter. I just wish they'd realize that what they're doing now with the all-too-often violent demonstrations and the calls for faux police reforms ignores the real plight that places black lives in danger in the first place. I wish instead that they would do something to help make our inner cities a safer place to live. I also wish they would realize that cops' lives, "blue lives," are also jeopardized every time an interaction between a police officer and a black youth turns ugly. We have a shared interest in ending these confrontations. Cops want them to stop too. Why aren't we working together?

On that subject, there are people who are both black and blue.

Less than a month before the one-year anniversary of Michael's death, an African-American St. Louis police sergeant was sitting in his car when he was ambushed and shot by a young, black male. Thankfully, his body armor saved his life.

I knew the sergeant involved before the shooting, and I have come to know him even better since. His story was the last column I wrote before the anniversary of Michael's death, and it ominously appeared in the August edition of the *Gendarme*.

It is a solemn reminder of the sanctity of both black and blue lives:

BLACK LIVES MATTER, EVEN WHEN THEY'RE BLUE[5]

In the wee hours of July 14, an off-duty St. Louis Police Sergeant sat in his personal car in full uniform working the secondary job that helped to make ends meet for he and his wife and their one-year-old toddler. Sarge, as I'll call him here to protect his identity, sat in that same spot many nights before, keeping sentry over the Central West End neighborhood occasionally targeted by burglars and car clouters.

That night felt very different than most, though. As it turned out, it would be different than any night Sarge had ever experienced or probably ever will.

It was a sweltering night even in those pre-dawn hours when reprieve is usually granted from the heat of a St. Louis summer. Sarge always wore his vest on duty and seldom took it off when he was moonlighting at his second job. But, he was coming off an eight-hour shift of working in the oppressive heat, so he did his rounds when he first arrived at the secondary gig, then shed his vest and tossed it in his back seat.

As a general rule, not much happened when providing security in this upscale neighborhood in the shadows of the lofty Chase Park Plaza. The streets were well lit and it was widely known by people that frequented the area that the business district was teeming with surveillance cameras. Add the presence of a hulking police officer in full uniform in his parked car, and only a fool would consider targeting the area for crime.

Unfortunately, we have no shortage of fools in St. Louis.

To pass the time when he was working secondary, Sarge would listen intently to the radio traffic on his police walkie-talkie. It was an uncharacteristically busy night for a Monday. Even for St. Louis, in a time when crime had spiked to near record levels, the volume and intensity of the radio traffic was disquieting for Sarge as he listened on. He described it as "a crazy, wild night on the radio. There were robberies; a car chase; a missing kid, just a bunch of crazy stuff going on."

Then Sarge spied two young men on foot in the neighborhood. It wasn't common at all to see pedestrians at that hour so Sarge took note of them. Cops just naturally have a heightened sense of awareness when they see something out of the ordinary, so his Spidey senses were tingling. As he described it, "The hairs on my neck stood up. Where'd they come from?" he wondered to himself.

Good cops learn as a matter of survival to trust their intuition, so Sarge did something that seemed simple and instinctive at the time. He didn't even really think much about it. He strapped his vest back on. That reflexive impulse very likely saved his life.

Then, a third pedestrian emerged and met up with the other two. The three then walked toward Kingshighway. This put the Sarge at ease. He thought maybe the first two had just been waiting for the third, or that maybe they were walking to the bus stop together since it was in the direction they were heading.

Moments later, a gray Ford rolled up out of nowhere, stopping right in front of Sarge's car. He recognized that three of the four occupants were the same men he saw walking in the neighborhood.

In the blink of an eye, a car door flew open and one of the occupants bailed out wearing a black bandana tied across his face.

Sarge reached for his gun, but it was too late. The man's feet barely hit the ground when he opened fire on Sarge. As lead punched through the windshield of his car, Sarge returned fire, unsure if his rounds would even pierce the windshield at point blank range. The noise of gunfire in such a confined space was deafening. Even when I sat down to interview Sarge a week later, his ears were still ringing. There is a sort of sensory overload that accompanies a shooting inside of a closed area like a car that can cause some people to simply shut down.

Not Sarge.

He was focused on surviving. As the man continued to fire, his bandana slipped down under his chin. "I've got to remember that face," Sarge thought to himself as the man glared at him with murder in his eyes.

The man stopped shooting, probably because he had emptied his clip, and he fled on foot as the car sped away in a different direction. Through his Swiss-cheesed windshield, Sarge was able to keep the shooter in sight as he chased him in his car. Amazingly, he was also able to put out the shots fired call on his radio while steering the car with his knee and reloading his sidearm. That ladies and gentlemen is the sort of unshakable intensity that characterizes a man like Sarge . . . the instinct to survive; the wherewithal to return fire; the urge to identify and apprehend his assailant before he hurts another cop or a civilian. This was literally a case of grace under fire.

The shooter slipped into a parking garage where Sarge lost him. Sarge thought that he might have hit the shooter with his return fire so he looked around for a blood trail that he could follow, but saw nothing on the ground.

By that time though, the cavalry had arrived. In what seemed like only seconds after he had put the call out on the radio, police cars and an ambulance were on the scene. Sarge described the response as amazing. Police cars from all across the city were on the scene in the blink of an eye. The paramedics on the ambulance were giving him the once over. He told them that as he was chasing the bad guy, "I realized something was wrong. I felt a burning in my chest like putting your hand on a hot oven."

The medics quickly determined that Sarge had been shot. As they desperately stripped his clothes off, the look of relief that he saw put Sarge at ease. The bullet, they concluded, had been stopped by Sarge's vest; the very same vest he had donned in the fleeting moments just before the shooting. Miraculous!

The ambulance crew assessed the blunt trauma to Sarge's chest and surveyed the rest of his body to see if he had been struck by any other rounds. They saw nothing; but nonetheless, they rushed him to nearby Barnes Hospital for a more thorough examination.

As Sarge lay on a hospital gurney, his wife and young son lay asleep at home in their beds.

His wife was an active member of the St. Louis Police Wives Association, so she woke up to "officer down" texts from other members of the SLPWA. She was accustomed, far too accustomed, to waking up to such calls. She and the other police wives would swing into action on such occasions and head to the hospital to see what support they could offer to the officer's family. She figured Sarge would be home soon from his ho-hum secondary job and she could leave their baby with him and head off to the hospital as she had so many times before.

That's not the way it would happen this time though. This police shooting was about to hit much, much closer to home.

It was just moments later that the notification call came from the department. Your husband has been involved in an "incident" they said. Sarge's wife had held the hands of many a police officer's loved ones as they waited for the two simple words that they desperately longed to hear, "He's okay." Those are exactly the words she heard with the second call and before she even hung up the phone, there were police officers at her doorstep ready to take her to the hospital.

Although there were only a few tenuous moments between finding out it was her husband that was shot and finding out he was okay, it seemed like an eternity. "That's a hard phone call to take," she recalled.

Even though she knew better than just about any police wife what to expect in a situation like this one, she still described the whole thing as "disconcerting and traumatic." She added "being on the receiving end of a call like that makes you rethink things."

While hearing the words "he's okay" was an indescribable relief, actually seeing it for herself when she arrived at the hospital was a hundredfold more relieving.

When I sat down with them, both the Sarge and his wife were tremendously appreciative of everything everyone did to help in the crucial moments and difficult days that followed the shooting. Sarge couldn't say enough nice things about all the officers that showed up at the shooting scene and particularly, about the ambulance crew. They both said the department administration was remarkably attentive to their every need and that the Chief kept them apprised every step of the way as the manhunt for the shooter unfolded. The SLPOA, FOP Lodge 15 and the Shield of Hope quickly bundled together about $2,500 in financial aid for the Sarge and his family. The SLPOA paid for a rental car that Enterprise Leasing provided at a reduced rate while their bullet-peppered car was being repaired. As it happened, they didn't need the rental car long because, with the help of the SLPWA, Glik's donated a company car to the family to keep to replace theirs.

An organization called Officer Needs Assistance USA went one step further and set-up a GoFundMe page to alleviate the financial burden of the Sarge not being able to work secondary for a while after the shooting. The page quickly raised over $2,000 and the tally continues to climb.

Sarge and his wife received dozens and dozens of calls from folks checking on their well-being. Among the callers were Darren Wilson and the St. Louis County Police Officer who got shot out in front of Ferguson City Hall in March.

As touched as the family was about the outpouring of support from their extended police family and people in the community outraged by the savage ambush, the one thing that bothered them was the lone protester that showed up at the shooting scene holding a sign asking the tastelessly callous question "how does it feel?"

The Sarge's wife said she'd like to tell that young man just exactly how she feels in the wake of her husband cheating death from a cowardly attacker provoked only by the color of the uniform her husband wore. "He just doesn't get it," she said shrugging off the hurtful remarks of the protester.

And, the Sarge and his wife both wondered where the "Black Lives Matter" organizers were. Those same folks that show up waving signs, canonizing young black men who die at the hands of the police even when the youth's own bad acts left the officer no choice but to use deadly force, were nowhere to be found when Sarge got shot.

You see, the Sarge is a black man himself. His wife, who is also black, asked rhetorically, "if this is the black lives matter movement, what about my husband? Doesn't his life matter?"

It's a fair question.

And, these two, more than most, have a right to ask it. The Sarge and his wife put their money where their mouths are. They are both very active in youth programs that cater almost exclusively to troubled black youths. Their mentorship is responsible for many, many youths at risk, black lives that matter very much to both of them, making the right decisions and putting their lives on the right path. In all too many situations, these are subtle choices that ultimately could've made a life and death difference for kids like Michael Brown, Vonderrit Myers, Kajieme Powell, and so many others.

While the cop haters, who never lifted a finger to help inner-city black youths make better choices despite the hopelessness and despair of being raised in neighborhoods plagued with failing schools, broken homes, violent crime, and substance abuse came out of the woodwork after the fact to lay claim to "Black Lives Matter" as a rallying cry for their ulterior agenda, the Sarge and his wife have lived that mantra day in and day out in the worst neighborhoods in St. Louis. A lot of the black cops I have known in my life give back to the community in the very same way, acting as role models for kids that live in neighborhoods devoid of anyone to look up to, neighborhoods where the dopeman, or the leader of the local gang are the closest thing to a success story.

Truly, every cop in St. Louis city has a claim they can stake to the Black Lives Matter mantra. They are the men and women that go to work every day in our diverse neighborhoods and place their lives on the line for the citizens of St. Louis, a city where blacks are dispropor- tionately the victim of violent crimes, a city that saw deadly spikes in gun crimes where blacks were almost exclusively the victims. All the while, local politicians elbowing their way to the national spotlight undercut and hobbled officers, making police officers' jobs virtually impossible to do without unrelenting criticism and interference.

You don't have to tell the Sarge and his wife, or any city cop I know that black lives matter. They live it every day and they don't deserve to be criticized for the handful of kids who decide that their own lives don't matter and turn deadly violence against the police. It's tragic when an officer has to take a life, and it weighs heavily on them when they do; but it doesn't mean that black lives don't matter to them. Quite the contrary, they wouldn't have been working in that neighborhood in the first place if black lives didn't matter to them.

Sarge's wife said that she is not unsympathetic to the Black Lives Matter movement, and she understands why they get mad when people counter with "All Lives Matter." As she pointed out, "ALL" hasn't always included black people in the history of this country.

She's right. Even though the Declaration of Independence said "ALL men are created equal . . . ," slavery was still legal for nearly a hundred years after those words were written. Even though the Pledge of Allegiance said "with liberty and justice for ALL," blacks struggled for voting rights and endured segregation for many years after slavery had ended. But, if the black lives matter mantra is to truly mean anything, we have to be honest and consistent, and we as a society can't devalue any lives. That includes the lives of blacks AND the lives of police officers.

As the Sarge's wife so succinctly put it, "Blue lives matter too."

Maybe the things I've said over the last year, and the words I've written in this book, will only further damage race relations. That isn't my intention. My desire is to set the record straight because I don't think we can move forward from any of this if we start out from the wrong place, the wrong premise. We have to be honest about what happened between Michael and Darren that day, or, we are simply embarking on a fool's errand.

I have been labeled a racist by the leaders of the protests in St. Louis and their online network of supporters nonstop since I stepped forward as a law enforcement spokesman after Michael's death.

It is an unfair characterization, to be certain.

I've tried to never judge another person based on his or her skin color. As I said before, the experience of going to an integrated elementary school at an early age forever instilled in me a sense that we all share the same hopes and dreams and disappointments and regrets. It ingrained in me that skin color shouldn't matter to anyone and certainly shouldn't matter to me.

I have worked with and been close to a lot of black people during my law enforcement and legislative careers, and I have seen the best of people of color who serve with distinction in both of those noble callings. I've also seen the worst of black people (and white) when I worked undercover narcotics, but I never thought their character defects were the result of their skin color, but rather, the predicaments they were born into and the choices they made.

Most important, I have three biracial nieces and nephews, and I love them and their mother just as much as I do everyone in our family. I want the best for them in their lives, and as long as skin color matters so much in our culture, I fear that they may someday suffer because of our failings as a society.

The black person who touched my life more than any other, though, was a woman named Doris Hoskins. "Mama Doris," as she was affectionately known, was in her eighties and of mixed Caribbean and African descent, with dark onyx skin that was as leathery as an old cowboy's saddlebag. She was feisty, to say the least, and you always knew where you stood with her. She was the only black resident of the tiny river town of Kimmswick, where I ended my law enforcement career as the chief of police and city administrator.

Mama Doris was distrustful of outsiders and kept me at arm's length when I initially took the job. She was downright ornery to me at first, thumbing her nose at everything I said, and openly criticizing me in front of our city clerk, who was a dear friend of hers. She would bring Kaye, the clerk, food and they would eat in front of me without offering a morsel. Finally, one day she said something churlish to me, and I told her playfully to "kiss my white ass." That was all it took to ingratiate myself to her. She chuckled and snorted and said, "You're all right, boy."

From there on, she always made a little extra of whatever she cooked to bring by city hall so that I could have a nip of her tasty treats. The fried catfish was the best. I can practically taste it now.

Doris lived in the ramshackle house that sat on the homestead her family had owned for over a hundred years. I would stop by to see her and buy whatever it was that she was hawking that day. Sometimes it was jellies she had canned; sometimes it was baked goods; sometimes it was the intricate gingerbread houses that she would make around the holidays. Whatever it was, it always smelled good, and I knew that she could use the money, so I always bought what she was selling, even if I wasn't going to eat it.

She enjoyed sitting in her driveway and sipping on a beer, although I never saw her drink more than one or two. I would grab a six-pack and stop by sometimes after work and sit at her side. We'd watch the world go by from her perch in our sleepy little town. She would regale me with stories of her life and stories of her grandparents, who had been slaves. She talked about how much the world had changed in the short span of her days.

One day, as I got up to leave, I leaned over to give her a hug. When I did, she kissed me on the cheek. Feeling obligated to return the gesture, I gave her a glancing peck on the cheek and barely made skin-to-skin contact.

She didn't say anything, but I could tell I had hurt her feelings. Her kiss was a real kiss; mine was an affront.

Let's face it; no young guy likes kissing an old lady. Whether it's your grandmother or your great-aunt or your Sunday school teacher, from a very early age, we all do it exactly the same way—a quick, passing cheek graze with un-moistened lips, not nearly powerful enough to penetrate the rouge and pancake makeup spackled on old Aunt Charlotte's face. It is a universal truth. Some are given to the opinion that it is genetically coded in our DNA. No doubt, Darwin could espouse a theory on how avoiding the dreaded "old lady kiss" allowed our progenitors to survive in the wild.

Yet for a young white man, the idea of kissing an elderly black woman is quite a different prospect altogether.

There is an ugly reality that most of us don't care to acknowledge. From a very young age, white children, especially boys, come to conclude that white skin is normal and that black skin is somehow stained, imperfect skin.

It is a simple, unsophisticated conclusion that most little boys of my race very much reach on their own. It is the collision of innocence and ignorance in an undeveloped mind. Like many childish concoctions, this one can go largely intellectually unchallenged. It is such a deep-seated, albeit misguided belief in the formative understandings of people who have darker skin than we do, that most who conjure it up in their imaginations will grow up with this concept rattling around unabated in their subconscious.

I had never given this notion a moment of cognizant consideration. I was no different from any other white man who had the same ill-conceived remnant of adolescent fancy buried deep below the surface of his conscious thought. If left unquestioned by reasoned analysis, the natural anticipation is this: kiss a black woman and the stain of imperfection will sully your lips just as soot stains a coal miner's face.

As I stood in her driveway, analyzing my deepest, most bigoted belief, an unexamined remnant of my earliest, silliest thoughts about race and skin color, I was ashamed . . . horribly, horribly ashamed. And I had hurt a dear friend whom I held in very high regard. At that moment, I questioned everything I believed and tried to unearth the other ill-formed implicit biases buried deep in my subliminal mind.

The next time I saw Mama Doris, I softly grasped her cheek and gently pulled her toward me. I wetted my lips and pressed them against her once-smooth skin in a full, un-retreating kiss. I could feel something nearly beyond description: a certain tenderness, a certain radiance, a certain energy, a certain galvanic response. It could only be described as, well, as love.

Doris felt it too.

And it felt glorious to us both.

In her graceful way, Doris never said anything to me about the way I had hurt her feelings when I spurned her kiss in the driveway that day. Likewise, she never said anything to me the day I made up for it with the loving embrace she so richly deserved. She just grabbed my hand and squeezed it tightly. That spoke volumes. I learned a lot about the world from the words Mama Doris spoke to me in front of her old family homestead. I learned even more about myself from the words she never spoke, the words she didn't have to speak.

Race is not an easy matter. It is something we all deal with consciously and unconsciously, regardless of our skin color. If it was easy to deal with, we'd be past all of this ugliness by now. We're not.

Mama Doris is gone now. I still drive by her house occasionally, and when I do, I smile and think about her and how she touched my life.

We need now more than ever to learn to touch each other's lives in ways that make us better, more understanding people. The acrimony of the last twelve months has taken its toll on us all and has damaged race relations in a way that this country hasn't seen in a long time.

So, go out and find someone different from you, someone with different skin color, someone with different life experiences, someone with a different frame of reference. Go out and find your own Mama Doris. Talk to them. Listen to them. Learn from them. And maybe you'll learn a little bit more about yourself.

After the year we've had, we could all use a little self-discovery.

THE UNDISCOVERED COUNTRY

We all know the "To be, or not to be" opening of *Hamlet*'s soliloquy, but Hamlet's introspection goes much deeper than the all-too-familiar commencement to what is perhaps the most famous monologue in literary history.

In weighing the familiar, albeit torturous, certainty of his instant predicament against the uncertainty of an alternate fate, Hamlet describes the unknown as "the undiscovered country."[1]

While Hamlet is clearly pondering the unknowable nature of the final destination of his soul, we could use the same expression to describe what comes next in a post-Ferguson world. What *undiscovered country* does the aftermath of this chapter in human history hold for us all?

I have to tell you: I take a modicum of solace in describing what comes next for all of us in such Shakespearean terms. The imagery of standing on the deck of an old, wooden clipper with its topsails unfurled in the trade winds sailing off into the unknown is a pleasing one to me. What's more pleasing yet is picturing the whole of humanity gathered on that deck beside me, staring longingly out into the horizon in shared hope for a better future and in mutual trepidation of the *slings and arrows* it might bring.

To eclipse that horizon, that is a true act of faith in the face of an unknown fate. There is safe harbor in our own current predicament. The waters are rocky, but at least we are not out to sea, where the crashing breakers might be tenfold more tumultuous.

Indeed, it takes courage and faith to set sail in search of that undiscovered country. But, it cannot be a solo voyage. Either we embark on this journey together, or we are doomed to be moored in this dismal port, shipwrecked in the travails of history that has stranded us here; stranded us at a place in time where young, black men have few prospects for happy, long lives, and police officers are constantly placed in harm's way by the failings of our social design and the violence bred by the hopelessness, haplessness, and helplessness visited upon the heirs to systematic disadvantage.

I say, cast off those hawsers and set course for the deep, blue expanse. Nobody knows what we may find when we finally come ashore at our ultimate destination, but that island paradise for which we all yearn cannot be charted until we put to sea in search of that *undiscovered country*.

So how do we get there?

No easy answers here, but the best one is probably "brutal honesty."

Until we have a frank, national conversation about what happened in Ferguson and elsewhere, and, more important, *why* it happened, we are damned to repeat these deadly showdowns over and over and over again. They won't always have the same outcome.

For those who cheer that encounter at Canfield as a triumph for law enforcement I say, hold your applause. Every one of these confrontations is a tragedy, not a triumph, for law enforcement. They won't all end like this. The more of these confrontations we have, the greater the chance that it is a police officer lying dead on a street like Canfield. Even if the police were to win every shootout, it is no happy occasion for a police officer to take a human life. It shakes a cop to the core, and none are ever the same after so doing.

Better that we conceive of a way to avoid these confrontations altogether. Better that we take an honest look at what makes interactions between police and inner-city youths so volatile. Better that we are forthright about the predicament in which both sides of these confrontations find themselves.

I hear people say about the Justice Department report alleging traffic court profiteering and racial profiling by the Ferguson Police, "Well, at least Michael didn't die in vain."

I am astonished when I hear those words because I believe just the opposite: Michael's death will have been utterly in vain if that grand political distraction is all we're left with from this whole chapter in American history.

Suppose this confrontation ended in a different way. Suppose that when Michael turned around and faced off against Darren Wilson, he decided to surrender rather than charge at the officer. Or, suppose Darren had said just the right word in that moment to convince Michael to submit. Or, suppose Dorian Johnson had shouted out to his friend, "Don't do it, Michael," and the angry, scared young man had snapped out of his rage. Or, suppose, just suppose, that Darren's final shots had hit Michael in the shoulder rather than the head and his forward momentum had stopped there and then.

Just suppose.

Suppose any happier outcome that you'd like that ends with Michael in handcuffs rather than a body bag.

For all intents and purposes, Michael's life, like it or not, would have still been over.

To go back to our friend Hamlet, "Ay, there's the rub!"[2]

Michael would have been facing a long, long prison sentence for the strong-armed robbery and the assault of a police officer. Even if he had surrendered without laying a finger on Darren, he would have likely been looking at jail time, or at the very least, a long stint on probation. He wouldn't have had Benjamin Crump for his attorney. He'd have gotten some fresh-faced public defender newly graduated from a second-tier law school. There would have been no marching in the street, no T-shirts, no rallying cries. There would have been only this: a day in court followed by an inevitable period of incarceration, and when he got out, he would've likely reoffended and spent the rest of his life in and out of the penal system, because that's what our prison system produces: reoffenders.

To have had a truly happier ending, we would have to travel back further, much further, in time. Back to before Michael tried to take Darren's gun. Back to before Michael stole those cigars. Back to before Michael was ever born. Because *this* is the sad and ugly truth of it all: Michael was placed on a collision course with that bloodstained pavement on Canfield Drive before he was ever brought into this world. Could he have made better decisions? Of course he could have; absolutely. But this was a young man who made better choices than most who share his lot in life. He graduated from high school. He was enrolled in technical school. He had given himself a fighting chance against odds that those of us born into the other America, white America, can barely imagine. The America that Michael lived in is a place that you could only comprehend if you've lived in it or policed in it.

I don't mean to sound like some Pollyanna, "everyone's a victim" apologist. Michael's fate was escapable. Many young men of color have broken free of the purgatorial confines to which they were born. We should celebrate those success stories all the more because it is no small mountain they have climbed. More important, we should recognize that the few who break free of the ghetto are the exceptions that make the rule.

Shouldn't we be honest with ourselves and admit that race still shapes the fate of people in America? Sure, there are people of color who rise out of the depths of despair into which they were born. Likewise, there are white Americans who are born into privilege, or in the very least, given more opportunities to succeed than kids in the inner city, yet squander those opportunities and succumb to the basest of human desires. When a white kid from a good family robs a liquor store or ODs on heroin, we don't think quietly to ourselves, *There goes another white kid getting in trouble*, or, *Well, he was just acting his color*, or whatever other callous, biased thought we might whisper to ourselves in the secluded confines of our subconscious inner monologue. We say, "My, my, I wonder where his poor parents went wrong," Do we have the same empathy when it's a black kid who screws up, or do we consider it a fait accompli?

Consider this: we learned from Darren Wilson's interview with the *New Yorker* that his childhood was no cakewalk. I could make a pretty strong case that Darren's childhood was tougher than Michael Brown's. We don't have to have that debate because we can all agree that they both had tough childhoods for the purposes of the analogy I want to make. Darren somehow found his way to a respectable career in law enforcement and fell in love with a wonderful woman he would ultimately marry. He made a life for himself, at least pre-Ferguson, that anyone would find reason to envy. Michael, on the other hand, fell in with companions on the streets of Ferguson who were sure to get him in trouble, and ultimately, turned to a life of crime; or at least, committed a crime on August 9 that led to his own demise.

So here is the analogy: what if Michael had been born white and Darren had been born black? Is there any reason to think that Michael wouldn't have been the one to conquer the challenges of his upbringing and that Darren wouldn't have turned to the thug life? Think about it. Whites in suburban America tend to get more opportunities to overcome the adversities visited on them while inner-city blacks are locked into a pit of hopelessness that is almost inescapable, a mountain of challenges that are practically insurmountable, an absence of opportunity that is nearly indomitable.

I don't say all of this because I think that we can hug and coddle our way to a happier outcome for those born into adversity. I believe firmly in personal responsibility, but we can't expect people to pull themselves up by the bootstraps when they don't have any boots.

Even if you don't care about the plight of the inner city and the disparate fate of people of color who wind up trapped within its invisible walls, care about this: as long as people are doomed to dwell in the crucible of urban poverty, crime, and hopelessness, we will continue to have a hyper-violent society. We will continue to endure drug trafficking for profit by young men who have no other path to financial success. Those who have nothing to hold on to and nothing to lose will continue to take from you the hard-earned possessions you hold dear. And the police who disrupt the misdeeds of the by-products of inner-city despair will continue to end up in deadly showdowns with the progeny of a system of racial and economic inequality.

Maybe you have a *depraved heart* and don't care about the outcomes of these deadly confrontations because the black teenager that you believe to be irredeemable is usually the one that ends up dead in the street. But I care; I care deeply because far too often, it is one of my brothers or sisters in blue that lies dead in the street. And frankly, I don't find young men of color irredeemable. You can't call yourself a Christian if you don't believe that every man and woman is capable of redemption.

So, as George Bernard Shaw once asked, "What price, salvation?"

The price is opportunity, not welfare, not handouts. The price is simply a fighting chance to raise oneself up from disadvantage, a brand-new pair of boots equipped with well-cinched straps, as it were.

Until we start providing every kid in America with more chances to make the right decisions, more opportunities to succeed, more hope for a bright future, then the next Michael Brown or Freddie Gray is destined for the front page of your newspaper or, worse yet, the back page when these deadly confrontations become so commonplace they stop being news.

So, here are my admonishments to you, America. Heed them well, or your town may be the next Ferghanistan:

WHITE AMERICA: Stop pretending that blacks in our country don't have a more difficult way to go than we do. There is real economic segregation at work in the United States. It is undeniable and we should stop pretending it doesn't exist. Blacks are disproportionately born into poverty because of their skin color. Blacks are disproportionately born into violent neighborhoods because of their skin color. Blacks are disproportionately arrested, jailed, and executed not because cops are racists, but because the socioeconomic conditions that have become an unfortunate birthright for far, far too many black Americans leads to a cycle of hopelessness, despair, and bad choices. And, yes, I say black Americans rather than African Americans because it really is about their skin color, not their nation of origin.

BLACK AMERICA: Stop pretending that cops are killing your kids. Your kids are killing your kids. Cops are in your neighborhoods in greater numbers to try to put a stop to the devastating loss of young lives that plagues your communities and our country. As a result of police intervention, sometimes your kids try to kill cops, too. That always ends badly. It always will. If you want the deaths of Michael Brown, Eric Garner, Freddie Gray, "and the rest" to have meaning, then use these tragedies as an opportunity to promote socioeconomic change by demanding the opportunities that have been denied to blacks for generations. If you allow the antigovernment anarchist to co-opt this moment in time, you have squandered a once-in-a-lifetime chance to make a real difference in the way America works. And, if you blow this opportunity, the handful of kids who die in confrontations with cops and the thousands more who die when the police aren't around to save their lives will have died meaninglessly. That would be the greatest tragedy to come out of all of this.

AMERICA: Stop pretending that we don't have a shared role in what led to the events of August 9, 2014, and the civil unrest that followed. We do. The best economy is one where nobody gets anything for free—except opportunity . . . abundant opportunity. As a nation, we have to provide more opportunities for those living in the rank poverty of the inner city to rise up and those who dwell in that poverty must be more willing to capitalize on these opportunities because poverty is our greatest national security threat, it abandons our urban neighborhoods to a legacy of violence, crime and despair and it places the police officers who patrol those urban war zones in imminent, deadly danger. If you want to do something to diminish the use of deadly force by cops, do something about poverty. If you want to do something about police officer safety, do something about poverty. Whether you're white, black, brown, biracial, whatever you are, stop pretending that you're blameless in all of this. We all have a stake in this. We all share fault in this. We have to act together in a candid, honest way about how we got to where we are and where we go from here. The kids and the cops who have died while we've done nothing should not have suffered a senseless fate that serves as a grim harbinger of the carnage and destruction to come. It is time for change. Embrace change and embrace each other.

✪ ✪ ✪

The two hardest things about writing a book are starting it and ending it. Leonardo da Vinci allegedly once said, "Art is never finished, only abandoned." Ostensibly, he meant that it is imperfect, incomplete, that it is doomed to its flaws when deserted by its creator.

We all feel that way sometimes, don't we—abandoned by our Creator, that is? We shouldn't. It is our imperfections and our flaws that make us unique and interesting. Likewise, we shouldn't resent our Creator for our finite time in this world. Without a beginning and an end, you can't have a middle, and that's where the real story is.

So, I committed to myself when I started writing this book that I would end it on the one-year anniversary of the shooting of Michael Brown by Darren Wilson. As I lay my head on my pillow on August 9, 2015, the streets of Ferguson are once again embroiled in violence and havoc. As I close my weary eyes, three people have already been shot this night, one of them a young, black man who fired his gun at police from point-blank range and was critically injured by the return fire from the officers. The eighteen-year-old gunman's name was Tyrone Harris Jr., and he was a classmate of Michael Brown's.

What little progress we've made in a year.

I thought it appropriate to close this book with a poem I wrote for the *Gendarme*. It is a bit melancholy, but it sums up exactly how I feel about Ferguson and its scorching aftermath. It embodies the idea that cops aren't the real problem, and that they are worthy of our support and understanding. It is meant, as is this entire writing, to be conciliatory and curative. It is more than anything else intended to be an honest expression of what I see going on around us.

I said at the beginning of this book that this isn't my story or Darren Wilson's story, but rather, my telling of law enforcement's story in the wake of the war on police that came to be known as Ferghanistan. Maybe it really is just my story, my words. Perhaps no one else sees things as I do or feels the way I feel. But somebody had to say the things I've said here. Somebody had to set the record straight.

Our community and our nation need healing after the events in Ferguson, Staten Island, North Charleston, Cincinnati, Cleveland, Baltimore, and so many other places where tragedy is yet to happen. Maybe my words don't soothe anybody; maybe they do nothing to heal us as a society. Maybe that all comes later. But first, before we can get past any of this, we have to be honest with ourselves and each other.

That's what I've tried to convey here . . . raw, brutal honesty about what happened in Ferguson and elsewhere. That's what this book is about; that's what my poem is about . . . ensuring that there are no more casualties of history. It is about doing what I do every day when I stand by the cops I represent and stand up for the truth about the work they do and the challenges they face.

I hope despite the pain we have inflicted on each other over the past year that we can all sail together on that voyage to that undiscovered country. I hope we can join together to embrace the truth so there might never again be another person standing in the shoes of Michael Brown or Darren Wilson.

Wouldn't that be nice?

WHO WILL YOU STAND BY?[3]

by Jeff Roorda

America,

Who will you stand by?

As reporters try

To vilify

And politicians criticize

And demonstrators demonize

The gals and guys

Who simply try

To protect lives

And just survive

Who will you stand by?

As bullets fly

The law's defied

As good folks die

And families cry

When the next drive-by

Takes a baby's life

Who will you stand by?

When hopeless times
Lead to demise
Of young men's lives
Who won't comply
When police draw nigh
Who just take flight
Or shoot or fight
Or pull a knife
Though live they might
Despite their plight
If they'd just comply

Who will you stand by?

As flames swirl high
Into the sky
While looters pry
A door at night
As riots rage
And people fight
When rules seem
Not to apply
When bad behavior's justified
When law and order's nullified

Who will you stand by?

I stand by
The kid who tries
And tries and tries
To do things right
But gets jumped by
A gang some night
And later dies
As his mother sighs
And cries and cries
And cries and cries

I stand by
That thin blue line
That's oft maligned
The gals and guys
With piercing eyes
Who see the things
That you and I
Shan't realize
And do the things
That you and I
Will dare not try

I stand by
That azure line

That thing divine

Whose badges shine

They'll not abide

Crime on the rise

Nor scoundrels

Who would victimize

Good people who epitomize

The reasons why

Cops lay their lives

On thin blue lines

And sometimes die

For you and I

That's who I

Stand by

Who will you stand by?

ACKNOWLEDGMENTS

THANK YOU TO . . .

My girls, Macie, Lydia, and Sophie, the best thing that ever happened to me

Nancy, the love of my life and an amazing mother to our children

Mom and Dad: I couldn't have done this, or anything else, without you

All of the friends and family who stood by me through all of this

Ruth and Arnold and all those who influenced me, but didn't live to see this

The St. Louis Police Officers Association and the Fraternal Order of Police,

particularly Joe and Kevin

The *Gendarme* and its editor, Martin, and publisher, Ron

My colleagues and friends in the Missouri Legislature who put the people first (you know who you are)

My "gal Fridays," Jaime, Leigh Anne, and Bret

Bob Goeggel for treating me like a son

Tim Meadows, Mark Bruns, and Neil Bruntrager for treating me like a brother

Frank Heine and all the other great teachers who inspire young minds

The "Narcs" that had my back: Coop, Sherm, Doug, Kenny, Hiram, Tug, Jeff, Roger, Bill, Luke, Bobby, Kelly, Murph, Tommy, Emmett, Sal, and especially Steve Strehl [RIP]

The Bulltown Boys and the MMUN Gang

Jamie and Churchie, "Truth Warriors"

My besties: Fred, Wayno, Mikey, Ripp-Dog, Bobby Z, Springo, Donnie, Gabe, Patrick, Hal, Douggie Fresh, Keith, Joe, Brian, Burkie, Jason, Ryan, Andy and especially, to Rick [RIP]

ABOUT THE AUTHOR

The War on Police is the first book by nationally recognized police spokesman and former Missouri state representative Jeff Roorda.

In the aftermath of the shooting of Michael Brown by Ferguson police officer Darren Wilson and other high-profile deadly encounters between police and suspects elsewhere, Roorda, the spokesperson for the Fraternal Order of Police in St. Louis, was propelled into the national spotlight. In hundreds of broadcast and print interviews, Roorda relentlessly defended police officers who he believed acted properly, and defiantly challenged what he called the "Hands up, don't shoot" myth that took hold in the wake of the Ferguson shooting. Roorda, a frequent guest commentator on CNN and Fox News Network, emerged as the most powerful pro-police voice during a time in history when law enforcement came under unprecedented and unwarranted criticism from protesters, the press, and politicians alike.

Roorda, a retired police chief and decorated undercover narcotics detective, was serving his last days in the Missouri House of Representatives due to term limits when hostilities broke out in

Ferguson. He spent his waning moments in public office criticizing Eric Holder, Barack Obama, and other members of his own party for their botched handling of Ferguson, and for fanning the flames of what he dubbed "the war on police." Roorda's un-retreating, bare-knuckles style comes bursting through the pages of his book as he sets the record straight with a sober, candid, and insightful examination of policing and race relations in America.

To learn more about the author, visit www.thewaronpolice.com.

NOTES

CHAPTER 1: FERGHANISTAN

1. See *Wikipedia*, s.v. "Ferguson unrest," accessed June 29, 2016, https://en.wikipedia.org/wiki/Ferguson_unrest.

2. See, for example, Philip Kennicott, "Images coming from Ferguson, Mo., reveal unfiltered, uncomfortable truths," *Washington Post*, August 14, 2014, https://www.washingtonpost.com/entertainment/museums/images-coming-from-ferguson-mo-reveal-unfiltered-uncomfortable-truths/2014/08/14/5235f68e-23df-11e4-8593-da634b334390_story.html

CHAPTER 2: MRS. O'LEARY'S COW

1. Elisa Crouch, "Michael Brown Remembered as a 'Gentle Giant'," *St. Louis Post-Dispatch*, August 11, 2014, http://www.stltoday.com/news/local/crime-and-courts/michael-brown-remembered-as-a-gentle-giant/article_cbafa12e-7305-5fd7-8e0e-3139f472d130.html.

2. CBS News, "Documents Describe Ferguson Officer's Version of Fatal Shooting," CBSNews.com, November 25, 2014, http://www.cbsnews.com/news/documents-describe-ferguson-officers-version-of-fatal-shooting/.

3. Paul Cassell, "Why Michael Brown's Best Friend's Story Isn't Credible," *The Volokh Conspiracy* (*WP* blog), December 2, 2014, https://www.washingtonpost.com/news/volokh-conspiracy/wp/2014/12/02/why-michael-browns-best-friends-story-is-incredible/.

4. "Police report in the Michael Brown case," LA Times, August 15, 2014, http://documents. latimes.com/police-report-michael-brown-case/.

5. Missouri Rev. Stat. §565.021.1(2).

CHAPTER 3: TONS OF ANARCHY

1. St. Louis Police Union Contract, art. 3, sec. 2, p. 5, online at https://issuu.com/ criminaljusticepolicy/docs/st_louis.

2. "Gun Sales Spike around Ferguson after 3 Days of Riots," RT, August 13, 2014, https:// www.rt.com/usa/180084-gun-sales-ferguson-protests/.

3. See the Revolutionary Communist Party, USA's publication Revolution, at http://revcom. us/movement-for-revolution/BAE/film.html.

4. "DAY FIVE WRAPUP: McCulloch blasts Nixon for replacing St. Louis County Police control," St. Louis Post-Dispatch, August 14, 2014, http://www.stltoday.com/news/ local/crime-and-courts/day-five-wrapup-mcculloch-blasts-nixon-for-replacing-st-louis/ article_0806541b-ed48-5d06-9267-323531ad6cf1.html.

5. Staff reports, "Day Five Wrapup: McCulloch Blasts Nixon for Replacing St. Louis County Police control," St. Louis Post-Dispatch, August 14, 2014, http://www. stltoday.com/news/local/crime-and-courts/day-five-wrapup-mcculloch-blasts-nixon-for-replacing-st-louis/article_0806541b-ed48-5d06-9267-323531ad6cf1.html.

6. Jeremy Kohler, "St. Louis Police Chief Says He Does Not Support Militarized Tactics in Ferguson," St. Louis Post-Dispatch, August 14, 2014, http://www.stltoday.com/ news/local/crime-and-courts/st-louis-police-chief-says-he-does-not-support-militarized/ article_b401feba-b49e-5b79-8926-19481191726f.html.

7. Albert Samaha, "Let the Dems keep hating: Jamilah Nasheed could pull off the political coup of the century," Riverfront Times, August 18, 2011, http://www.riverfronttimes. com/stlouis/let-the-dems-keep-hating-jamilah-nasheed-could-pull-off-the-political-coup-of-the-century/Content?oid=2495766.

8. Elliott Davis, "Armed man tries to carjack MO State Senator Nasheed," Fox2now, November 22, 2014, http://fox2now.com/2014/11/22/armed-man-tries-to-carjack-mo-state-senator-nasheed/.

9. Pema Levy, "Ferguson Prosecutor Robert P. Mcculloch's Long History of Siding with the Police," Newsweek, August 29, 2014, http://www.newsweek.com/2014/09/12/ ferguson-prosecutor-robert-p-mccullochs-long-history-siding-police-267357.html.

CHAPTER 4: THE MAN WHO SHOT LIBERTY VALANCE

1. Jake Halpern, "The Man Who Shot Michael Brown," New Yorker, August 10 and 17, 2015, issue, http://www.newyorker.com/magazine/2015/08/10/the-cop.

2. AFI's 100 Years . . . 100 Movie Quotes Nominees, http://www.afi.com/Docs/100Years/ quotes400.pdf

CHAPTER 5: MICHAEL AHERN REINCARNATE

1. Jeff Roorda, "The Rest of the Story," *Gendarme* 44, no. 9 (September 2014): 4.

CHAPTER 6: BROKEN ARROW

1. For the lyrics, go to: http://www.metrolyrics.com/mind-riot-lyrics-soundgarden.html. A performance can be seen at: https://www.youtube.com/watch?v=FajC1lvV6MQ.
2. "Los Angeles Riots: 20 years later," *Los Angeles Times*, April 28, 2014, http://www.latimes.com /la-me-los-angeles-riots-sg-storygallery.html.
3. Joel Currier, "St. Louis police release video, audio of deadly police shooting," St. Louis Post-Dispatch, August 20, 2014, http://www.stltoday.com/news/local/crime-and-courts/ st-louis-police-release-video-audio-of-deadly-police-shooting/article_9326e02a-2a60- 5baa-b63a-9c77b8b81bab.html.

CHAPTER 7: NO BIKO

1. Lyrics can be seen at http://www.metrolyrics.com/biko-lyrics-peter-gabriel.html; a YouTube performance can be viewed at https://www.youtube.com/watch?v=iLg-8Jxi5aE.
2. Jeff Roorda, "The Thick Blue Line," *Gendarme* 44, no. 10 (October 2014): 1.

CHAPTER 8: ". . . AND THE REST"

1. "Friend of Officer Darren Wilson: 'Ferguson Effect' is real," Fox News, June 4, 2015, http://video.foxnews.com/v/4275345512001/friend-of-officer-darren-wilson-ferguson- effect-is-real/?#sp=show-clips
2. Jeffrey Roorda, "The Shaw Shoot Redemption," *Gendarme* 44, no. 11 (November 2014): 5.

CHAPTER 10: BEHIND BLUE EYES

1. Jeffrey Roorda, "Darren Wilson's War," *Gendarme* 44, no. 12 (December 2014): 1.

CHAPTER 11: WAITING FOR AN IGNORAMUS

1. Jenny Jiang, "Transcript: St. Louis County Prosecutor Robert McCulloch's Statement on the Grand Jury's Decision in the Michael Brown Case–Part 2" (et. al) December 2, 2014, *WTF? (What the Folly?)* (news/analysis blog), http://www.whatthefolly.com/2014/12/02/ transcript-st-louis-county-prosecutor-robert-mccullochs-statement-on-the-grand-jurys- decision-in-the-michael-brown-case-part-2/. This transcript exists in nine parts on this blog, with a link to each part. The citation begins in Part 2 but is continued on separate pages.
2. See Sasha Goldstein, "Michael Brown's Stepfather, Louis Head, Is Being Investigated for Inciting Ferguson Riots by Yelling 'Burn This B---h Down': Report," *New York Daily News*, December 2, 2014, http://www.nydailynews.com/news/crime/michael-brown- stepdad-eyed-ferguson-riots-report-article-1.2030219.

3. Jeffrey Roorda, "Zach Hoelzer: Unknown Soldier?" *Gendarme* 45, no. 5 (May 2015): 1.

CHAPTER 12: RAMIFICATIONS

1. Justin Baragona, "Keith Olbermann Names Darren Wilson Supporter Jeff Roorda World's Worst Person in Sports," *Politicus Sports* (blog), December 1, 2014, http://sports.politicususa.com/2014/12/01/keith-olbermann-names-darren-wilson-supporter-jeff-roorda-worlds-worst-person-in-sports.html.

2. Brett Smiley, "Jon Stewart Rips Police over Response to Rams players' 'Hands Up, Don't Shoot' Gesture," *TheBuzzer* (Fox Sports blog), December 3, 2014, http://www.foxsports.com/buzzer/story/jon-stewart-rams-daily-show-120314.

3. Christine Byers, "Man charged with making online threats to kill St. Louis police," St. Louis Post-Dispatch, January 1, 2015, http://www.stltoday.com/news/local/crime-and-courts/man-charged-with-making-online-threats-to-kill-st-louis/article_6e4157cc-607e-5be8-930a-dd38af1edb38.html.

4. Jeffrey Roorda, "A Grave New World," *Gendarme* 45, no. 1 (January 2015): 4.

CHAPTER 13: CHARACTER CZOLGOSZING

1. Jeffrey Roorda, "No Muzzle for This Pit Bull," *Gendarme* 45, no. 3 (March 2015): 4.

CHAPTER 14: GET YOUR RED-HOT BURRITOS

1. See Eric Tucker, "In Ferguson, Scathing US Report Brings Pressure for Change," Aol. News, March 4, 2015, http://www.aol.com/article/2015/03/04/in-ferguson-scathing-us-report-brings-pressure-for-change/21149595/.

2. "Attorney General Holder Delivers Update on Investigations in Ferguson, Missouri," United States Department of Justice website, March 4, 2015, https://www.justice.gov/opa/speech/attorney-general-holder-delivers-update-investigations-ferguson-missouri.

3. Ibid.

4. See political commentator Mike Gallagher's revealing discussion on this in his article "'When did 'Hands up, don't shoot!' become 'Don't write me a ticket?'" The website of Mike Gallagher, March 13, 2015, http://www.mikeonline.com/when-did-hands-up-dont-shoot-become-dont-write-me-a-ticket/.

5. The following text from this interview, aired March 6, 2015, is a combination of the transcript as shown on CNN's Transcript page, at http://edition.cnn.com/TRANSCRIPTS/1503/06/acd.01.html (note that, among numerous other errors and omissions, this transcript incorrectly identifies me as "JEFF FLORIDA"), and Lindsay Toler's report titled "Jeff Roorda Calls DOJ Ferguson Report a 'Flimsy Tortilla,' Anderson Cooper Can't Even," on the *Riverfront Times* news blog, March 9, 2015, http://www.riverfronttimes.com/newsblog/2015/03/09/jeff-roorda-calls-doj-ferguson-report-a-flimsy-tortilla-anderson-cooper-cant-even, which fills in some of the gaps from CNN's flawed transcript. The video of the interview is embedded in Toler's article.

6. See Toler, "Jeff Roorda Calls DOJ Ferguson Report a 'Flimsy Tortilla'"; Jeff Roorda, Facebook, https://www.facebook.com/roordaformo.

7. Toler, "Jeff Roorda Calls DOJ Ferguson Report a 'Flimsy Tortilla.'"

8. See United States Department of Justice, Civil Rights Division, *Investigation of the Ferguson Police Department* (United States Department of Justice, March 4, 2015), 65, https://www.justice.gov/sites/default/files/opa/press-releases/attachments/2015/03/04/ferguson_police_department_report.pdf.

9. Missouri Attorney General's Office, "Vehicle Stops Report," https://ago.mo.gov/home/vehicle-stops-report.

10. US Department of Justice Civil Rights Division, "Investigation of the Ferguson Police Department," March 4, 2015, https://www.justice.gov/sites/default/files/opa/press-releases/attachments/2015/03/04/ferguson_police_department_report.pdf, p. 6.

11. Ibid., 62.

12. See ibid., 4–6.

CHAPTER 15: US V. THEM

1. See United States Department of Justice, Civil Rights Division, *Investigation of the Ferguson Police Department* (United States Department of Justice, March 4, 2015), https://www.justice.gov/sites/default/files/opa/press-releases/attachments/2015/03/04/ferguson_police_department_report.pdf, 2, where Ferguson's law enforcement are accused of allowing their law enforcement practices to be shaped by the city's "focus on generating revenue."

2. Public Papers of the Presidents of the United States: Lyndon B. Johnson, 1967, [Sept. 14, 382], p. 833.

3. United States v. Darby 312 U.S. 100.

4. U.S. Code Title 42, Chapter 136, Subchapter IX, Part B, § 14141, "Cause of action," https://www.law.cornell.edu/uscode/text/42/14141.

5. United States Department of Justice, *Investigation of the Ferguson Police Department*, 2.

6. Ibid., 3.

7. Ibid., 4.

8. Jared Taylor, "New DOJ Statistics on Race and Violent Crime," American Renaissance, July 2, 2015, http://www.amren.com/news/2015/07/new-doj-statistics-on-race-and-violent-crime/.

9. See ibid., pages 5–6, where Ferguson's approach to law enforcement is blamed for "community distrust."

10. COPS, "Collaborative Reform Initiative for Technical Assistance," accessed July 5, 2016, http://www.cops.usdoj.gov/pdf/2015AwardDocs/crita/CRI-TA_one-pager.pdf.

11. Simone Weichselbaum, "Policing the Police," The Marshall Project, May 26, 2015, https://www.themarshallproject.org/2015/04/23/policing-the-police#.0pKqx7FiT.

12. Eric Lichtblau, "Bush Sees U.S. as Meddling in Local Police Affairs," *Los Angeles Times*, November 29, 1997, http://articles.latimes.com/2000/jun/01/news/mn-36333.

13. Simone Weichselbaum, "A Rural Sheriff Stares Down the Justice Department ," The Marshall Project, October 6, 2015, https://www.themarshallproject.org/2015/10/06/a-rural-sheriff-stares-down-the-justice-department#.WCNrEUsWd.

14. United States Department of Justice, *Investigation of the Ferguson Police Department*, 9, 15.

15. See ibid., 50.

16. See ibid., 16–28.

17. Ibid., 79.

18. Ibid., 80.

19. Ibid., 90.

20. Julian P. Boyd, ed., *The Papers of Thomas Jefferson*, vol 1: *1760–1776* (Princeton: Princeton University Press, 1950), 243–47.

CHAPTER 16: THERE WILL BE BLOOD

1. "Roorda: Some protesters want 'dead cops'," CNN, http://www.cnn.com/videos/tv/2015/03/12/lead-intv-roorda-police-react-ferguson-shooting.cnn

2. Daily News 24, "Ferguson Police Rep: Protestors 'Finally Got What They Wanted — Dead Cops'," Mar 12, 2015, https://www.youtube.com/watch?v=wZTTiuewd5U.

3. Jeff Roorda, "Ferghanistan: The War On Police Draws Blood," *Gendarme* 45, no. 4 (April 2015): 1.

CHAPTER 17: WE ARE DARREN WILSON

1. Jeff Roorda, "Identifying Cop," *Gendarme* 45, no. 7 (July 2015): 1.

CHAPTER 18: PROJECT MAYHEM

1. *Fight Club*, directed by David Fincher (1999; Century City, CA: 20th Century Fox,2000), DVD.

2. Jennifer Medina, "Rodney King Dies at 47; Police Beating Victim Who Asked 'Can We All Get Along?'"

3. Eric Bradner, "Obama: 'No excuse' for violence in Baltimore," CNN Politics, upd. April 28, 2015, http://www.cnn.com/2015/04/28/politics/obama-baltimore-violent-protests/index.html,

4. Michele McPhee and Sara Just, "Obama: Police Acted 'Stupidly' in Gates Case," ABC News, July 22, 2009, http://abcnews.go.com/US/story?id=8148986&page=1.

5. Byron Tau, "Obama: 'If I Had a Son, He'd Look Like Trayvon,'" *Politico44 Blog*, March 23, 2012, http://www.politico.com/blogs/politico44/2012/03/obama-if-i-had-a-son-hed-look-like-trayvon-118439.

CHAPTER 19: CASUALTY OF HISTORY

1. See, for example, Jim Myers, "11 Facts About the Eric Garner Case the Media Won't Tell You," NewsMax, July 6, 2016, http://www.newsmax.com/Newsfront/eric-garner-chokehold-grand-jury-police/2014/12/04/id/611058/.
2. Ibid.

CHAPTER 20: A TALE OF TWO CITIES

1. Jeff Roorda, "Scorn on the Cob," *Gendarme* 45, no. 2 (February 2015): 4.

CHAPTER 21: IN LOCO PARENTIS

1. "The cost of a nation of incarceration," CBS News, April 23, 2012, http://www.cbsnews.com/news/the-cost-of-a-nation-of-incarceration/
2. Allie Bidwell, "How States Are Spending Money in Education," U.S. News & World Report, January 29, 2015, http://www.usnews.com/news/blogs/data-mine/2015/01/29/how-states-are-spending-money-in-education.

CHAPTER 22: MAMA DORIS

1. National Institute or Justice, "Racial Profiling and Traffic Stops," January 10, 2013, http://www.nij.gov/topics/law-enforcement/legitimacy/pages/traffic-stops.aspx.
2. Jared Taylor, "New DOJ Statistics on Race and Violent Crime," American Renaissance, July 1, 2015, http://www.amren.com/news/2015/07/new-doj-statistics-on-race-and-violent-crime/
3. FBI Uniform Crime Reporting Program, "Law Enforcement Officers Assaulted and Injured," 2013, https://ucr.fbi.gov/leoka/2013/tables/table_90_leos_asltd_and_injured_age_group_of_known_offender_by_race_and_sex_2013.xls.
4. See Maria Puente, "Darren Wilson: 'No Way' Brown Had His Hands Up," *USA Today*, November 25, 2014, http://www.usatoday.com/story/life/tv/2014/11/25/stephanopoulos-lands-first-interview-with-ferguson-cop-darren-wilson/70100712/.
5. Jeff Roorda, "Black Lives Matter, Even When They're Blue," *Gendarme* 45, no. 8: 4.

CHAPER 23: THE UNDISCOVERED COUNTRY

1. William Shakespeare, *Hamlet*, 3.1.86. References are to act, scene, and line.
2. Ibid., 3.1.72.
3. Jeff Roorda, "Who Will You Stand By," *Gendarme* 45, no. 6 (June 2015): 5.

INDEX

A

ABC, 92, 93, 139, 229

AC-360 (CNN news show), 46, 147, 151

Ahern, Michael (journalist, *Chicago Republican*), 48–49, 66

Ahlbrand, Kevin (president, Missouri FOP), 41–42

Alamance County Sheriff's Department (NC), 167

Al Jazeera America, 42

Allen, Thomas, 80

All in the Family, 244–45

Allman, Jamie, 139

Allman Report (news-talk show), 139

America, author's admonitions to, 270–71

AP (Associated Press), 124

Arnold Police Department (MO), 82, 141

arson, 4, 9, 37, 38, 121, 197, 224

Attucks, Crispus, 65

Audacity of Hope (Obama), 85–86

author's admonitions to America, 270–71

B

Baltimore, Maryland, xiii, 25, 166, 194, 203, 210, 213, 220, 222, 223–25, 236, 272

BBC America, 42

Belmar, Jon (St. Louis County police chief), 19, 29, 30

Biko, Stephen, 63–64, 65, 66

Black America, author's admonitions to, 270

Black Lives Matter, ix, 23, 165, 201, 209, 251–52, 257–58

blacks, statistics on, 247–48

bounded rationality, 78

Brown, Michael, xiv–xvi, 2, 4–15, 18, 21–22, 27, 34, 35, 36–37, 39, 40, 42, 51–53, 55, 58, 62, 64–67, 71, 73, 74, 76, 77, 79, 81, 88, 94, 96, 98, 101, 104, 108, 111, 113, 114, 116, 123, 124, 125, 126, 135–36, 138, 141, 143, 144, 147, 151, 152, 154, 163, 176, 178, 181, 182, 190, 193, 204, 209, 214, 217, 223, 224, 225, 227, 228, 230–31, 237, 241, 242, 249–50, 251, 252, 257, 259, 266–67, 268, 269, 270, 271–72, 273, 279

No publisher in the world has a higher percentage of *New York Times* bestsellers.

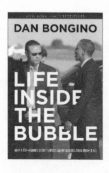
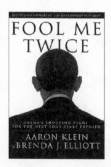

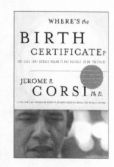
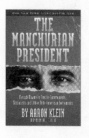

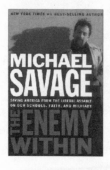
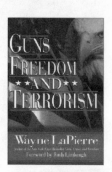
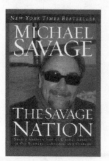

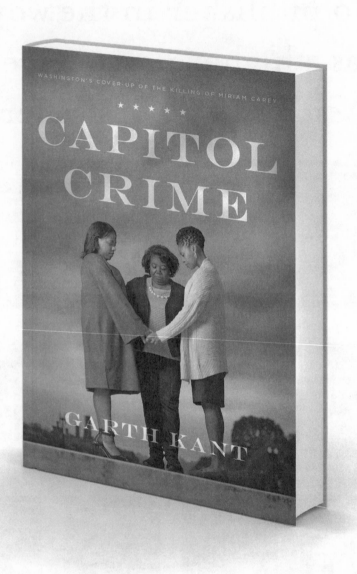

Miriam Carey became the black life that didn't matter when she was gunned down by elite federal forces in plain view of the entire nation in front of the Capitol in Washington DC. CAPITOL CRIME follows the dogged investigative reporting of veteran journalist Garth Kant, who after months of probing, questioning and filing FOIA lawsuits, finally put together the shocking pieces of the puzzle.

WND Books • WASHINGTON DC • WNDBOOKS.COM

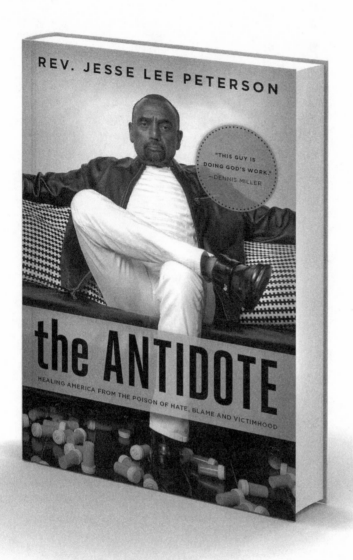

REV. JESSE LEE PETERSON

"THIS GUY IS DOING GOD'S WORK."
—DENNIS MILLER

the ANTIDOTE

HEALING AMERICA FROM THE POISON OF HATE, BLAME AND VICTIMHOOD

For a half century or more, black people have labored under the spell of what Jesse Lee Peterson calls the alchemists. These are the race hustlers, media hacks, politicians, community organizers and the like who promise to fundamentally transform America. The transformation they promise, however, produces only fool's gold unearned benefits like welfare, food stamps, subsidized housing, payouts from lawsuits, and maybe one day even reparations. Worse, to secure these counterfeit goods, recipients have to sacrifice something of infinite value: the sanctity of the two-parent family. It is a devil's bargain.

WND Books • WASHINGTON DC • WNDBOOKS.COM